The National Institute of
Economic and Social Research

EMPLOYMENT, OUTPUT AND INFLATION
The National Institute Model
of the British Economy

The National Institute of Economic and Social Research is an independent,
non-profit-making body, founded in 1938. It has as its aim the promotion
of realistic research, particularly in the field of economics. It conducts
research by its own research staff and in cooperation with the universities
and other academic bodies. The results of the work done under the
Institute's auspices are published in several series, and a list of its recent
publications will be found at the end of this volume.

EMPLOYMENT, OUTPUT AND INFLATION
The National Institute Model of the British Economy

Edited by
ANDREW BRITTON

HEINEMANN

Heinemann Educational Books Ltd
22 Bedford Square, London WC1B 3HH

Heinemann Educational Books Inc.
4 Front Street, New Hampshire 03833

ISBN 0 435 84089 4

Typeset in IBM Press Roman 10/11pt. by the Castlefield Press of Northampton
Printed in Great Britain by Biddles Ltd, Guildford, Surrey

Contents

List of tables

List of charts

Preface

The model described in this book has been developed by a team of economists on the Institute's staff over a period of many years. It would be impossible therefore to mention by name all those who have contributed to this book either directly or indirectly. I would like, however, to acknowledge with special gratitude the contribution of my predecessor, David Worswick. Much of the work reported here was indeed completed under his direction before I arrived at the Institute. Special thanks are also due to Fran Robinson who prepared the text for the printer.

Since 1966 the Social Science Research Council has made grants towards the cost of research and forecasting in macroeconomics at the Institute and HM Treasury has also made a substantial contribution to the funding of model development. I would like to take this opportunity of expressing our appreciation for this support.

AJCB

London, June 1983.

Introduction
Andrew Britton

In this book we report the most recent results from a programme of research at the National Institute which began with the first *Economic Review* in 1959. We now use a medium-sized macroeconomic model of the British economy for both forecasting and policy analysis. The sectors of that model provide the structure for Part One of the book, the eight chapters each being related to one set of mathematical equations describing some aspect of economic behaviour. The purpose is not just to describe the model, but also to give an account of the research that underlies it and its basis in theory and empirical data. The second part of the book includes a chapter on the use made of the model in forecasting, a chapter describing some of the properties of the complete model as they are revealed by simulation results and a chapter on its interpretation of the events of the last few years. In this introduction I shall try to provide an overview of macroeconomic modelbuilding, not just at the National Institute. As a branch of applied economics it has developed a methodology of its own and even threatened at times to break away and become a subject in its own right. My first aim will be to relate modelbuilding to economic theory, my second to describe in broad outline the distinguishing characteristics of the theory embodied in a sub-class of macroeconomic models, for which the Institute model may serve as representative.

The first macroeconomic models were built in the late 1950s and early 1960s, exploiting the rapid growth and development of economic statistics in the decade after World War Two.[1] The main purpose of such models was, and is, to explain fluctuations in the level of economic activity, to make them more predictable and, perhaps, therefore, more susceptible to control. Over the years the models have proliferated rapidly: more and more models have been estimated and many of those models have become large and complex, aiming to explain more and more aspects of economic behaviour.[2] In the 1960s confidence in modelbuilding grew, and its influence was extended. Econometrics never replaced judgemental or time-series methods altogether, but the modelbuilders did establish a position of intellectual superiority over other kinds of forecasting. The results of their work came to have a real influence on policymaking in many countries, Britain perhaps more than any other, and in the international organisations, especially the OECD. This period of intellectual dominance was curtailed in the 1970s by the general experience of rising inflation and by a concurrent revival of interest in neo-classical economics and particularly in monetary theory. During that decade modelbuilding continued to flourish and to develop in many interesting ways, but the spotlight of public attention was focused elsewhere. Now, as we move further into the 1980s, the propositions of neo-classical economics do not seem to provide an adequate guide to practical forecasting or policy-making. The ground is clear for modelbuilders in the earlier tradition to recover their lost influence. But they will not do so unless they can show that they have adequate answers to the criticisms that have been made of their methodology, and that they have taken account of the limitations which the events of the 1970s exposed in their understanding of economic behaviour.

Modelbuilding and economic theory

Models are designed not just as an aid to forecasting but as an aid to understanding. They claim to represent, in a much simplified form, the actual rules of behaviour which economic agents follow. The consumption function, for example, is supposed to reproduce, in outline at least, the process of decision-taking followed by a typical consumer in the real world; he actually does, it is claimed, consider what his current income is and what wealth or credit he has readily available and base his spending decision on that information. If this claim is justified then the model will predict correctly even if the actual level or rate of growth of personal sector income is very different in the future from that observed in the period over which the relationship was estimated. If the claim is not justified then there is no reason to expect stability in the relationship when circumstances change. In other words the models have a theoretical basis which should mean they explain the behaviour of the past and do not merely describe it.

This claim has been challenged, especially by neo-classical economists, but also more widely by economists in the tradition of microeconomics rather than macroeconomics. The expression used, as a term of abuse, is *ad hoc*. A model is *ad hoc* if the theory which it embodies is no more than a rationalisation of behaviour observed in the data it seeks to explain. As such it is little, if at all, better than a description of the data; real understanding, it is claimed, requires a secure basis in independent reasoning or observation. Few modelbuilders would claim that all the relationships in their models are unscathed by this line of attack.

There is room for plenty of disagreement, however, as to what constitutes independent reasoning or observation in this context.

Most economic theory, perhaps all pure theory in economics, is derived from the assumption of rationality in economic behaviour. It involves a process of deduction about the way a rational agent ought to act in pursuit of consistent aims in changing circumstances. Macro-economic models have been criticised because they are not always based on an explicit process of optimisation of this kind; they do not go back to first principles, but tend rather to take it for granted that regularities of behaviour will persist simply because they have been observed consistently for some time. To take just one example, a model may indicate that export prices normally remain unchanged in terms of the exporter's currency when the exchange rate changes. This may be an accurate description of the period of observation on which the model is based, but that may not be good enough for forecasting or for a real understanding of how the economy works. We need also to ask why exporters have set their prices this way in the past; if there is simply a convention that this is the way trade is conducted, we must ask why that particular convention has become established. Only then, it is argued, will one know what will happen if the exchange rate changes in some entirely new way, rising rapidly for example after a long period of slow decline.

There is no doubt that some modelbuilders, and some less expert users of models, have tended in the past to treat the economy as more mechanical than it is, to assume that the conventions or 'rules of thumb' established for a decade or two will last for ever. But the nature of the lessons to be learnt, apart from the need for humility, is more debatable. It may be true that behaviour has in fact been governed by conventions rather than by decisions taken continuously by a totally rational process, with all agents free to work out their optimum strategy, making a fresh start each day. If so, then we must be grateful to economic theory for warning us that these conventions are likely to change and sometimes even telling us a little about how they may change. But we will gain nothing at all from turning back to the data and trying to estimate the relationships of our model as if the conventions had not held in the past. The best we can hope for is a model of the past which embodies the rules of behaviour which agents had in mind at the time. That is all that the data can provide. But the critics are right to say that this on its own is not enough; it should be complemented by an account of the reasons for those rules of behaviour based on a process of deduction (allied to introspection) because without that there is no way of telling how robust the relationship will be.

The debate over rational expectations is just one aspect of this wider issue about the treatment of conventions and rules of behaviour. In retrospect that debate seems to have been concerned with two very different propositions. The first, the strong proposition, is that agents in the past have behaved as if they already knew the structure, and even the parameters, of the models now being built to describe their behaviour. It is surprising how seriously this view has been put forward. It seems to imply that the public has access to quantified knowledge of the economy, free of all systematic bias, which is not available to professional economists.

The second, or weaker, proposition is that the public use the information available to them in a logical and consistent way when they attempt to forecast, learning from their mistakes as they go along. This proposition is a special case of the general appeal to rationality, which is, as we have said, the ultimate basis of all economic theory. Its practical use to the modelbuilder is not immediately obvious. We know, from experience, that the logical and consistent application of knowledge to economic forecasting is a hazardous business and that it takes years, if not decades, to learn from one's own mistakes.

A possible outcome from the debate over expectations may be a much wider use by modelbuilders of the direct evidence about expectations. In this country there are now several forecasting organisations (the National Institute is one) which have been producing forecasts for many years. The general public may not always accept these forecasts at face value, but they do have some influence and may also be in some sense representative of the expectations held by the public at large. We also have long data series for expectations and plans reported by firms to the Confederation of British Industry (CBI), which may be adapted to the needs of macroeconomic modelbuilding. Such direct information may be used to study the effect of information on expectations and also to study the effects of expectations on behaviour. This in turn may lead to a deeper understanding than can be achieved by looking at the effects of information on behaviour, without considering the intermediate stage of forming expectations.

Economic modelbuilding needs a sound theoretical structure because it is necessarily based on a relatively short run of empirical data. When the results of a research project are presented it may appear that only a small proportion of the statistical degrees of freedom available for the investigation has been used. However, the final equation is often selected after the examination of scores, or even hundreds, of rather similar alternatives. This search is commonly, but perjoratively, described as 'data-mining'. There can be little doubt that the apparent precision of many of the equations in macroeconomic models owes a great deal to the patience of researchers (and the speed of computers) rather than the rich information actually contained in the data available to them. If one goes on looking long enough one is almost bound to find something which fits the data well; but unfortunately that does not guarantee that one has at last discovered the model which explains how the data were generated. The test comes when new data are generated which were not available when the model was selected and which can be compared with the prediction of the estimated equation. The great strength of model-building, and the basis for its claim to be a science rather than an art, is the straightforward way in which it is continually exposed to falsi-fication — even though the time taken to establish that conclusion may often be lengthy.

Whilst data-mining is a constant source of unreliable equations, it would be wrong to suggest that a data-miner with sufficient diligence will always find evidence to confirm his presuppositions. It may be a fact that monetarist or Keynesian researchers, for example, are statisti-cally more likely to find (or to report) monetarism or Keynesianism respectively in the data, but it is also a fact that keen and competent researchers, who have spent years in search of confirmation for their theoretical presuppositions, have sought in vain. No-one, for example, has found clear evidence of a substantial effect of real interest rates on industrial investment in this country, although many have looked for one. No-one has yet shown investment to have a measurable effect on productivity, although almost everyone expects the effect to be there. Many researchers approach the trade statistics expecting to find that substitution is easy between manufactures produced in different countries, yet the estimated elasticities remain obstinately low. The market for government securities seems to confound all attempts at quantified explanation. These failures, although regrettable, are never-theless reassuring, because they demonstrate that the process of model selection is not overwhelmingly weighted in favour of the preconceptions with which the researcher approached his task.

This contrast enhances the interest of the successes which can also be reported. Perhaps one indication of the success of modelbuilding is the fact that many of the specifications that were adopted by the pioneers in the late 1950s still seem appropriate today. It is rather striking that one can look back to the first quarterly model of the United Kingdom economy[3] estimated by Klein, Ball, Hazlewood and Vandome, using data for the period 1948 to 1956, and find there a basic structure not unlike that of the models now used by their successors in such places as Cambridge, the London Business School, the Treasury, the Bank of England, and the National Institute. The treatment of the consumption functions, the trade equations, the determination of prices, of un-employment, all show a high degree of stability and continuity from one generation of models to another. But this is alongside a record of relative uncertainty and instability associated with some other relationships such as those determining fixed investment, stockbuilding, interest rates and now the exchange rate.

Another way of assessing the success of modelbuilding in general is to look at the accuracy of the forecasts that have been made with the aid of models.[4] Some groups, including the National Institute, have been producing forecasts now for many years, using broadly the same methodology. The consensus view seems to be that forecasts using structural models have done better than could be expected on the basis of good luck alone, whilst nevertheless not achieving the precision required for fine tuning of the economy. It is a more open question to what extent that limited success has been the result of the judgemental adjustments made to model forecasts by all professional forecasters and to what extent it reflects the parameter estimates of the models that have been used.

Post-mortem analysis of forecasting errors suggests, for this country, that an average absolute error in total output a year ahead would be about 1 to 1½ per cent. Thanks to some major unexpected events, especially two dramatic increases in the world price of oil, the size of those average errors seems, if anything, to have increased in the 1970s. Forecasts more than a year ahead would generally be less accurate. Modelbuilders cannot claim to have a full understanding of fluctuations in economic activity; room must always be left for a multitude of unique and random events of a kind which models do not try to explain and also for shifts in the relationships which capture such knowledge as we have. The aim of modelbuilding cannot be, and never has been, to devise a machine which will deliver a forecast free from error. The aim is to understand the systematic relationships which influence employment, output and inflation consistently over the years. The forecasting record suggests that some progress has been made towards that aim.

Employment, output and inflation

Many of the macroeconomic models in regular use for forecasting and policy analysis share the same theoretical structure. There are important differences between these models in their treatment of certain relationships, in their size and in the aspects of the economy on which they concentrate most attention (and in the policy conclusions their progenitors draw from them). A few models adopt a fundamentally different structure throughout.[5] Nevertheless, it is the similarities rather than the differences which are more striking. The common theoretical structure derives from Keynes; but it would be wrong to credit Keynes with all the insights it contains, or to blame him for its limitations. In this section some of the common features of these models will be described; where they are particularly controversial some supporting evidence or theoretical explanation will be attempted.

Most macroeconomic models are designed on the assumption that expenditure plans of all agents are realised (except to the extent that lags in expenditure equations may reflect normal supply limitations). The cyclical fluctuations in the level of economic activity are interpreted as fluctuations in demand for goods and services, not in supply. Supply is treated as passive in response to these fluctuations, producers are assumed to make what they expect to sell. They do not adjust their selling price continuously in such a way as to keep supply and demand in line over the cycle; on the contrary they price largely on the basis of a fixed mark-up on costs. This structure must be contrasted with new or neo-classical models in which it is assumed that market equilibrium is maintained continuously by an adjustment of prices.

The supporting evidence for the disequilibrium approach to cyclical fluctuations is not confined to the work of the modelbuilders themselves. Casual observation shows procyclical movements, closely matching those of output, in such indicators as orders on hand, capacity utilisation, vacancies and the proportion of firms experiencing shortages of skilled labour or raw materials. Profit margins relative to trend costs show little change in response to cyclical fluctuations, although it is possible that they are reduced by a fall in demand which is expected to be permanent. There are, of course, exceptions: in the markets for food and raw materials, prices are much more flexible and an assumption of continuing equilibrium would be much more appropriate. Theoretical models do exist to explain the relative rigidity of margins in most industrial and service sectors. For example, where there is monopoly, oligopoly or merely imperfect competition, the extra sales to be won by price cutting may not justify the loss of margin per unit.[6] If the change in demand is believed to be temporary and the response to price believed to be slow, the interests of the individual firm may best be served by an inflexible pricing rule. Producers seem to prefer price stability if it is attainable, even when the consequence must be some instability in volume of production; where prices are sensitive to market forces, their instability seems to be resented by producers.

Two points are worth emphasis. First, a structure which does not assume continuous market clearing may nevertheless be consistent with agents behaving rationally. Second, the pricing behaviour we observe may reflect conventions appropriate to the kind of fluctuations in demand typical of the 1960s and 1970s. Those conventions would not necessarily hold if the amplitude and frequency of these fluctuations changed.

The centrepiece of the earliest models was the consumption function. Subject to many qualifications, the theory is that spending depends on the flow of income instead of, or as well as, the stock of wealth. Some models treat company expenditure on investment, dividends or even stocks in much the same way, relating them to profits or cash flow. Such behaviour would not be entirely logical in a household or firm which had access to credit, or accumulated savings. If readily available cash is no problem, current spending will relate to current income only to the extent that current income is regarded as a good guide to 'permanent' income or wealth. Before dismissing cash flow effects as illogical, however, one must reflect that there may be good reasons why credit is limited to most individuals and why many households, at some period of their lives, hold very small balances of financial assets.

Modelbuilders have never had any difficulty in establishing a relationship between cash flow and spending. This is certainly true of consumption and, to a lesser extent, of investment also. Other influences on expenditure are less easy to identify. Theory would suggest that both consumption and investment might be sensitive to changes in the level of interest rates (or better, of real interest rates). The evidence on this point is far from conclusive. If anything akin to market-clearing is to occur for aggregate goods and services, even in the long run, then expenditure decisions must respond (directly or indirectly) to the price level. When models in the Keynesian tradition were first estimated, such effects were totally absent and the level of output was determined solely by demand, even in the long run. More recent work has identified an effect of prices on consumer spending. Nevertheless, the concept of a market equilibrium for the economy as a whole is not very securely grounded in the experience of recent economic behaviour and it is not necessarily the most useful way of describing the properties of macroeconomic models. These points are well illustrated by the simulations of the National Institute model in the final chapter of this book.

In most models the level of employment is determined by demand, which fluctuates in response to the cyclical movements in output. The evidence against continuous equilibrium in labour markets includes the procyclical movement of vacancies, skill shortages, and overtime working as well as the anticyclical movement of unemployment. The movements in the real hourly wage rate are not easy to interpret and are confused by the effects of successive phases of incomes policy but, on balance, the evidence now seems to point to some increase in real wages when the pressure of demand in labour markets is high. One cannot be more confident than that on this crucial issue in the present state of knowledge.

A partial explanation of the sluggishness of real wages may be available in terms of market structure. Unions, like firms, prefer stability and seem most reluctant to accept that lowering their wage claims may result in better employment prospects for their members in the foreseeable future. The existence of social security benefits, which provide a floor to real wages, is another factor which limits the flexibility of the labour market. From the firm's point of view also, stability of wages may have its attractions as the process of changing wages involves a protracted and sometimes costly process of collective bargaining. In other contexts economists may conclude that the process of wage (or price) setting needs reform to make it more flexible; but for the model-builder the relevant fact is that the process has been, and remains, relatively inflexible and that is therefore the system he must model.

In most models employment is treated as a consequence of output, since output determines the demand for labour. Attempts to elaborate on this by allowing for the influence of fixed capital, or relative factor prices, have not produced clear-cut results. The case is not proven, despite its theoretical plausibility, that an increase in real wages will lead employers to substitute capital for labour. It is true, nevertheless, of many models that higher real wages mean less employment in the long run, if not the short. The argument is that employers will pass their labour costs on to consumers, at home or abroad, who will then buy cheaper goods produced elsewhere. That in turn will reduce output and hence reduce employment. The mechanism is rather slow acting but in some models it seems very powerful.

Modelling the labour market is also a necessary step in explaining inflation. Many of the early models treated the growth of earnings as exogenous and prices as a fixed mark-up on costs. Since exchange rates in those days were fixed, this meant that the models had little or nothing to contribute to the understanding of inflation, which was to become one of the most serious of the problems that beset this country, and others, in the 1970s. More recently, it seems that some advance has been made in explaining the growth of earnings and relating it to the pressure of demand for labour. It should still be recognised, however, that our understanding of the determinants of the inflation rate is not nearly as securely based as our understanding of short-term movements in output and employment.

The other main link between output and inflation in an open economy is through the balance of trade and the exchange rate. The trade equations in most models are specified, like the expenditure equations, to emphasise demand rather than supply. An alternative view, which would be as appropriate to a small open economy and perhaps of relevance to the British case, would regard trade as tending to equilibrate supply and demand for tradeable goods in the domestic market. In that case one might explain an increasing trend in imports by a low level of profit or investment in domestic industry. As trade is currently modelled such factors are taken into account only to the extent that they are reflected in the relative price of home and overseas production. The elasticities of substitution as estimated tend to be rather low.

Over the past ten years attention has shifted from the detailed modelling of the current account of the balance of payments to an attempt to explain capital flows and the exchange rate. Here we have to deal with a very different kind of market structure and a different set of problems with specification and with data. The data problems arise because the measurement of capital account transactions is so incomplete and inaccurate, and because only data for the last decade are relevant, that is, since the formal abandonment of fixed exchange rates in 1972. This is a relatively new area of modelling and it is to be hoped, therefore, that a better understanding will come with experience. For the United States economy this uncertainty may be an inconvenience; for the United Kingdom it is a more serious worry and should be taken as an important qualification to all forecasts and simulations in which the exchange rate is treated as floating freely.

The National Institute model, like many others in the same tradition, does not look to movements in the monetary aggregates to provide an explanation of inflation. As originally conceived, macroeconomic models took little or no account explicitly of financial or monetary relationships at all. This position was once thought defensible, and might still be defended by some economists. The argument would be that saving and borrowing decisions are the necessary obverse of spending decisions, and that an adequate model of spending must imply an adequate model of its financial implications. The main weakness of this defence of the neglect of finance is that the composition of the financial assets and liabilities may influence future spending decisions. A joint decision may be needed involving at least two choices amongst three or more possible uses of income and wealth: for example, to spend, to invest long term, or to stay liquid. There seems little reason in theory why any one decision should be taken independently of the others.

Most models now contain financial or monetary sectors of some complexity. Typically, these relate to the private sector as a whole and therefore net out many familiar transactions, such as household investment in equities or pension funds, in the process of aggregation. The emphasis is rather on transactions in public sector debt, bank lending and bank deposits. This means they can form some kind of bridge between forecasts of income and expenditure on the one hand and forecasts or assumptions about monetary aggregates on the other. In the United Kingdom the emphasis in the 1970s was on the link with £M3, the target variable adopted by the monetary authorities.

The addition of a financial or monetary sector does not make a model any more or less monetarist in its theoretical structure. In many macroeconomic models the monetary aggregates have no behavioural role to play at all, they are strictly 'output only', at a dead-end in the flow chart. Some models do allow for a feedback from a monetary aggregate to expectations, for example in the exchange rate equation. Such a device recognises the fact that many people did take monetary aggregates very seriously for part at least of the period of estimation; it does not mean they were right to do so, except in the limited sense that incorrect views can be self-fulfilling for some time.[7] Other models do give real behavioural significance to monetary aggregates by including them in the equations which describe spending decisions.[8] But as the difficulties of measuring any monetary aggregate consistently over time are recognised, this practice seems likely to decrease.

There remains, therefore, some uncertainty about the role which monetary modelling is to play in the overall structure of macroeconomic models. There is little point in devoting a great deal of effort to this difficult area unless the results have a significant effect on the properties of the system as a whole. That effort will be rewarded in this way only if parallel work on the determination of expenditure shows that financial variables are important to those relationships. Once that has been established the motivation for financial modelling will be much clearer. It will also be clearer which aggregates have real significance for forecasting and policy analysis.

It should be added that the work carried out, although imaginative and painstaking, has not been very successful in its own terms. The demand for public sector debt remains very difficult indeed to predict in any formal way, perhaps because here, as in the foreign exchange market, speculation is an essential element. Models of bank lending have been little more successful, perhaps because of the frequent changes in control methods adopted by the monetary authorities.

The addition of a monetary sector means that it is possible computationally to solve the whole model for fixed values of a monetary aggregate and then report the results of forecasts and simulations as being a description of the consequences for the economy as a whole of following a given monetary rule. The wish to perform such calculations is indeed one reason why monetary sectors were developed. But strictly all that these calculations can show is the effects of *trying* to hit monetary targets, since the authorities do not have any means of controlling the aggregates at all precisely. If, nevertheless, it is decided to treat the money supply as if it were an exogenous variable, the models can be used to simulate the effects of a change in the money supply and trace through its effects on output and prices. Such experiments have been carried out to see how significant in practice are the differences between the views embodied in Keynesian models and those held by empirical monetarists on the basis of direct observation of movements in money and prices.

The answers to that question are not easy to interpret, especially as the simulation results are very different when different means are used for bringing about the change in the money supply; if fiscal policy is involved the effects tend to be larger than if interest rates are used. In general the answer seems to be that the models contain no mechanism which will cause prices to respond rapidly when policy is changed and that the effect on output is proportionately large and long-lived. Some monetarists expect a more rapid response of prices and a more limited and transient effect on output. Insofar as the recent history of both the United Kingdom and the United States provides a fair test, the evidence is currently favouring non-monetarist structural models on this important point.

The National Institute model

The model described in this book is the one brought into use at the Institute for forecasting and policy simulation in the first half of 1983. (It is referred to as Model Six in the Institute's series.) Its introduction followed a comprehensive programme of re-estimation over the preceding year, which had resulted in significant changes in the way that some of the relationships were specified. The chapters in this book describe not only the specification that was finally chosen but also some of the experiments which were conducted in the course of re-estimation. Many of these are of interest in their own right and an account of the work done indicates rather well the range of methodological and empirical problems which concern modelbuilders at the present time.

The criteria that have been used to select equations for the model reflect its various uses. The model is continually being subjected to test by its use to produce forecasts. This means that the equations we select must fit the data well, especially perhaps the data for the recent past. Our aim is to have a model which can be used in the preparation of forecasts for publication without a great deal of residual adjustment or tuning. At the time of writing, most of the relationships reported here do have that desirable property, even in some hazardous areas like earnings or the exchange rate.

A good fit over the estimation period on its own does not give grounds for confidence. We also look at the stability of the relationships over time. We prefer them to have a convincing basis in economic theory, since only then is there reason to believe that they will perform well in circumstances different to those of the estimation period. It is important that the model as a whole should give a coherent and convincing account of the way that the economy would behave in response to policy changes. That is one reason for carrying out a variety of simulations of the kind reported in the second part of this book.

Certain features of the model distinguish it from its predecessors and from close relations to be found in other centres of modelbuilding in this country. Consumer spending in our model responds moderately strongly to a change in the rate of inflation. This property seems to fit well with recent experience. For stockbuilding, we believe we have identified some powerful effects from the availability or cost of finance to companies, although the equations currently in the model do show an asymmetry between manufacturers' and distributors' stocks in this respect. We interpret the behaviour of exports and imports as consistent with a response to price competitiveness that is relatively weak, but also relatively rapid. The new equation for wage inflation suggests that there is a considerable response, both to the level and to the rate of unemployment. Clearly this finding is in line with recent experience, although its stability may be questioned given the difficulty of applying a common explanation to wages over an estimation period which includes many phases of incomes policy. Similar difficulties arise in estimating an exchange rate equation, given the many changes that there have been in the rules governing monetary policy. Nevertheless, we have an exchange rate equation which gives a reasonably coherent account of the dramatic rise and subsequent weakness of sterling since the late 1970s. Together, these two equations largely determine the extent to which the model predicts that inflation, as well as output, will be reduced as a consequence of fiscal deflation. Typically, the simulations reported in this book suggest that the costs, in terms of lost output and employment, of reducing inflation by these means are heavy and prolonged. This does not seem to conflict at all with recent experience although the precise numbers involved must remain extremely uncertain.

Conclusion

A practitioner may not be the best person to offer a detached summing up. If, nevertheless, I were to attempt this task, I would conclude that macroeconomic modelbuilding is in good heart and sound health.

As a means of understanding or forecasting short-term fluctuations in employment and output, it has emerged from the tests of the last decade substantially vindicated. Increasingly, progress is being made also in understanding short-term movements in the rate of inflation. In their present form, however, the models do not explain many of the longer-term trends in the economy, the slower growth of output in the 1970s for example. Slower-moving developments are necessarily more difficult to explain by time-series analysis. As the passage of time produces longer runs of data the explanatory power of models should increase.

The empirical basis of macroeconomic models needs to be supported by theoretical reasoning. As the microeconomic foundations of the subject are explored, it could be that a more constructive exchange may develop with the neo-classicists who are now becoming increasingly interested in the empirical exceptions to their presumption of market equilibrium and rapid adjustment.

These themes, and above all the continuing fascination of research in applied macroeconomics, are, I believe, well illustrated in the chapters which follow.

Notes

[1] For a brief account of the pre-history of modelbuilding see, Samuelson, P. A., 'The art and science of macromodels over 50 years' in Fromm, G. and Klein, L. R. (eds), *The Brookings Model: Perspective and Recent Development*, London, North Holland, 1975.

[2] The literature on the subject has also proliferated rapidly. For accounts of some leading United States models see, Fair, R. C., *A Short-run Forecasting Model of the US Economy*, Lexington, Mass, D.C. Heath & Co., 1971; Hickman, B. G. and Coen, R. M., *An Annual Growth Model of the US Economy*, Amsterdam, North Holland, 1976; Fromm and Klein, (eds), *The Brookings Model: Perspective and Recent Developments, op. cit.; Intriligator*, M.D., *Econometric Models, Techniques and Applications*, Amsterdam, North Holland, 1978; Klein, L. R. and Young, R. M., *An Introduction to Econometric Forecasting and Forecasting Models*, Lexington, Mass, Lexington Books, 1980; Cooper, J. P., *Development of the Monetary Sector, Prediction and Policy Analysis in the FRB – MIT – Penn Model*, Lexington, Mass, Lexington Books, 1974. For the United Kingdom see, Renton, G. A. (ed), *Modelling the Economy*, London, Heinemann, 1975; Hilton and Heath-field (eds), *The Econometric Study of the United Kingdom*, London, Macmillan, 1970; Pearce, I. F., Trivedi, P. K., Strombuck, C. T. and Anderson, G. J., *A model of output, employment, wages and prices in the UK*, Cambridge University Press, 1976; Surrey, M. J. C. (ed), *The Analysis and Forecasting of the British Economy*, Cambridge University Press, 1971; Barker, T. S. (ed), *Economic structure and policy with applications to the British economy*, London, Chapman and Hall, 1976; HM Treasury, *Macroeconomic Model Technical Manual 1982;* Holden, K., Peel, D. A. and Thompson, J. L., *Modelling the UK Economy, an Introduction*, Oxford, Martin Robertson, 1982; Arestis, P. and Hadjimatheou, G., *Introducing Macroeconomic Modelling, An Econometric Study of the UK*, London, Macmillan, 1982; Ormerod, P. (ed), *Economic Modelling, Current issues and problems in macroeconomic modelling in the UK and US*, London, Heinemann Educational Books, 1979.

[3] See Klein, L. R., Ball, R. J., Hazlewood, A. and Vandome, P., *An Econometric Model of the UK*, Oxford, Basil Blackwell, 1961.

[4]For assessments of the accuracy of forecasts see, Ash and Smyth, *Forecasting the UK Economy,* Lexington, Mass, Lexington Books, 1973; Zarnowitz, V., *An Appraisal of Short-term Economic Forecasts,* National Bureau of Economic Research, 1976; Spivey, W. and Wrobleski, W., *Econometric Model Performance in Forecasting and Policy Assessment,* Washington, D.C., American Enterprise Institute, 1979; McNees, S. K., 'The accuracy of macroeconometric models and forecasts of the US economy' in Ormerod, P. (ed), *Economic Modelling, op. cit.;* Britton, A. and Campbell, A., *Treasury Forecasts, Outturns and Policy Adjustments,* Government Economic Service, 1982; Osborn, D. R. and Teal, F., 'An assessment and comparison of the NIESR econometric forecasts', *National Institute Economic Review,* no. 88, May 1979; Chow, G. C. and Corsi, Paolo (eds), *Evaluating the Reliability of Macroeconomic Models,* Chichester, J. Wiley, 1982; Savage, D., 'The assessment of the National Institute's forecasts of GDP, 1959–82', *National Institute Economic Review,* no. 105, August 1983. Estimates of average errors are given with all forecasts published by the Treasury. An account of the methodology used will be found in the *Economic Progress Report,* June 1982.

[5]For the purpose of this chapter the Treasury model, the Bank of England model, the LBS model, the two Cambridge models and the National Institute model described in this book are all in the mainstream. The Liverpool model is not.

[6]See, especially, Okun, A. M., *Prices and Quantities: A Macroeconomic Analysis,* Washington, D.C., Brookings Institute, 1981.

[7]This is the position in the Treasury model (1982).

[8]This is true of the current National Institute model, since £$M3$ is used in the derivation of personal sector liquidity, which is an influence on consumption.

PART ONE: MODELBUILDING

1 Consumer Spending
K. Cuthbertson

The consumption function has been examined theoretically and empirically more, perhaps, than any other macroeconomic aggregate. Prior to the 1970s, consumption was thought to be a rather stable and predictable variable but in the high inflationary period of the 1970s existing equations failed to predict consumption accurately as the saving ratio rose rapidly (chart 1.1).

Chart 1.1   Saving, income and inflation

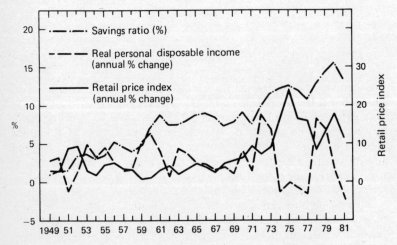

Source: Economic Trends, CSO Monthly Digest of Statistics.

This chapter begins with a discussion of the theory of consumption, emphasising the role of liquidity and inflation; this is followed by a brief review of some recent empirical work. The National Institute equations for non-durable and durable consumption are then described.

Theories of consumption

Saving is the difference between current disposable income and current consumption: for any given level of income the decision to consume more is also a decision to save less. Consumption decisions are, therefore, inextricably bound up with decisions about the level of financial or real assets or the level of liabilities. Decisions about savings can also be seen as decisions about the allocation of consumption over time.

According to the life cycle hypothesis of saving (LCH) the individual is assumed to maximise a utility function which depends upon all current and future consumption, subject to a lifetime budget constraint (which equates discounted expected labour income $_tY^e_{t+i}$ plus initial wealth W to discounted future consumption). With suitable restrictions on the utility function (for example, an additive homothetic function) and assuming a perfect capital market, constancy in the real interest and pure time preference rates, one obtains the result that desired consumption C^* is proportional to lifetime resources R. The constant of proportionality k is independent of the level of resources but depends on the parameters of the utility function (that is, tastes), the rate of time preference p, the real interest rate r and the remaining lifespan of the individual L:

$$C^*_t = k(r, p, L)R_t \tag{1}$$

where

$$R_t = Y_t + \Sigma^L_{t+} \, _tY^e_{t+i}/(1+r)^{i-t} + W_{-1} \tag{2}$$

The behaviour suggested by the permanent income hypothesis is very similar but it is expressed in terms of permanent income, which includes both expected future labour income and the return on wealth and which can be seen as an annuity of value equivalent to R_t. The LCH and the permanent income hypothesis focus attention on expected future income and on wealth. Changes in current income affect consumption only to the extent that they lead to (or are associated with) changes in expected income over the lifetime as a whole.

In principle one can use an auxiliary equation to generate estimates of expected future income. This series may then be used as an independent variable in the consumption function, or alternatively, we may include variables that determine expected income in the function directly. However, Hall [14] has shown that if permanent income is generated according to the rational expectations hypothesis then the LCH predicts that lagged consumption will reflect permanent income more accurately than an extrapolation of past income levels. Thus, in the absence of adjustment costs, no other variables dated at $t-1$ or earlier, other than lagged consumption, should influence current consumption and only the unanticipated or surprise component of current income should affect consumption. These striking conclusions from the RE-LCH are in sharp contrast with existing consumption relations including those in the National Institute model. Tests of the RE-LCH consist of a regression of consumption on lagged consumption and an additional set of other lagged variables. If the latter are statistically significant this is taken as evidence against the hypothesis. An additional refinement is to include surprises in current income as measured by the residuals from an auxiliary regression with current income as the dependent variable. Muellbauer [18] finds that support for the RE-LCH on United Kingdom data is far from conclusive.

These theories do not take account of risk and they assume perfect capital markets (that is, no borrowing constraints, equal lending and borrowing rates and zero transactions costs). Thus, in principle, one pound's worth of additional income received today has the same effect on consumption as an increase of one pound in the value of (discounted) future income, as one extra pound added to holdings of liquid assets or to the value of a house, or the reduction of one pound in the stock of consumer debt: casual observation suggests that such restrictions are unrealistic.

Yaari [24] has investigated the implications of the LCH when there is uncertainty as to the time of death together with a competitive insurance-annuity scheme. Nagatani [19] considers uncertainty in income expectations and finds that consumption is not independent of the time profile of income. Hey [16] provides a useful summary of the consumption-saving choice when future income and interest rates are subject to uncertainty. However, in general, these extensions do not produce tractable estimating equations or unambiguous *a priori* results and we do not discuss these formal models of uncertainty further. Precautionary saving may nevertheless be important and the use of less formal models may be preferable to ignoring the problem altogether. Uncertainty surrounding *future* real income prospects may depend on such factors as the uncertainty about the rate of inflation (which might be proxied by the actual rate of inflation) and the probability of becoming unemployed (which may be proxied by recent changes in unemployment).

Liquidity

In the simplest form of the LCH there is no role for liquidity, since all assets can be bought and sold at zero cost. In the real world there are market imperfections which include transactions costs, uncertainty and disequilibrium. Pissarides [20] extends the model of Flemming [11] and deals with the first of these. He incorporates transactions costs into the life cycle model by assuming that the borrowing rate exceeds the lending rate and that there is a fixed transactions cost attached to moving out of illiquid long-term assets prior to maturity. The high borrowing rate could be described as the cost of moving out of illiquid human wealth.

The utility of lifetime consumption is maximised subject to a lifetime budget constraint which now includes borrowing and lending rates and transactions costs. The latter variables enter the determination of optimal consumption but in a very complex way. Two general and important qualitative results follow. First, the value of an individual's lifetime resources is a highly subjective quantity, being determined not only by the time profile of the income stream, but also by the asset market structure. This casts doubt on the usefulness of the various market measures of wealth used in empirical work. Secondly, an unexpected fall in current income, even if it is believed to be merely transitory, will lower the consumption to wealth ratio if liquid assets are insufficient to cover the whole of the fall in income. For that reason, it is probably better to use current income and a measure of liquidity such as the liquid assets to income ratio, rather than wealth, as independent variables in the consumption function.

Inflation

In the simplest form of LCH expected inflation may influence consumption, for example through its effect on the expected real interest rate, but the direction of this effect is indeterminate *a priori*. Theories of asset demands suggest that a higher stock of consumer *durables* will be held as their relative yield, including appreciation, increases. We might, therefore, expect a positive relationship between the durables stock (and hence replacement purchases) and the expected rate of inflation, if nominal interest rates are not expected to reflect inflation in full.

Inflation may also influence consumption, particularly in the short run, because consumers use simple (but non-optimal) rules for generating estimates of their permanent income. For example, if individuals have accurate information on past incomes but poor information on past prices, they may (in effect) estimate (the log of) their real permanent income, y_t^p, by deflating past nominal income by the current period price index $y_t^p = a(y_t' - p_t) + b(y_{t-1}' - p_t)$ where y' is the log of nominal income and p_t is the log of the price level. Using $p_t \cong g_p + p_{-1}$ (where g_p = quarterly rate of inflation) we obtain $y_t^p = ay_t + by_{t-1} - bg_p$ where $y_{t-1} = y_{t-1}' - p_{t-1}$ is real income as conventionally measured. Hence estimated permanent income and therefore actual consumption depends negatively on the rate of inflation.

Bulkley [3] argues that fixed contract periods for wage increases, even under perfectly anticipated inflation, result in the saving ratio depending upon the *acceleration* in inflation. For example, an annual wage contract period implies that real wages are gradually eroded over the year and to smooth out consumption the individual must save relatively more in the early part of the year than he would have needed to had his weekly real income been constant over the year. Aggregation over individuals with staggered contracts yields no additional saving when inflation is constant but, when (anticipated) inflation is increasing, the extra saving by those who have recently gained wage awards will more than offset the reduction in saving of those nearing the end of their nominal wage contract.

Deaton's [10] rational money illusion hypothesis is based on the assumption that the consumer has inadequate information on *relative* prices, especially in inflationary periods. Correctly perceived relative prices affect the allocation of total consumers' expenditure between alternative goods but not the total itself. The consumer purchases goods sequentially and has imperfect knowledge of their relative prices. If the actual price level p_t exceeds the expected price level, $_{t-1}p_t^e$, then the consumer may forego the purchase of, say, a transistor radio because it seems expensive relative to other goods. Thus, an unanticipated increase in the price *level* $p_t - {}_{t-1}p_t^e$ leads to lower consumption. But $(p_t - {}_{t-1}p_t^e) = (p_t - p_{-1}) - ({}_{t-1}p_t^e - p_{-1}) = (\dot{p}_t - {}_{t-1}\dot{p}_t^e)$ and therefore an *unanticipated* increase in *inflation* also reduces consumption. Deaton's is a disequilibrium hypothesis and may, therefore, augment any equilibrium theory, for example, the life cycle hypothesis.

In Hendry and von Ungern Sternberg (HVUS) [15] inflation is introduced into the analysis by assuming that the individual measures his disposable income net of any losses on money-fixed assets (and these are taken to be net liquid assets). The income variable used is thus $Y_t^* = (Y_t - \dot{p}LA_{t-1})$ where Y is real personal disposable income as conventionally measured and LA is the stock of real net liquid assets. The consumption function is of the form

$$\Delta_1 C_t = \theta_0 + \theta_1 \Delta_1 Y_t^* + \theta_2(C_{t-1} - Y_{t-1}^*) + \theta_3(LA_{t-1} - Y_{t-1}^*) \quad (3)$$

which, in a steady-state equilibrium, results in the ratio of consumption to adjusted income depending on the liquid assets to adjusted income ratio and therefore on the rate of inflation.

Some recent empirical work
In the context of the LCH, Deaton [9] finds evidence that the total of net financial wealth has an influence on consumer spending. Thomas [21], on the other hand, finds little evidence of effects from illiquid

assets, but his study does support the inclusion of liquid assets in the consumption function. One reason for the difficulty of establishing a simple relationship between consumption and total wealth may be the existence of state and occupational pension schemes (see, for example, Green [13] and Threadgold [22]).

Considerable attention has been devoted to the dynamics of consumption functions and the form of the lagged response of spending to income. The use of adaptive expectations and simple partial adjustment in earlier studies has been shown by Davidson *et al* [7] to be over-restrictive and they suggest the use of an error correction model where the change in consumption responds to the change in income and previous errors in the (cumulative) consumption—income ratio. Davidson *et al* and also Bean [2] find evidence that both the rate of change and the acceleration of prices influence spending. This is interpreted by Bean as the consequence of an inflation loss on 'money fixed' assets. Bean, also finds that precautionary saving may be related to the change in unemployment. Other empirical work surveyed in Cuthbertson [6] and Davies [8] provides an econometric evaluation of the main United Kingdom consumption functions for non-durables expenditure.

Non-durable consumption in the National Institute model (*see Appendix (1.1)*)

After some preliminary experimentation, we followed the approach of Hendry and von Ungern Sternberg (see above) and incorporated into the definition of income an estimate of the inflation loss accruing to holders of liquid assets. Hendry and von Ungern Sternberg use an inflation adjusted income variable in which a fraction b of the inflation loss on liquid assets is deducted from measured real personal disposable income, Y. The value of b is estimated iteratively. Use of the variable $Y^* = (Y - b\dot{p}L)$ (where $\dot{p}$ is the rate of inflation and L is the stock of liquid assets) and its lagged values, implies that the responses of expenditure to a change in RPDI and in the inflation loss on liquid assets have similar time profiles. This seemed unduly restrictive and, in the National Institute equation, the inflation loss was included as a separate variable with the *a priori* presumption that the response of consumers' expenditure to a change in income would have a shorter time lag than that arising from a change in the inflation loss on liquid assets.

HVUS also consider that consumers have a constant desired liquid assets to *inflation adjusted* income ratio (that is, $L/Y^* = k$) and *disequilibrium* in this ratio leads to changes in consumption. The National Institute equation, as first estimated, also included terms in a liquid assets to income ratio but these were found to be statistically insignificant, as were *changes* in real liquid assets. Neither we nor HVUS consider additional variables, such as interest rates, as determinants of desired liquid assets.

The unrestricted equation which we estimated was of the form $\ln C = a_0 + \Sigma_1^4 a_j \ln C_{-j} + \Sigma_0^4 b_j \ln Y_{-j} + \Sigma_1^3 c_j \ln IL_{-j} + \Sigma_0^5 d_j (\Delta_4 \ln P_j/4)(L_{-j}/Y_{-j}) +$ three seasonal dummies + two budget dummies. After experimentation using seasonally unadjusted data[1] the best equation was re-run on adjusted data to give

$$\Delta_4 \ln C = -0.088 \ln(C/Y)_{-4} + 0.46 \Delta_4 \ln Y + -0.072 IL \qquad (4)$$
$$\quad (5.2) \qquad\qquad (13.9) \qquad\qquad (3.4)$$

$6501 - 8103$, $\bar{R}^2 = 0.75$, $SEE = 0.010$, $DW = 1.9$, $CHI(8) = 13.1$, $LM(4) = 14.1$ where the inflation loss on liquid assets IL is given by $IL = [\frac{1}{4}(\Delta_4 \ln P_{-3})(L_{-4}/Y_{-3}) + \frac{1}{4}(\Delta_4 \ln P_{-4})(L_{-5}/Y_{-4})]$ and CHI and LM are the Box-Pierce and Lagrange multiplier tests for serial correlation.

The equation has a standard error of 1 per cent and there is some evidence of negative fourth order residual autocorrelation[2] which may be indicative of omitted variables. It has a long-run solution for constant growth rates; $\Delta_4 \ln Y = g_Y$, $\Delta_4 \ln L = g_L$, $\Delta_4 \ln P = g_p$ of:

$$\frac{C}{Y} = \exp\left(-6.1 g_Y - 0.41 g_p \cdot \frac{L}{Y}\right) \qquad (5)$$

This equation has the now familiar properties that the static long-run income elasticity is unity and that an increase in the rate of growth of income or in the rate of inflation increases the savings ratio. A 1 per cent increase in the rate of inflation, *ceteris paribus,* increases the savings ratio by about 0.4 percentage points after 4 years. Compared with other recent studies, our inflation elasticity is rather low. Davis [8] reports other estimated inflation elasticities in the range of 0.5 to unity. The response of consumption to a change in real income is 0.4 in the current quarter. The unrestricted estimates of the terms in the inflation loss on liquid assets indicate that the response of consumption to a loss of real income due to the erosion of the real value of liquid assets is, as expected, far more sluggish than that due to changes in measured real personal disposable income (RPDI).

The static and dynamic single equation residuals for the non-durables equation are satisfactory. For the estimation period as a whole the equation error is only 1 per cent. However, the static and dynamic prediction errors for the recession years of 1980–1 are quite large: the equation fails adequately to pick up the rapid rise in the saving ratio over this period. Overall, the equation's dynamic predictions over eight (and sixteen) quarters ahead are good.

Expenditure on consumer durables in the National Institute model (*see Appendix (1.3)*)

Measurement of the *stock* of consumer durables, except in the case of cars, is often difficult (see [4]). To obtain a satisfactory measure of the aggregate stock of *all* durable goods, which includes many heteregeneous groups, poses even greater problems. In our recent research at the National Institute, therefore, (Cuthbertson [5]) we decided to concentrate directly on the determination of expenditures rather than on the stock of durable goods and to attempt to model the effects of changes in the stock on expenditures without using actual stock data.

Consumers are assumed to derive satisfaction from the flow of services from durables and to make additional purchases both to replace the ageing stock and to keep up with a fast changing market based on high technology and rapid design development. At the simplest level (and ignoring all factors other than real personal disposable income, Y) we might hypothesise that in equilibrium the desired ratio of durables expenditure, C, to income, increases both with the level of income and its rate of growth, $\ln Y$:

$$C/Y = f(\Delta \ln Y, Y) \tag{6}$$

In modelling the dynamic response of durables expenditure to changes in income we must acknowledge the importance of the existing stock and the age structure of the stock. In a consumer boom or after the introduction of a widely purchased new product (for example, colour TV sets, tape cassettes, freezers), the ratio of expenditure to income would be higher and there would be a lowering of the average age of the capital stock. In subsequent periods we may expect lower replacement expenditure and thus a lower rate of growth of durables expenditure. For similar reasons, we would expect that, starting with any given value for the expenditure—income ratio, an increase in the ratio would be followed by a lower growth rate of durables expenditure. Finally, we expect that whatever the existing disequilibrium in the expenditure to income ratio, an increase in the rate of growth of income causes an increase in the rate of growth of expenditure. This dynamic stock adjustment process may be written:

$$\Delta \ln C = a_0 - a_1 \ln(C/Y)_{-1} - a_2 \Sigma_{j=2}^{m} \ln(C/Y)_{-j} - a_3 \Delta \ln(C/Y)_{-1}$$
$$+ \Sigma_{j=0}^{n} b_j \Delta \ln Y_{-j} \tag{7}$$

with a_j and $b_j > 0$. Although equation (7) embodies one plausible adjustment process, it is by no means the only representation possible: the data may indicate equally plausible dynamic responses of durables expenditure to income. We started by estimating a general equation of the form

$$\ln C = b_0 + b_1 \ln C_{-1} + \ldots + b_j \ln C_{-j} + d_0 \ln Y + \ldots d_j \ln Y_{-j} \qquad (8)$$

to see whether our *a priori* view expressed in equation (7) (which is a restricted form of (8)) is consonant with the data. In equation (7) influences on new purchases and replacement purchases of durable goods are not separately identified. Moreover the dynamic structure of the equation may also reflect the formation of expectations about permanent income as well as any lagged adjustment of actual to desired expenditure.

Hire-purchase credit terms are assumed to operate through changes in d, the minimum deposit rate and m, the maximum monthly repayment period. They are represented by the term, $HP = d + (1 - d)/m$. This form of variable to represent HP control is more likely to be exogenous to expenditure than the frequently used flow of hire-purchase credit. The flow of credit is chosen by consumers simultaneously with expenditures and both are presumably influenced by the degree of restrictiveness of d and m. We expect that, for a liquidity constrained individual, an increase in d would entail higher savings per period and thus a delay in purchases and that, therefore, the HP variable will have a transitory effect on the level of durables expenditure (see [1] and [12]).

At the outset it was thought that liquid assets would play some part in determining expenditures on durables. However, terms in the (smoothed) liquid assets to income ratio and the inflation loss on liquid assets proved insignificant (see Cuthbertson [5], p. 68). The *change* in (gross) liquid assets was the only statistically significant liquid assets term.

Since the introduction of 'Competition and Credit Control' in 1971, bank advances have not been subject continuously to quantity constraints imposed by the monetary authorities, and the price of advances may have become more important. A switching weights model of the influence of bank advances and interest rates on durables expenditure achieved reasonable results (see Cuthbertson [5], pp. 64–5, 67). But the equation included in the model is a simpler one in which the influence of bank credit on expenditure is represented by the use of a real interest rate variable.

The unrestricted version of our preferred equation included up to four period lags on durables expenditure CD and income, Y; three period lags on the HP term, real liquid assets, L, the rate of inflation $\Delta \ln P$ and the nominal interest rate on local authority temporary debt, RLA. After simplifying restrictions, the preferred equation using seasonally unadjusted data was re-estimated on adjusted data to give

$$\Delta \ln CD = -3.6 - 0.52 \ln(C/Y)_{-1} + 0.39 \Delta_4 \ln Y + 0.23 \ln Y_{-4}$$
$$ (4.0) \quad (5.1) \phantom{\ln(C/Y)_{-1}} (1.4) (3.2)$$
$$ -0.039 LPER + 1.4 \Delta_2 \ln L_{-1} - 0.010 RR + \text{budget}$$
$$ (2.8) (2.6) (3.1) \text{dummies} \qquad (9)$$

SEE $= 0.048$, CHI$(10) = 24.5$, LM$(8) = 16.3$ where the real rate of interest RR is given by $RR = (RLA_{-3} - 200\Delta_2 CPI_{-1})$ and $LPER$ is a $(0,1,2)$ dummy variable used as a simplified representation of the HP variable. The equation has a standard error of about 5 per cent, which seems adequate for such a volatile quarterly series as consumer durables. The residuals showed some sign of negative second order autocorrelation but re-estimation subject to common factor restrictions showed that the autocorrelation parameter was not statistically significant.

The long-run income elasticity is about 1.5 and a 1 per cent change in either the nominal interest rate or the annual rate of inflation eventually leads to a 2 per cent change in expenditure. As expected, the dynamic terms in (C/Y) appear to model the stock-adjustment process adequately.[3] The hire-purchase credit dummy variable $LPER$ has a powerful short-run and a zero long-run effect on expenditure.

The static and dynamic single equation errors for durables expenditure are satisfactory. The (within sample) static residuals for 1979–81 show no marked deterioration as compared with earlier years, even though in this period the behaviour of durables expenditure was rather volatile (rising by 28, 3 and 1 per cent in 1979, 1980, 1981 respectively). The dynamic residuals are also reasonably satisfactory, although there is a tendency to overpredict the latter half of the 1970s, particularly the recession year of 1980.

Our results reported here may be contrasted with those obtained by Bean [2], who finds that net liquid assets and the real rate of interest are statistically insignificant in durables equations. This difference may arise from his use of a more restrictive dynamic structure than that used here.

Notes

[1] The unadjusted equation estimated using instrumental variables passed the usual diagnostic tests (for example, Lagrange multiplier test for autocorrelation and the Chow and post-parameter constancy tests for stability) over the last eight quarters of data). K. Wallis [23] suggests using unadjusted data when testing dynamic models.

[2] Estimation of the equation subject to a fourth order common factor restriction gave a statistically significant value for the autocorrelation coefficient with the equation passing the likelihood ratio test of the common factor restrictions. However, the coefficients and standard errors were changed very little (see Mizon and Hendry [17]).

[3] The dynamic adjustment term $\Delta\ln(C/Y)_{-j}$ was significant when using seasonally unadjusted data but insignificant with adjusted data.

References

[1] Allard, J., 'Credit restrictions and the lag distributions on consumer durables equations', *Applied Economics*, vol. 11, no. 2, 1979.

[2] Bean, C. R., 'The determination of consumers' expenditure in the UK', Government Economic Service Working Paper no. 4, 1978.

[3] Bulkley, G., 'Personal savings and anticipated inflation', *Economic Journal*, vol. 91, no. 361, March 1981.

[4] Central Statistical Office, 'The stock of consumer durables in the UK', *Economic Trends*, March 1978.

[5] Cuthbertson, K., 'The determination of expenditure on consumer durables', *National Institute Economic Review*, no. 94, November 1980.

[6] Cuthbertson, K., 'The measurement and behaviour of the UK savings ratio in the 1970s', *National Institute Economic Review*, no. 99, February 1982.

[7] Davidson, J. E. H., Hendry, D. F., Srba, F. and Yeo, S., 'Econometric modelling of the aggregate time series relationship between consumers' expenditure and income in the UK', *Economic Journal*, vol. 88, no. 4, 1978.

[8] Davies, E. P., 'The consumption function in macroeconomic models: a comparative study', Bank of England Discussion Paper, Technical Series, no. 1, August 1982.

[9] Deaton, A. S., 'Wealth effects on consumption in a modified life-cycle model', *Review of Economic Studies*, 32, (120), October, 1972, pp. 443–53.

[10] Deaton, A. S., 'Involuntary saving through unanticipated inflation', *American Economic Review*, 67, 1977, pp. 899–910.

[11] Flemming, J. S., 'The consumption function when capital markets are imperfect: the permanent income hypothesis reconsidered', *Oxford Economic Papers*, XXV, 1973, pp. 160–72.

[12] Garganas, N. C., 'An analysis of consumer credit and its effects on purchases of consumer durables', in Renton, G. A. (ed), *Modelling the Economy*, London, Heinemann, 1975.

[13] Green, F., 'The effect of occupational pension schemes on saving in the UK: a test of the life cycle hypothesis', *Economic Journal*, vol. 91, no. 361, June 1981.

[14] Hall, R. E., 'Stochastic implications of the life-cycle permanent income hypothesis: theory and evidence', *Journal of Political Economy*, vol. 86, 1978.

[15] Hendry, D. F. and von Ungern Sternberg, T., 'Liquidity and inflation effects on consumers' expenditure', *forthcoming* in Deaton, A. (ed) *Essays in the Theory and Measurement of Consumers' Behaviour*.

[16] Hey, J. D., *Uncertainty in Microeconomics*, Martin Robertson, Oxford, 1979.

[17] Mizon, G. E. and Hendry, D. F., 'Testing dynamic specification in a model of the demand for consumer durables in Canada', *Review of Economic Studies*, vol. 47(1), no. 146, 1980.

[18] Muellbauer, J., 'Surprises in the consumption function', Birkbeck College Discussion Paper no. 126, 1982.

[19] Nagatani, K., 'Life cycle saving: theory and fact', *American Economic Review*, vol. 62, no. 3, June 1972.

[20] Pissarides, C. A., 'Liquidity considerations in the theory of consumption', *Quarterly Journal of Economics*, 82, 1978, pp. 279–96.

[21] Thomas, R. L., 'Wealth and aggregate consumption', *Manchester School*, June, 1981.

[22] Threadgold, A. R., 'Personal savings: the impact of life assurance and pension funds', Bank of England Discussion Paper no. 1, October 1978.

[23] Wallis, K. F., 'Seasonal adjustments relations between variables', *Journal of the American Statistical Association*, vol. 69, 1974, pp. 18–31.

[24] Yaari, M. E., 'Uncertain lifetime, life insurance and the theory of the consumer', *Review of Economic Studies*, vol. 32, April 1965.

2 Investment and Stockbuilding
S.G.B. Henry and S. Wren-Lewis

Investment

Some background theory

In this section we provide a brief sketch of some of the theoretical issues relevant to an appraisal and discussion of the model equations. We will not attempt even a partial survey of the voluminous literature on the theory of investment decisions and its application to empirical aggregate investment equations. An admirable discussion of the theory of investment decisions by individual firms, together with a survey of relevant empirical evidence, is provided by Nickell [17], while useful, if slightly outdated, surveys of the empirical macroeconomic literature are provided by Rowley and Trivedi [18] and Helliwell [9].

It is convenient to distinguish between two main theoretical approaches to aggregate investment behaviour, the accelerator model and the pure neo-classical theory. At its simplest, the flexible accelerator relates the desired stock of capital K^* to expected output Q^e and assumes that firms partially adjust their capital stock towards this desired level. If we make the additional assumption that a proportion δ of the capital stock needs replacing each year (but for a critical discussion of this assumption see Feldstein and Rothschild [6]), we have

$$I_t = \beta(K_t^* - K_{t-1}) + \delta K_{t-1}$$
$$= \beta f(Q^e) - (\beta - \delta)K_{t-1} \qquad (1)$$

and $K_t = K_{t-1} + I_t - \delta K_{t-1}$

If the data on the past capital stock were unavailable or unreliable (see Griffin [8]), by manipulating lags and differencing we could transform this equation into one where investment was a function of the level and the change in (expected) output alone, that is, an accelerator. (An alternative method of substitution is provided by Bean [2].)

The assumption of partial adjustment of the capital stock towards its desired level was originally *ad hoc,* but it would be fairly easy to formalise it in terms of quadratic adjustment costs on much the same lines as the model of employment derived in Chapter 4. (In this case the rate of capital utilisation, rather than hours, might be the other variable within the production function.) Analysis along these lines would emphasise the importance of (possibly fairly long-term) expectations in any investment equation. This approach could also be generalised to include the costs of adjusting other factors, yielding the interrelated factor demand model.

The flexible accelerator model does not allow for substitution between labour and capital in meeting some expected output level. A possible theoretical justification for this lack of factor substitution is provided by Garegnani [7]. The model pioneered by Jorgenson (see, for example, Jorgenson and Stephenson [12]) is more neo-classical in focusing on factor substitution following changes in factor prices, yet it continues to include output as an independent variable. It is based on firms who maximise a future stream of discounted profits, where profits in period t are given by

$$\pi_t = p_t Q_t - w_t L_t - q_t I_t \tag{2}$$

where p_t, w_t, q_t are *exogenous* output prices, labour costs and the price of investment goods respectively. The firm faces two constraints: the production function and the need to replace the proportion δ of the capital stock that has depreciated. If we assume the production function to be of the Cobb-Douglas type, then a first order condition for maximisation yields

$$K^* = k^\sigma (p/c)^\sigma Q \tag{3}$$

where σ is the elasticity of substitution, k is the distribution parameter in the production function and c, the cost of capital, is given by

$$c_t = q_t - (1 - \delta) q_{t+1}/(1 + r) \tag{4}$$

where r is the constant discount rate. (Here we abstract from the complications caused by taxation. For a more detailed treatment see Jorgenson (*op. cit.*) and Feldstein and Flemming [5].) Incorporating (2) within the cost of adjustment framework gives us a model similar to (1), but where the function $f(\ldots)$ would now include the cost of capital as well as output.

There are a number of difficulties associated with this approach. Profit maximisation for a price taker implies that both factor demands and output are endogenous and it is unclear, therefore, why output should appear in an investment equation derived from this model of the firm. Instead, the desired capital stock should depend on the price of capital and the price of the product. This is still true even if we relax the assumption of perfect competition and instead base our model on monopolistic firms who face an exogenously given demand curve. On the other hand, if output is assumed to be completely exogenous to the firm, then investment should depend on relative factor prices rather than the price of capital relative to the price of the product.

It has also proved extremely difficult to estimate significant cost of capital effects in models of the form given by (3) in the United Kingdom. Bean, *op. cit.*, on whose work the equations in the Treasury model are based, could only estimate relatively weak effects in the *change* of the cost of capital or interest rates. No cost of capital terms appear in the accelerator type models of the Bank of England, the Cambridge Economic Policy Group, the London Business School or the National Institute.

The simple version of the neo-classical model also requires the assumption of a perfect capital market, in which investment can be financed to any scale for an individual firm at the going interest rate (see Modigliani and Miller [16]). A model based on neo-classical lines which avoids some of these assumptions is Tobin's 'q' theory, in which firms increase their capital stock if their valuation ratio is above its equilibrium value. Jenkinson [11] provides some interesting empirical tests of this theory on United Kingdom data. However, the principle source of investment funds for United Kingdom firms is neither debt nor new issues but retained profits. In practice, the firm is unlikely to be indifferent between these three sources of raising finance (see, for example, Wood [19], King [13] and Nickell [17]).

A number of models have attempted to allow for quantitative financial constraints on investment (that is, non-price constraints) by including terms in liquidity or profitability within the accelerator framework. (For a survey of United States studies see Clark [4], while the £$M3$ term in the London Business School model could also be interpreted in this way.) A recent example along these lines is provided for the United Kingdom by Gordon Anderson [1].

Data
Chart 2.1 plots manufacturing investment at 1975 prices against manufacturing output and a measure of real profits. The investment series is clearly very cyclical and there is also a tendency for the cycle in investment to lag behind the cycle in output. However, movements in profitability also tend to lead to changes in investment, with one clear example being the recent recession. Both output and profitability play an important role in the National Institute model equation.

Chart 2.2 shows the relationship between private investment in dwellings and one measure of short-term nominal interest rates. As the

Chart 2.1   Manufacturing output, investment and profitability

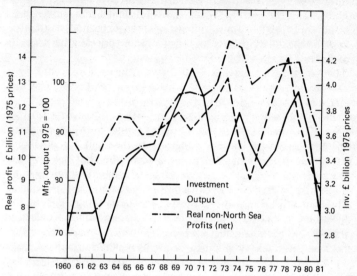

Chart 2.2   Investment in dwellings and interest rates

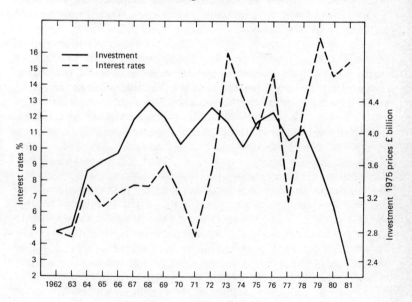

equation discussed below suggests, the relationship between this category of investment and the cost of finance is likely to be complex, involving, for example, price expectations and the availability of building society funds, but the chart nevertheless suggests an inverse relationship between these two series.

The National Institute model of investment

There are nine investment categories in the National Institute model but six of these are treated as exogenous. These are local authority dwellings; investment by mainly public industries and services; fees; shipping; oil and natural gas; and iron and steel. The decision to treat these as exogenous was based on two considerations. Firstly, most of these investment activities are carried out within the public sector. They have often been influenced by wider considerations such as demand management or the proper size of the public sector, as well as or instead of the economic factors considered above. Secondly, other items in this list, such as shipping, are characterised by substantial, discrete, changes. Such 'lumpiness' in certain forms of investment has long been recognised as posing peculiar problems in capital theory and again is difficult to model econometrically. The remaining three categories of total investment are endogenous in the model. These are private dwellings, manufacturing and other private investment. An outline of each of these sectors follows.

Private dwellings (see Appendix, equation (2.1))

Investment in private dwellings is explained by a demand function for housing. Here the main determinants are the cost of house purchase, the relative rate of return on investment in housing and the real flow of funds into building societies. The cost of house purchase is expressed in terms of the real, net of tax, mortgage repayment. Since interest payments on mortgages of up to £25,000 (before April 1983) are allowable against income tax, the mortgage interest cost is expressed after tax at the standard rate. Despite high transactions costs owner-occupied housing is frequently treated by households as an investment as well as a consumption good. This aspect of demand is represented by the relative rate of return in the short run on new housing. Another possibility is that this variable is also reflecting the response of the *supply* of new housing to interest rates. The final variable is the real flow of funds into building societies, which represents in part the influence of rationing by the building societies. (This incorporates a special low interest government loan which was made to building societies in 1974—5 in an attempt to hold down interest rates.) The equation makes no allowance for any changes following the recent marked increase in mortgage lending by banks. In this equation *QDKPD* is investment in private dwellings and *PNH* is the price index for new houses.

Manufacturing investment (*see Appendix, equation* (2.5))

The dependent variable in this equation includes new capital equipment leased by the manufacturing sector but owned elsewhere and excludes investment by the iron and steel industries. The two main independent variables are the change in output, representing an accelerator type effect, and companies' cash flow, which introduces an influence from past profitability. The lagged value of the capital stock was insignificant in estimation but capacity considerations are incorporated to some extent through the CBI survey capacity utilisation variable (*UTIL*), which modifies the accelerator term. This variable is also included in the Treasury model equation for manufacturing investment, although in this case it is entered separately from the accelerator terms.

The cash flow variable (*CF*) is defined as the real level of non-North Sea post-tax profits net of stock appreciation. The long lags involved before a change in cash flow has its full effect on investment (after allowing for the large lagged dependent variable) suggest that this variable is not representing the influence of short-term liquidity constraints on firms alone but a slower-acting and longer-lasting effect from the availability of internal finance. The equation implies that, *ceteris paribus*, about 7 per cent of any increase in profits will be added to investment.

Other private investment (*see Appendix, equation* (2.6))

This category of investment is also modelled by an accelerator type equation but, since this sector comprises largely service and distributive trades, the activity variable used is consumers' expenditure (*QCE*) rather than output. The lagged capital stock for this sector (*QKOTH*) was significant in estimation and the equation is, therefore, of the flexible accelerator variety. The estimation method uses autoregressive least squares and the results are shown in the Appendix.

Stockbuilding

As Alan Blinder has recently observed (Blinder [3]), although inventory behaviour has received relatively little attention in the literature, it appears to play a crucial role in the propagation of business cycles. The interaction of stock adjustment with the output multiplier may be one important factor behind the apparently systematic cyclical behaviour of the United Kingdom economy since the war. An adequate modelling of stockbuilding behaviour is therefore crucial to the overall properties of any econometric model of the economy.

There are a large number of reasons why a firm might hold stocks, either in the form of inputs (for example, raw materials) or outputs (finished goods). Production may be continuous and yet it may be economically sensible to purchase raw materials or deliver products in discreet batches. This type of behaviour is analogous to simple transactions models of the demand for money. Equally, production of a single product may take considerable time, so that at any point in time there will be a considerable stock of work in progress. Indeed work in progress represents about a third of total manufacturers' stocks. In models based on these ideas, stocks are clearly related to the scale of production and also to the relative cost of holding stocks compared with costs of delivery and storage.

The fact that production takes time and that production may be temporally and spatially separated from sales are key elements in the buffer stock model of stockholding (see, for example, Mills [15]). This precautionary demand for stocks recognises that demand is uncertain and is based on the idea that producers do not want to be unable to satisfy an unexpectedly large demand for their product (producing a stockout). Here the desired stock level not only depends on their relative holding cost and the expected level of sales but also on the expected variability of sales. This model also illustrates that movements in finished goods stocks may be involuntary. Thus if sales are exogenous to the firm in the identity *output – finished goods stockbuilding = sales,* then for given production plans an unexpected increase in sales will lead to a corresponding involuntary fall in stocks.

The choice between changing output and changing stocks following a change in sales is also at the heart of the production smoothing model of stockholding (see Holt *et al* [10]). Even if changes in sales are anticipated, they may be expected to be only temporary. If changing output levels involves important costs of adjustment (such as the costs in changing employment discussed in Chapter 4), then it may be sensible to allow the temporary fluctuation in demand to be met from stocks rather than by changing output. An important implication of this model is that desired stocks will depend not only on expected sales in the immediate future, but also on more long-term sales expectations. Costs in adjusting output also imply that desired stocks cannot be obtained immediately (if this involves altering production level) and stocks will, therefore, only partially adjust towards their desired levels. Expectations about sales and lagged adjustment are therefore likely to be key elements in any stockbuilding model.

There are yet more motives for holding stocks which we will not consider here, such as speculation or attempts to reduce delivery date delays (see Maccini [14]). A comprehensive survey of theoretical studies up to the mid-1970s is provided by Rowley and Trivedi [18]. The transactions, precautionary and production smoothing models of stock-building can be summarised in the following equation: $S_t = aS_{t-1} + b(X_t^e - X_t) + f(X_t^e, X_{t+1}^e, \ldots) + g(Z_t, Z_t^e, Z_{t+1}^e, \ldots) + cY_t$ where S are stocks, X sales, Y output and Z a vector of other variables including the opportunity cost of holding stocks. In the following equations Z comprises nominal interest rates and the rate of inflation, where their difference, real interest rates, is taken as the opportunity cost of holding stocks. The parameter b is designed to pick up involuntary stockbuilding and the parameter c elements of stockbuilding like work in progress. Clearly we can use the stockbuilding, sales, output identity to eliminate either output or sales from this equation. To complete the model we need some hypothesis about expectations behaviour and here we adopt the convenient, if restrictive, assumption that the expected value of any variable is some unspecified function of lagged values of that variable.

This formulation of stock behaviour in terms of current and lagged sales or output, interest rates and inflation, lies behind most of the stockbuilding equations in large econometric models. However, both the Bank of England and the London Business School models include additional financial variables besides interest rates (a term related to profits, and £$M3$ respectively) and the Treasury model contains a (non-estimated) system for allocating disequilibrium in company liquidity to real variables like stockbuilding. Although the National Institute stockbuilding equations do not contain any effects of this kind, the large nominal interest rate term in one of the equations below could be interpreted as a proxy for such liquidity effects. Possible theoretical reasons why disequilibrium in firms' financial positions might influence variables like stockbuilding, employment or investment, have been discussed elsewhere but it remains true that as yet the inclusion of effects of this kind in econometric equations remains rather *ad hoc* and unrelated to formal theory.

Stockbuilding in the National Institute model is divided into three sectors: manufacturing, distribution (comprising retailers and whole-salers) and 'other stockbuilding'. This last category comprises a wide variety of quite dissimilar stocks and the model equation simply relates it to stockbuilding in the other two sectors.

Manufacturing (see Appendix, equation (3.1))
Chart 2.3 plots the stock—output ratio for manufacturers against manufacturing output. The series suggest that as output begins to decline the stock—output ratio rises, since some of the fall in sales is absorbed by building up stocks. Once output reaches its trough, however, firms adjust the stock—output ratio back towards equilibrium by meeting any increase in sales by running down stocks (perhaps involuntarily at first).

Chart 2.3   Manufacturers' stock—output ratio and output

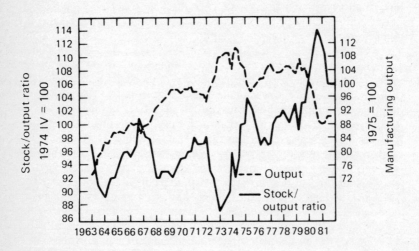

In between these two points stockbuilding is likely to intensify the cyclical behaviour of output as firms reduce their output in an effort to reduce their stocks.

One other feature of the stock—output series is the upward trend that appears to develop in the mid-1970s. This may well be associated with the stock relief scheme introduced in 1974, which removed corporation tax from the stock appreciation element of profits. In the model equation this effect is captured by a simple dummy variable.

This equation represents a restricted form of a more general equation including two additional lags on stocks itself and up to five lags on output. These additional lags could easily be excluded from the equation, although output lagged five quarters was almost significant. Despite the presence of the negative coefficient on output lagged two quarters, the response of the stock level to a sustained increase in output is fairly smooth, largely because of the implicit large lagged dependent variable in the level of stocks. The small positive constant implies a slight tendency for the equilibrium stock—output ratio to fall as output increases.

The stock relief dummy is both significant and extremely large in the long run and a less *ad hoc* modelling of the effects of the stock relief scheme would clearly be desirable. The levels of both interest rates and inflation were insignificant and incorrectly signed when included in equations like that above, as were variables related to company profitability, a three day week dummy or a time trend. One interesting feature of the equation is that it tracks the exceptional (but within sample) 1980–1 recession period fairly well.

Distribution (*see Appendix, equation (3.2)*)

This equation presented more difficult problems. The stock–sales ratio for this sector (see chart 2.4) clearly shows a pronounced upward trend throughout the estimation period. When trend terms were included in the equation for distributors' stocks they were always highly significant. In this equation these trends, as well as terms in interest rates and inflation, are scaled by the level of consumption, so that the stock–sales *ratio* is a function of interest rates, inflation and a trend. (Scaling these terms in this way was always more successful than entering the variables on their own.)

Chart 2.4   Distributors' stock–sales ratio

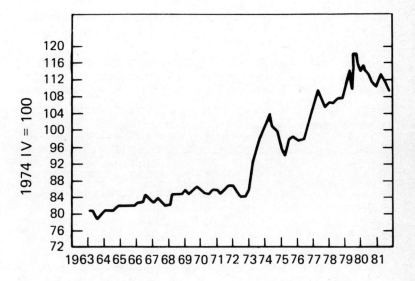

The term in nominal interest rates is far larger and more significant than the term in inflation (and therefore, implicitly, than the real interest rate effect). A one point rise in the local authority three month rate (which performed slightly better than the bank lending rate) will reduce stocks in the long run by nearly £500 million, compared with a total stock of currently around £9 billion. Another potentially implausible feature of this effect is that it only begins after a four quarter lag. The level of consumption has no immediate impact on stockbuilding, partly perhaps because of initial involuntary destocking. Thereafter the response in the stock level to higher consumption is fairly smooth, although the significant positive constant implies that the stock–sales ratio will, in the long run, tend to fall as consumption rises, a tendency which, over the period as a whole, partially offsets the influence of the positive time trend. One final worrying feature of this equation is the substantial serial correlation indicated by the *LM* statistic. One possible explanation for some of these difficulties is that consumption, while being the appropriate sales measure for retailers, is less appropriate for elements of wholesalers' stockholding, such as stocks of building materials for example.

References

[1] Anderson, G., 'A new approach to the empirical investigation of investment behaviour', *Economic Journal,* vol. 91, 1981.

[2] Bean, C., 'An econometric model of manufacturing investment in the UK', *Economic Journal,* vol. 91, 1981.

[3] Blinder, A., 'Inventories in the Keynesian macro model', *Kyklos,* vol. 33, 1980.

[4] Clark, P. K., 'Investment in the 1970s: theory, performance and prediction', Brookings Papers on Economic Activity, no. 1, 1979.

[5] Feldstein, M. and Flemming, J., 'Tax policy, corporate saving and investment behaviour in Britain', *Review of Economic Studies,* vol. 38, 1971.

[6] Feldstein, M. and Rothschild, M., 'Towards an economic theory of replacement investment', *Econometrica,* vol. 43, 1974.

[7] Garegnani, P., 'Notes on consumption, investment and effective demand', *Cambridge Journal of Economics,* 2(4) December 1978 and 3(1) March 1979.

[8] Griffin, T., 'The stock of fixed assets in the UK: how to make the best use of the statistics', *Economic Trends,* October 1976.

[9] Helliwell, J. (ed), *Aggregate Investment,* Penguin Modern Economic Readings, 1976.

[10] Holt, C., Modigliani, F., Muth, J. and Simon, H., *Planning Production Inventories and Work Force,* Englewood Cliffs (N.J.), Prentice-Hall, 1960.

[11] Jenkinson, N., 'Investment, profitability and the valuation ratio', Bank of England Discussion Paper no. 17, 1981.

[12] Jorgenson, D. and Stephenson, J., 'Investment behaviour in US manufacturing, 1947–1960', *Econometrica,* vol. 35 April, 1967.

[13] King, M., *Public Policy and the Corporation,* London, Chapman-Hall, 1977.
[14] Maccini, L., 'An empirical model of price and output behaviour', *Economic Inquiry,* vol. 15, 1977.
[15] Mills, E., *Price, Output and Inventory Policy,* New York, John Wiley, 1962.
[16] Modigliani, F. and Miller, M. H. 'Cost of capital, corporate finance and the theory of investment', *American Economic Review,* vol. 48, 1958.
[17] Nickell, S., *The Investment Decision of Firms,* Welwyn, Jones Nesbet & Co, 1978.
[18] Rowley, J. C. R. and Trivedi, P. K., *Econometrics of Investment,* London, Wiley & Sons, 1975.
[19] Wood, A., *A Theory of Profits,* London, Cambridge University Press, 1975.

3 Exports and Imports
S. Brooks

The relationships commonly used to model the volume of trade flows have a similar basic structure, although there are many differences of detail. For both exports and imports, the trade flow depends on an activity variable and a relative price variable. In the export equations the activity variable is a measure of world trade (world exports) — the exact measure varies from equation to equation — while in the import equations the activity variable is total final expenditure in the United Kingdom. On the export side, volumes traded depend also on a measure of the average price of the type of exports in question relative to the world price of similar goods or services; on the import side, volumes depend on the average price of the imported goods or services relative to an average price of United Kingdom goods or services.

Disaggregation is mainly for statistical reasons and does not reflect any belief that explanations differ fundamentally between commodities. As the form of the equations is the same, the equations for exports and imports can be reduced to a standard equation for the volume of a trade flow. All those volume equations can best be interpreted as demand equations. The import equations describe the United Kingdom's demand for foreign goods; the export equations describe the rest of the world's demand for United Kingdom goods.

The theory of export demand

The export equations in the model are all versions of what has become the standard export equation of macroeconomic models. This is of the form $\ln QX = a_0 + \Sigma_i a_{1i} \ln QA_{-i} + \Sigma_j a_{2j} \ln RP_{-j} + u$ where QX is the volume of exports, QA is an activity variable and RP a measure of competitiveness. Within this framework a choice must be made of an appropriate activity variable, an appropriate competitiveness index and the right form of lag distribution. In the National Institute equation for exports of manufactured goods (excluding erratic items), the activity variable is the volume of world exports of manufactures and the competitiveness variable is the ratio of United Kingdom export prices to an index of world export prices. In both cases 'world' refers to the main manufacturing countries.

The equation can be seen as an imperfect embodiment of a more precise demand theory. Consider the position of a French importer of manufactured goods. Suppose he makes his decision to import from the United Kingdom in two stages: first he decides what to spend on all imports of manufactured goods; then he decides how to allocate this expenditure amongst the various competing exporters. The first decision can be considered to depend on his total expenditure and the average price of imported manufactures compared with other available goods. In the second stage the allocation of expenditure to United Kingdom exports depends only on the total expenditure available for all imported manufactures and on the price of United Kingdom goods relative to that of the exported manufactures of third countries. On the assumption that all Frenchmen are alike, a demand curve for imports into France from the United Kingdom can be derived: $q_F = a_F M_F + b_F RP_F$ where M_F is the total of all imports into France and RP_F is the relative price of United Kingdom exports to exports from other countries.

Similar exercises can be carried out for all the countries importing manufactures from the United Kingdom. Aggregating over countries gives $q = \Sigma_F q_F = \Sigma_F a_F M_F + \Sigma_F b_F RP_F$. Now, on the assumption that all countries are alike this becomes $q = a\Sigma_F M_F + b\Sigma_F RP_F$. $\Sigma_F M_F$ is total expenditure on imports of manufactures by those countries which import from the United Kingdom and as such is appropriately represented by world exports — that is the exports of the main manufacturing countries. Similar aggregation of the RP terms is possible only if the exports of each country are considered in exactly the same way by each importing country. That is, the weights used in the construction of the RP indices are identical (a) in one country, across the prices of imports from other countries and (b) for the exports of one country, across the demand functions of the importing countries — that is, there is a single weight, w, applied to all price indices in all countries. This difficulty of aggregation arises because the numerators of the RP terms include different sets of export prices. Some relaxation of these conditions would be possible if each RP term contained the same set of prices. This might be true if the index in each case were to include domestically produced goods as well as imports. If this change were to be made, then the world trade variable would have to be replaced by world production (which equals world expenditure on all manufactures), and this raises no particular difficulty in principle. However, a serious difficulty arises in practice because export prices often differ from domestic prices by substantial amounts for substantial periods of time.

Given the rather stringent assumptions which must be made in building up United Kingdom exports from an aggregation of other countries' demands, it must be accepted that the equation actually estimated could well prove unstable. The problems are exacerbated by the requirement that the individual demand curves be linear if the aggregate demand curve is to have the same functional form. In fact the estimated equation is linear in its logs and cannot be derived exactly from the aggregation of individual country curves of whatever form. The log-linear specification has been adopted rather uncritically by most modellers.

If it is argued that this form of demand curve (aggregate and log-linear) is the most appropriate form statistically, then it is doubtful whether world trade is the most appropriate activity variable to include. For if the rest of the world is treated as a single country then the choice facing residents of this composite country is between domestic production on the one hand, which is measured by world manufacturing output, net of United Kingdom manufacturing output, and on the other imports from the United Kingdom. Thus the natural expenditure variable to use in the equation would be world manufacturing output less United Kingdom demand for United Kingdom output. However, this specification suffers from the inappropriate assumption that output is homogeneous. World trade in manufactures has grown much faster than world output of manufactures, suggesting that production patterns within manufacturing have shifted in favour of exporting industries. If this increased specialisation continues, then it seems more sensible, on pragmatic grounds, if a choice has to be made, to link United Kingdom exports to world exports rather than world production.

Exports of manufactured goods

Most macroeconomic models, including those of the National Institute, the London Business School, the Treasury and the Bank of England, do not disaggregate below the level of manufactured goods. This being the case, exports of manufactures are by far the largest component of exports of goods and services and modelbuilders put most of their research effort into estimation of equations for this category. There are also more highly disaggregated studies of exports which make it possible to check the validity of the assumption that a stable aggregate relationship exists at the level of exports of manufactures as a whole. In the United Kingdom valuable work of this kind has been done by Winters [6] and [7].

However, Winters' painstaking work with ten categories of exports to sixteen markets — distinguishing therefore 160 export flows — revealed large differences in coefficients, thus casting doubt on the wisdom of aggregation. In Winters [7], the author approaches the problem of disaggregation explicitly. A full account of his methods is beyond the scope of this chapter, but his main conclusions are of interest. First, the derived aggregate own-price elasticity was very sensitive to the degree of disaggregation. Secondly, in terms of within-sample fit simple more aggregated models explained the total better than sets of disaggregated equations. Overall, Winters' work does not point conclusively to any particular degree of disaggregation: it does serve as a reminder — if one were needed — that the very notion of a correct level of aggregation has to be approached with a certain scepticism.

The equation for exports of manufactured goods (excluding erratic items) used in the current version of the National Institute model has a world trade elasticity of over 0.6 and a competitiveness elasticity of nearly 0.5. Compared with other similar research these elasticities are at the lower end of the range, although they represent an increase on those of the corresponding equation used in earlier versions of the model. The equation is shown in the Appendix (4.1).

The main novel feature of this equation is the treatment of the lag on the price of exports relative to competitors' prices, *PRPEX5*. The estimating equation allows for a longer lag — up to seventeen quarters. The lag weights are at first negative, then become positive, before becoming negative again. The reported equation, the one used in the model, utilises only the negative weights from the beginning of the distribution. This decision was taken after extensive research had shown that the long-run competitiveness elasticity was more or less unaffected by ignoring all lags after the seventh and that the out-of-sample forecasting performance of the equation was improved by their omission.

This decision was a by-product of a research project established for the systematic econometric comparison of export equations. Some of the results of this study have been published in Brooks [3]. To summarise a lengthy argument: experimentation with both the National Institute's relative export price model and the Treasury's relative normalised unit labour cost model consistently produced lag distributions that had two modes, the first after one to two years, the second after about three years. This lag shape could be constrained to be unimodal but usually at great cost to the error statistics of the equations, in particular the indicators of autocorrelation. This was particularly marked in the National Institute model; however, the total contribution of the positive and negative values of the lag distribution after the first mode was normally negligible and omitting these weights tended to improve the forecasting performance of the equation. Now a reasonably low degree of polynomial may well have great difficulty in accommodating a lag distribution that is smooth to start with, but also includes one or two apparently significant (but probably spurious) coefficients at the end of the distribution. Overall, the evidence is considered sufficient to exclude all the later lags.

Table 3.1 Exports of manufactured goods in the main forecasting models of the UK economy

Model	World trade		Competitiveness variables			Trend	Other Variables
	Elasticity	Max lag	Type	Elasticity	Max lag		
NIESR	0.625	0	Relative export prices	− 0.485	7	−	−
HMT	0.852	1	Relative normalised unit labour cost	− 0.825	17	− 0.008	UK spare capacity indicator
BOE	0.781	0	Relative normalised unit labour cost	− 0.507	16	− 0.021t+ 0.00006t²	−
LBS	0.68	a	Relative costs	− 0.46	b	−	Share of manufacturing in GDP (UK) Relative interest rates

[a]95 per cent adjustment is achieved in 6 quarters.
[b]95 per cent adjustment is achieved in 14 quarters.

Source: NIESR – National Institute Model 6; February 1983; HMT – Treasury Macroeconomic Model Technical Manual 1982 (November 1982); BOE – Bank of England Model Manual, Spring 1983; LBS – London Business School Quarterly Econometric Model of the United Kingdom Economy: Relationships in the Basic Model as at December 1982.

The final equation is compared with those of the main United Kingdom forecasting models in table 3.1. When making comparisons it is important to remember that the relative price and relative unit labour cost variables behave quite differently: the change in competitiveness since 1975, measured by prices, has been much less than the change measured by relative normalised unit labour costs. Also the sizes of the elasticities are very sensitive to the inclusion of time trends (see Brooks [3] and the references cited therein).

Exports of non-oil non-manufactures

This category of exports includes a rather heterogeneous collection of goods: food and live animals; beverages and tobacco; crude materials (that is, unprocessed ones, wood, rubber, etc); animal and vegetable oils; and fuels excluding crude oil. This being the case, it is unlikely that a single equation will be satisfactory. In fact the equation used in the model is very simple (see Appendix (4.7)).

The world trade elasticity is very similar to that of the exports of manufactures equation (although the measure of world trade is of course different). The most notable feature of the model is the absence of any competitiveness effect. It is, however, extremely difficult to arrive at a satisfactory world price variable for this composite category, so that its value in identifying a competitiveness effect is far from decisive. On the other hand, some goods in this category, the (unprocessed) foods, are traded in non-competitive markets and have low price elasticities of demand in consumption.

Exports of services

The importance of exports of services is often underrated. In 1981, for example, services amounted to 25 per cent of the total of exports of goods and services. As is the case with the previous category, services comprise a large number of not very similar items. The CSO statistics distinguish sea transport, civil aviation, travel; financial services; government services and 'other' services. Other services is, of course, the largest single item. None of the main forecasting models make much use of this disaggregated data: the National Institute and the London Business School do not disaggregate at all; the Treasury and the Bank of England distinguish only between sea transport and all other services.

The equation used in the National Institute model (see Appendix (4.11)) is similar to the other export equations: the activity variable is total world trade in goods; competitiveness is measured as the ratio of the deflator for exports of services to the deflator for imports of services. This is on the assumption that the United Kingdom is a price taker as far as its imports of services are concerned. The activity effect is spread over two quarters; the long-run competitiveness elasticity is the highest for any of the endogenous components of exports and greatly enhances the effect of exchange rate changes on the volume of exports of goods and services.

The theory of import demand

The explanation of imports has always been particularly troublesome in models of the United Kingdom economy. Until recently the problem was to explain the apparently chronic tendency for import penetration to rise. Typically, the problem was solved by using a demand for imports equation with a very high activity elasticity or by attributing a substantial part of the growth to a time trend. The discovery of strongly positive trends in import equations and strongly negative trends in export equations then supports extreme pessimism in trade forecasts for the medium or longer term.

The stylised facts that trade equations have to cope with are first, that United Kingdom exports have grown much less quickly than world exports and secondly, that United Kingdom imports have grown much more quickly than United Kingdom demand. There is also a third fact: United Kingdom exports have grown much more quickly than United Kingdom output. If the discrepancy between the rate of growth of exports and the rate of growth of the economy can be treated as exogenous to the United Kingdom (an aspect of the much greater growth of *world* trade than *world* output) this third fact does itself suggest that import penetration will rise. If the balance of trade is to be constant on average an exogenous fast growth of exports relative to output must imply a fast growth of imports relative to output. In part the increase in the United Kingdom's degree of import penetration reflects the international increase in specialisation in the production of traded goods and in particular of manufactured goods. A direct measure of specialisation based on the ratio of world exports to world production has occasionally been used (see, for example, London Business School [5]).

This measure of specialisation, like the use of time trends, is intended as a modification to a basic (log-linear) demand equation for imports to allow for the fact that imports increase even in the absence of growth in total final sales and with competitiveness unchanged. A more fundamental change to the theory reflects the view that goods are imported mainly because domestic supply of these goods is insufficient to meet the level of domestic demand. If demand increases and domestic supply is fixed, the margin of demand is satisfied by imports: the appearance of a high elasticity of demand for imports is really evidence of a low elasticity of supply of import substitutes. In United Kingdom macroeconomic models this sort of approach has been used by the Bank of England (see Bank of England [1]) whose model uses conventional demand equations for most categories of goods but imports of finished manufacturers are calculated as the difference between demand for these goods and their domestic supply.

As already indicated, the logarithmic form of the equation, although standard, is not necessarily appropriate. Consider a logarithmic equation like $QM = QD^{\alpha}$ where QM is the volume of imports and QD is some measure of demand. The degree of import penetration θ is then $QM/QD:\theta = QD^{(\alpha-1)}$. It follows at once that if θ increases as QD increases α must exceed unity. However, suppose instead that the equation is linear: $QM = a + bQD$. In this case $\theta = b + a/QD$ and $d\theta/dQD = a/QD^2$. This is positive as long as a, the intercept in the demand equation, is negative. Now anyone with knowledge of the data will have some pre-suppositions about the likely sizes of α and b but not about a. If the properties of the estimated log-linear equation seem implausible because in fact a high value of α is needed to track the increase in import penetration, a switch to a linear equation may well provide a more acceptable result, since in this form of equation the rate of change of import penetration is independent of the marginal propensity to import.

The import equations in the National Institute model are based on the view that neither high demand elasticities nor time trends are a satisfactory way of accounting for the increase in import penetration; they are therefore based on linear rather than log-linear functional forms. On the other hand, other arguments suggest that the marginal propensity to import will depend on the state of competition. This suggests a hybrid equation of the form $QM = a + bQTFE + u$, $b = \alpha + \beta COMP + v$, where, in addition to the notation already defined, $COMP$ is a measure of the competitiveness of imported goods relative to domestic supply and u and v are error terms. The equations are estimated together by substituting the second equation into the first. This gives $QM = a + QTFE(\alpha + \beta COMP + v) + u = a + \alpha QFTE + \beta COMP\,QTFE + w$ where $w = vQTFE + u$. It is difficult to argue that the error w will be classical but if the equation is transformed by dividing by $QTFE$ the new error has all the usual desirable properties.[1] This is the form in which the equation was estimated.

Finally, before estimating the various equations, the expression for the marginal propensity to import was made more elaborate. The final form adopted was $b = \alpha + \Sigma_i\beta_iCOMP_{-i} + \Sigma\gamma_iD_i + \delta_iOMF/QTFE$ where $D_1 = QPAC/QTFE$, $D_2 = QDK/QTFE$, $D_3 = QDS/QTFE$, $D_4 = QEX/QTFE$. The D_i terms are the shares in total final expenditure of general government current expenditure ($QPAC$), gross investment (QDK), stockbuilding (QDS), and exports of goods and services (QEX). OMF is the index of output of the manufacturing sector.

The use of a distributed lag on the competitiveness indicator is entirely conventional and needs no further discussion. The D_i variables are intended to investigate the dependence of the marginal propensity to import on the structure of demand. The negative effect of manufacturing output (OMF) is included to allow for circumstances in which domestic output falls (for reasons unconnected with measured competitiveness) and in which imports rise to meet the resulting excess demand.

Imports of manufactured goods

Much of the difficulty in explaining total imports can be attributed to the behaviour of imports of manufactured goods. For this reason our category of imports of goods excluding oil was divided into imports of manufactures (*QMMF*) and imports of non-oil non-manufactures (*QMOTH*). The final equation for *QMMF* may be found in the Appendix (5.1).

As expected the intercept was strongly negative. The long-run coefficient on competitiveness, defined as the ratio of the unit value index for manufactures, adjusted for tariffs, divided by the United Kingdom wholesale price index for manufacturing output, is small, as is usual in studies of imports. What is unusual is the very long lag: the maximum lag is thirteen quarters but there is no effect at all of a change in competitiveness for the first year. In the Treasury model, by contrast, the competitiveness effects in the four equations which together account for manufactures all have maximum lags of five to eight quarters.

The D_is varied considerably. After a certain amount of experimentation it was decided to divide investment into investment in plant and machinery (*QDKPM*) and all other investment (*QDK* – *QDKPM*). The final marginal propensities to import by category of expenditure (assuming the terms in *COMP* sum to zero) are shown in table 3.2. The low propensities calculated for *QPAC* and (*QDK* – *QDKPM*) are not surprising. The figure for stockbuilding is no higher than that for consumer spending.

No evidence was found, over the estimation period as a whole, that imports of manufactured goods were especially strongly linked with stockbuilding. This hypothesis is often advanced, nevertheless, to explain the very low level of imports in the 1981–2 recession.

Table 3.2   Marginal propensity to import by category of expenditure (manufactures)

Consumers' Expenditure	QCE	0.356
Public Consumption	QPAC	0.0
Investment (excluding plant and machinery	QDK – QDKPM	0.0
Investment in plant and machinery	QDKPM	0.780
Stockbuilding	QDS	0.356
Exports of goods and services	QEX	0.478

Imports of non-oil manufactures

As is the case with the corresponding category of exports, this aggregate included several very different subcategories. The same approach was used as for manufactures. The equation in the model is shown in the Appendix (5.2). In this case the anticipated sign on the output of the manufacturing sector is positive, reflecting the derived demands for

Table 3.3 Marginal propensity to import by category of expenditure (non-oil non-manufactures)

Consumers' Expenditure	QCE	0.0
Public Consumption	QPAC	0.065
Investment	QDK	0.13
Stockbuilding	QDS	0.0
Exports of goods and services	QEX	0.065

industrial inputs. The competitiveness effect is of the right sign, although indirect terms in the lag distribution are not well defined; competitiveness is here defined as the ratio of the deflator for imports to the market price deflator for GDP. In this equation the marginal propensities may call for comment; in particular the marginal propensity of zero attached to consumption. However, it must be remembered that the consumption goods in this category consist largely of food and drink and tobacco, which are known to have low elasticities of demand.

Imports of services
In contrast with the case of exports of services a simple analogue of the models used for imports of goods was not very successful for analysing imports of services. There is little evidence of a rising import propensity and a simple log-linear specification has a long-run elasticity on QTFE very close to unity (see Appendix (5.5)).

Prices of exports and imports
The prices of exports and imports are treated differently in the National Institute model. All import prices are considered as determined on world markets and exogenous to the United Kingdom in terms of foreign currency; the sterling prices are obtained from the foreign prices by dividing by the exchange rate. This formulation is controversial especially in respect of finished manufactures. Two points are at issue. First, do foreign exporters vary the price they charge to United Kingdom importers according to market conditions in the United Kingdom? Secondly, are changes in the exchange rate entirely 'neutral' even in the short term?

Impressionistic evidence certainly supports the view that exchange rate changes do at least have some transitory effect. The evidence in favour of market pricing of United Kingdom imports is mixed. For a study of this problem see Bond [2].

Export pricing is treated differently. Equations are used to determine the sterling prices of exports of manufactured goods and of non-oil non-manufactures. The price of exports of oil (in United States dollars) is considered an exogenous variable. United Kingdom exporters are assumed to compete in imperfect markets in which they do not lose all their sales if they raise their prices above those of their competitors. Simple equations summarise their dilemma of finding a selling price that is appropriate to both their competitors' prices and their own costs. In the recent past United Kingdom exporters, selling from a high inflation, low productivity-growth economy, have been faced with the problem of pitching their prices low enough to maintain sales and high enough to make some profits.

The equation for the prices of exports of manufactures assigns equal weights to the domestic and foreign prices and, although unconstrained in estimation, the coefficients on domestic and foreign prices sum to unity in the long run. The equation for non-oil non-manufactures shows the first property but not the second: the sum of the long-run elasticities applied to domestic and foreign prices is about 1.2. The standard error of this equation is also a good deal larger than that of the previous one. It is much more difficult to find satisfactory price and cost measures for this category of goods. In particular, the dependent variable includes the prices of fuels other than crude oil whereas the world price variable omits them. Also, no suitable domestic cost or price variable is available to cover a sector that includes agricultural goods, processed foods, crude materials and some fuels. The use of a general wholesale price variable can only be justified as a rather crude proxy.

The equation for the prices of exports of services is of the same style but here the data problems are even more acute both because of the heterogeneous nature of the product and because of the difficulties involved in estimating the price and volume components of the recorded flows. The use of the price of imports of services as a measure of competitors' prices involves some rather extreme assumptions about the homogeneity of trade in services. Although the weight of domestic and foreign prices is of the same order of magnitude in the short run, the weight of foreign prices is very small (just 0.17) in the long run. The condition that the long-run elasticities sum to unity is imposed in this equation but this restriction was not rejected by the data according to the usual statistical tests.

There are two main problems with this kind of export price equation. The first is that prices are determined wholly by other prices with no direct reference either to sales or to the margin of capacity. The second concerns the assumption that exporters treat a variation in their competitors' price in exactly the same way whether it arises from a change in the foreign price itself or from a change in the exchange rate. It might be expected that producers would not change their prices so much following an exchange rate change if they believed that its effect on competitiveness would be short-lived. Both the Bank of England model (see Bank of England [1]) and the Treasury model (see HM Treasury [4]) do make such a distinction and find it to be significant.

For non-manufactures the position is rather different, since United Kingdom production is generally smaller relative to world production and so less capable of influencing world market prices. Yet we find that domestic prices still have some role to play in the formation of the overall export price for this sector. In practice it seems that much of the output of this sector is not exposed to much foreign competition: trade in agricultural goods is controlled by EEC regulations; coal prices are effectively set by the degree of subsidy granted by the government. As explained above, no role for competitiveness could be isolated in the equation for the volume of exports of non-oil non-manufactures. Under these circumstances it is surprising that the domestic cost determinants of export prices do not have even greater weight.

Note

[1] $QM/QTFE = a/QTFE + \alpha + \beta COMP + w'$

where $w' = w/QTFE = v + u/QTFE$. Consider the error term w'. If $QTFE$ is non-stochastic $E(w')$ is zero provided that $E(v)$ and $E(u)$ are both zero. The variance of w' is more complicated.

$$Ew'^2 = E\left(v + \frac{u}{QTFE}\right)^2 = E(v)^2 + \frac{E(u)^2}{QTFE^2} + \frac{2}{QTFE}E(uv)$$

There is no reason to suppose that the errors u and v are correlated; furthermore, there is no reason to assume that the error v is anything other than a classical error term. So if w' is to be a classical error term it is necessary that $E(u)^2/QTFE^2$ is a constant, say $\sigma^2 u$. This is a reasonable assumption and is much to be preferred to the assumption that u itself is a classical error term.

References

[1] Bank of England, Bank of England Model Manual, Spring 1983.
[2] Bond, I., 'The determination of UK manufactured import prices', Bank of England discussion paper no. 16, 1981.
[3] Brooks, S., 'Systematic econometric comparisons: exports of manufactured goods', *National Institute Economic Review*, no. 97 August, 1981.
[4] HM Treasury, Macroeconomic Model Technical Manual, 1982.
[5] London Business School, Quarterly Econometric Model of the United Kingdom Economy: Relationships in the Basic Model as at December 1982.
[6] Winters, L. A., *An econometric model of the export sector*, Cambridge Studies in Applied Econometrics – 4, Cambridge University Press, 1981.
[7] Winters, L. A., 'Aggregation in logarithmic models: some experiments with UK exports', Oxford Bulletin of Economics and Statistics, February 1980.

4 Employment
S. Wren-Lewis

Some theoretical issues

Employment equations in the United Kingdom, in both the academic literature and large econometric models, have generally used output as their main independent variable. (O'Brien [19] provides a critical summary of some of the more important studies.) However, before discussing the theoretical model on which this approach is normally based, we should note some important exceptions to this rule.

The employment equations in the London Business School model, for example, are based on variables related to labour supply as well as, or instead of, labour demand. In particular, manufacturing employment depends in the long run on the population of working age, the female participation rate and the ratio of industrial production to GDP, and only the last of these can be considered as influencing labour demand. If the labour market cleared in each period, so that labour supply was always equal to labour demand and employment, we could in principle model employment either from the demand or the supply side. However, in the labour market the assumption of continuous market clearing is extremely strong, as Solow [24], for example, forcefully argues.

Unfortunately, the correct procedure for modelling quantities when markets do not clear is somewhat uncertain. Rosen and Quandt [21] assume that employment is the minimum of demand and supply in each period, whereas Beenstock and Warburton [1] have employment gradually adjusting towards its market clearing equilibrium value. However, most studies have, at least implicitly, assumed that employment is always equal to labour demand and have therefore ignored supply side influences or the possibility that firms may in some periods have faced systematic labour shortages. An alternative procedure, explored by Muellbauer and Winter [14] and also Challen and Hagger [5], is to combine data on employment and unfilled vacancies to obtain a better representation of labour demand.

Within labour demand models, a fundamental distinction lies between those based on profit maximisation and those that confine themselves to cost minimisation. In profit maximisation models output is endogenous along with employment, and if output and employment decisions are made concurrently and yet output is included as an independent variable, the employment equation will suffer from simultaneity bias. The relevant exogenous variables for a profit maximiser in an environment of perfect competition are *real* factor prices, that is, factor prices divided by the output price. Studies that eschew output in favour of real factor prices are relatively rare, but two important recent examples are Sargent [23] for the United States and Symons [25] in the United Kingdom.

In a more realistic environment of oligopolistic or monopolistic competition, the profit maximisation approach runs into the difficulty that shifts in the firm's demand curve may be at least as important in determining employment as movements in real factor prices, yet modelling these shifts may be potentially complex. One way of avoiding this difficulty is to assume (somewhat arbitrarily) that output expectations or plans are predetermined when firms formulate their demand for labour, which reduces the profit maximisation problem to one of cost minimisation for a predetermined level of output.

Cost minimisation models have generally focused on substitution between employment and hours worked. Typically the cost function involves two key non-linearities. The first stems from the fact that if hours worked are above some 'normal' level overtime premia will be incurred, while if hours worked are below normal levels employees may still be paid for a standard week and so the cost to the employer for each effective hour rises. The second non-linearity involves incorporating costs of adjusting employment levels, due to training costs, redundancy pay and so on. These adjustment costs are normally assumed to be quadratic, which implies that the marginal cost of adjusting employment varies positively with the scale of the adjustment. (It also implies that these costs are symmetrical, which is more questionable.) These two considerations suggest a cost function of the form

$$C_t = w_t j(h_t, N_t) + a_t(L_t - L_{t-1})^2/2 \tag{1}$$

where C_t are costs at time t, w is the wage rate (per hour), h is hours worked, N is normal hours, and L is employment. The function $j(\ldots)$ is designed to pick up the extra costs incurred if hours deviate from normal levels. (For a discussion of the shape of this function, see Wickens [27] or Muellbauer [15], for example.) For the moment we shall assume that normal hours are unobservable.

The firm is assumed to face a production function in hours and employment and for simplicity we shall take hours and employment to be perfect substitutes, that is,

$$Y_t = f(h_t L_t) \tag{2}$$

Minimising discounted costs over all future periods subject to (2) for given levels of output gives us two first order conditions besides (2), which when combined with various assumptions about the form of the functions $j(...)$ and $f(...)$, chosen for convenience as much as for realism, can be used to derive a linear, second order difference equation in employment, with output as the independent forcing variable.

Solving this in terms of a decision rule for employment in the current period T as a function of employment and output last period gives

$$L_T = c_1 L_{T-1} + c_2 \hat{Y}_T \tag{3}$$

where $\hat{Y}_T$ is a function of current and future output of the form

$$\hat{Y}_T = Y_T + c_1 Y_{T+1} + c_1^2 Y_{T+2} + c_1^3 Y_{T+3} + \ldots \tag{4}$$

and $0 < c_1 < 1$. (For details of this derivation, showing the relationship between the various parameters, see Henry and Wren-Lewis [11]. For an analysis along similar lines, see for example, Tinsley [26], Nickell [18], Muellbauer [15] or Sargent [23].)

There are two important properties of (3) and (4) that are worth noting at this stage. The first is that c_1, the coefficient on lagged employment, will be positively related to a_t, the cost of adjusting employment. This leads us to the intuitively plausible result that as these adjustment costs rise, the more inertia there will be in employment movements. However there is an important corollary; from (4) we can see that, as c_1 increases, expectations about output in the relatively distant future also become more important. In these circumstances it would be quite wrong to replace $\hat{Y}_T$ by Y_t in (3). Secondly, in the long-run steady-state in which both employment and output are constant, the long-run coefficient on output in (3) will reflect the parameters of the production function (2). In particular, if we rewrite (3) and (4) in terms of the logarithms of employment and output, constant returns to scale for employment in a Cobb-Douglas production function will imply a long-run output coefficient of unity, and anything below unity suggests increasing returns to labour in the long run.

To base estimation on equations (3) and (4) we must assume that aggregation is possible across all firms. We must also specify some model of how output expectations are formed. The most common assumption is that expectations are generated by some unrestricted function of lagged values of output, by an nth order Markov process

$$Y_{t+1}^e = \beta_1 Y_t + \beta_2 Y_{t-1} + \beta_3 Y_{t-2} + \ldots + \beta_n Y_{t-n+1} \tag{5}$$

Combining (3), (4) and (5) gives us a reduced form in which employment depends on lagged employment and current and lagged output, where the lags on output stretch $n-1$ periods into the past;

$$L_T = c_1 L_{T-1} + \gamma_1 Y_T + \gamma_2 Y_{T-1} + \gamma_3 Y_{T-2} + \ldots + \gamma_n Y_{T-n+1} + dt + u_T \tag{6}$$

The trend in this equation is included to pick up trend productivity growth, due, for example, to technical progress. Equation (6) is the maintained hypothesis on which our estimated employment equations are based.

We can use a similar procedure to derive an equation for hours as a function of lagged hours and current and lagged output, that is,

$$h_T = g_1 h_{T-1} + \delta_1 Y_T + \delta_2 Y_{T-1} + \ldots + \delta_n Y_{T-n+1} + ft + v_T \qquad (7)$$

In this case, although we would expect the initial values of δ_i to be positive because at least part of any increase in output will be met by extra hours, as employment adjusts to higher output hours worked will fall and so subsequent δ_i should be negative. In fact, because hourly wage costs are always at a minimum when normal hours are worked (that is, $j(\ldots) > h$ when $h \neq N$), in the long run hours should be completely independent of output. In (7) movements in normal hours are proxied by a time trend.

Equations similar to (6) and (7) form the basis of the employment and hours equations in the Treasury and Bank of England models as well as in the National Institute model. The Treasury model equations do not contain any lagged dependent variables, but they do include an explicit (although exogenous) variable measuring trend productivity growth. In forecasting manufacturing employment the Bank of England have one equation for total man-hours as a function of output and another that relates employment to normal hours and total man-hours. (For a detailed discussion and evaluation of these and other equations see O'Brien [19].)

One obvious way of elaborating this simple cost minimisation model is to include measures of relative prices or other factors of production. Even if we restrict ourselves to substitution between hours and employment, we can attempt to model changes in the function $j(\ldots)$ in equation (1) by including variables related to normal hours and the relative cost of extra hours in relation to the cost of employment in equation (6) or (7). The main limitation here is the difficulty of obtaining relevant data series, although the results reported in Henry [10] are encouraging. Hart and Sharot [7] consider the role of non-wage labour costs, while Bosworth [2] considers some of the complications arising from shiftworking.

The cost function (1) assumes that there are no adjustment costs involved in changing hours rather than employment. Once we allow for adjustment costs in more than one factor of production the mathematics of the optimisation problem become more difficult, involving, for example, fourth order difference equations. Nevertheless, one fairly general result is that employment not only depends on the lagged value of itself, but also on the lagged value of these other factors of production. (Morrison and Berndt [13] develop a similar model based on the change in quasi-fixed factors appearing in the production function.) These may include hours (see again Henry [10]), but a more familiar example comes from the interrelated factor demand model of Nadiri and Rosen [17], in which employment depends on the lagged value of the capital stock. Briscoe and Peel [3] estimate this model on United Kingdom data. The interrelated factor demand model can also be extended to include stockbuilding decisions, where sales rather than output is predetermined. More speculatively, disequilibrium in company sector financial variables may also have implications for the dynamic path of employment. (For some survey evidence that suggests this, see *National Institute Economic Review,* no. 99, February 1982, p. 26.)

In the interrelated factor demand model, disequilibrium in the capital stock influences employment because of the constraint imposed by the production function. In addition, the relative price of capital to labour may also influence employment in the long run. There are theoretical problems in translating the simple capital labour substitution model to a complex production economy (see Garegnani [6]) and there are also severe difficulties in correctly measuring the cost of capital. Substitution may also be possible between labour and raw materials or energy, implying that this relative price should enter the employment equation. (See for example Bruno and Sachs [4], and Roy and Wenban-Smith [22].) An additional complication is that, as for output, it is expectations about future values of these relative prices that actually appear in the employment decision rule. Given the many problems of measuring (expected) relative factor prices, it is tempting to abandon the attempt to incorporate them explicitly. The next best solution may be to take account of the output price by including (expected) *real* labour costs in the employment equation.

Models based on adjustment costs inevitably involve expectations about future variables, so the estimated employment equation will involve some hypothesis about expectations as well as the employment decision rule. This is equally true whether we assume profit maximisation or cost minimisation. In Sargent [23], for example, employment is a function of expected real wages, where expectations follow a Markov process in much the same manner as (5). In the case of expected output (and possibly for the United Kingdom real wages as well, see Henry and Wren-Lewis [12]), this particular expectations model can be criticised as naive and unrealistic, in that it excludes other variables (like international price competitiveness) that almost certainly influence output in the real world, and that might well, therefore, influence output expectations. We could simply add such variables into the employment reduced form, but the *ad hoc* nature of these additions and the consequent lack of *a priori* restrictions on the parameter estimates in that equation will increase the chances of spurious correlation and reduce the efficiency of the parameter estimates.

One way of attempting to avoid this situation and yet improve on the simple specification embodied in (5), would be to use actual data on output expectations in (3) and (4). The answers to various CBI survey questions are likely to involve firms' output expectations, although possibly only of a somewhat short-term nature. An alternative source of data that could be used as a proxy for expectations would be published forecasts (for example those of the National Institute).

In the absence of any satisfactory direct measurement one method of constructing expectations data (either explicitly or implicitly) is to use the rational expectations hypothesis. Three recent studies of employment have used this approach in the context of the cost minimising model set out above. In Nickell [18], expected output depends on real share prices and the growth in $M3$, while in Henry and Wren-Lewis [11] output expectations are generated from past values of international price competitiveness and a fiscal policy variable. (The two models are compared in Henry and Wren-Lewis [12]). In both cases it is assumed that current employment is a function of output expectations which are based on information available in the previous period and therefore independent of current period output. (This assumption has the advantage of avoiding problems of simultaneity outlined below.) In Muellbauer [15] and Muellbauer and Mendis [16] firms do react to surprises in current period output and this assumption allows the authors to derive a particularly simple and elegant form for the employment decision rule.

One other key element in any employment equation based on labour demand will be the production function. This is typically taken to be of a Cobb-Douglas type, but Hazledine [8] argues that a more plausible short-term production function would allow labour productivity to rise with output to some peak rate (representing the technically efficient operating level) and fall thereafter. The difficulty with this approach is in measuring changes in this peak level, although modelling trend productivity changes in equation (6) by a simple time trend may be equally problematic. Hazledine [9] contains some suggestions for improving this situation (p. 156), and also provides a recent, critical survey of some of the theoretical problems in modelling employment.

Data

In the National Institute model total United Kingdom employment is divided into four subsectors: manufacturing, 'other private' which includes services, construction and agriculture, 'mainly public' (which includes all non-manufacturing SICs which contain any public corporation) and, finally, public services. Quarterly data on hours is only available for operatives in the manufacturing sector. (For employment equations at a more disaggregated level, see Peterson [20].)

Chart 4.1 plots output, output per head (productivity) and hours

Chart 4.1   Manufacturing employment, hours and output

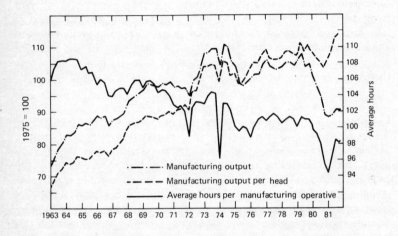

Source: Economic Trends.

worked for the manufacturing sector from 1963 to 1981. The cycle in output is reflected in both hours and productivity, although in the hours series the underlying trend is downwards. The cycle in productivity is more damped than the cycle in output, but is nevertheless quite distinct. (Much the same is true for the 'other private' sector.) This is exactly what the presence of important adjustment costs in changing employment would suggest; a fall in output is only partially met by a fall in employment because hours also fall. In some cases, however, such as in 1975 or 1981, the movements in productivity appear to be at least as sharp as those in output. As we shall see, our equations have difficulties in tracking both of these periods. The behaviour of productivity in the last two years of the data period is particularly unusual in that the fall in productivity in 1980 is far less severe than the decline in output.

The other notable feature of the productivity series is the underlying upward trend. However, whereas the data appeared to cycle around a fairly constant *exponential* trend between 1963 and 1973, developments since then have made the position far less clear. For this reason alone, it is as yet impossible to say whether very recent improvements in productivity represent any permanent change in underlying trend.

Apart from the restricted coverage of the data, we should note that measured hours are unlikely to correspond to the rate of utilisation of labour (which is the relevant concept in a production function) because of variations in the intensity of work effort. There is a distinct downward trend in the hours series, which we would associate with a decline in normal hours. However, the published series for normal hours has been almost constant from 1966 to 1980. This suggests that the recorded series may not correspond with the concept of normal hours used above, that is, the minimum of the hours function $j(\ldots)$ in equation (1).

Estimation

All the equations in this section were estimated by ordinary least squares. This involves one problem which remains unresolved. As we have already noted, profit maximisation implies that output is endogenous to the employment decision and that therefore an employment equation that includes current period output (as all the equations below do) will suffer from simultaneity bias. Another source of simultaneity bias may arise because increases in income are generated by extra employment and this leads to additional consumption and higher output in the same period. We have made no attempt to correct for any simultaneity bias in the equations below, although some results using instrumental variable techniques are included in O'Brien [19].

Our maintained hypothesis for employment is equation (6). There, the maximum lag on output (that is, n) remains unspecified, but experimentation with lags up to eight quarters suggest that only a few short lags on output were significant. Only one lag on employment appears in equation (6), but there are a number of theoretical reasons why longer lags might be expected. For example, if disequilibrium in other variables, such as the capital stock or stockbuilding, influences employment, but these variables are not included in the equation, then some of these effects may be picked up by additional lags on employment. Planning periods longer than one quarter, or the existence of more than one type of labour, would also generate additional lagged dependent variables. In the case of both manufacturing and the 'other private' sector, the data strongly suggested including more than one lagged dependent variable in the employment equation.

Manufacturing (see Appendix, (7.1))
The model equation includes two lags on employment and output, as

well as current period output and a time trend. *EMPMF* is manufacturing employment and *OMF* an index of manufacturing output. The data easily reject the inclusion of an extra lag on output and employment ($F(2,62) = 0.15$), or indeed any additional lags on either variable. (An example of a general equation including eight lags on output and employment, estimated over a slightly shorter data period, is given in Henry and Wren-Lewis [11], p. 12.)

The model equation embodies the important restriction that the long-run coefficient on output is unity. (The apparently odd ratio terms in the equation are required to impose this restriction.) This restriction is accepted, with an F test giving $F(1,63) = 2.8$ compared with a critical 5 per cent value of about 4. Without this restriction, the long-run coefficient on output is about 0.6, which suggests increasing returns to labour in the short *and* long run. This increasing returns phenomenon is a well-known characteristic of United Kingdom data (see, for example, Hazledine [8]). The model equation imposes constant returns to labour in the long run, but in the short and medium term increasing returns persist; for example a sustained 1 per cent rise in manufacturing output will increase employment by 0.5 per cent after one year, 0.7 per cent after two, 0.8 per cent after three years, and so on.

In the previous section we noted the unusual behaviour of productivity in the last two years of the estimation period. An obvious question is, therefore, whether the model equation would remain stable if re-estimated over a period that ended in 1979 rather than 1982. At first sight the results are reassuring, in that the parameter estimates on the employment and output terms remain very similar. However, there are two major problems. Firstly the unity restriction on the long-run output coefficient would be rejected in the equation whose estimation period ends in 1979. Secondly, a Chow test for stability gives an F statistic over three, compared with a 5 per cent critical value of around two and so, by this criteria, stability is rejected. This result simply reflects the model equation's inability to predict employment movements in 1980 and 1981. The equation's residuals from 1980(II)–(IV), in percentage terms, are $- 0.2, - 0.6, - 0.1$, reflecting a failure to pick up the speed of the decline in employment during the recession. One interesting point is that a very similar overprediction of employment occurs in the previous recession, when from 1974(III) the equation's residuals are $- 0.5, - 0.0, - 0.5$ and $- 0.2$ per cent.

There are a number of explanations for this predictive failure. One possibility, which links this with the problem of increasing returns to labour, is explored in Henry and Wren-Lewis [11]. This suggests that the parameters on output are biased towards zero because they measure output expectations imperfectly and that, furthermore, output expectations were revised downward sharply during 1980, leading to unusually rapid falls in employment. This hypothesis finds some support, although as yet the evidence is far from conclusive. (A similar idea is discussed in Muellbauer and Mendis [16].)

The model equation also has important implications for productivity that are worth noting. The time trend in the equation implies a trend productivity growth rate of around 3 per cent per annum. However, the equation also implies that the level of output per head is related to the rate of growth of output. We can see this by examining the model equation in a steady growth equilibrium in which output growth equals (at a quarterly rate) g and the level of productivity is p. Using the trend rate of productivity growth above to relate the growth of employment to g, we can write the equation as $0.26g = 0.088 - 0.008(0.31) - 0.00014t + 0.02p$. If the annual growth rate in output rises by 1 per cent, this equation implies that in the long run output per man will rise by just over 3 per cent.

Theory suggests a number of additional variables that might be included in the employment equation besides output and we therefore tried including some of these in equations similar to the one above. Normal hours were always insignificant and wrongly signed, confirming our doubts about the published series noted above. Lagged values of actual hours were also insignificant. Various measures of relative prices were included, but the only variable to achieve any significance was the ratio of raw material prices (using the Department of Industry's input price index) to labour costs. However, this was only significant when lagged exactly eight quarters, suggesting the possibility of spurious correlation.

Other private sector employment (see Appendix (7.2))

The model equation for other private sector employment is very similar to that for manufacturing, the only difference being the exclusion of output lagged two quarters. In this equation $OOTH6$ is the index of output for the other private sector. In a more general equation there was some evidence of a term in employment lagged four quarters (which partially accounts for the high Box-Pierce statistic), but it had a t value near unity and so its exclusion was not rejected.

Constant returns to labour are again imposed in this equation and this restriction is just accepted, with $F(1,60) = 3.2$. However, without this restriction we get the opposite result to manufacturing, with a long-run coefficient on output near three! The trend rate of productivity growth implied by the model equation for this sector is only ½ per cent per annum. The equation completely fails to pick up the decline in employment in 1980 and 1981, producing negative residuals in every quarter. In this case, however, there is no similar pattern during 1974/5.

Mainly public employment and employment in public administration (*see Appendix* (*7.3*) *and* (*7.4*))

In the public services output is measured in terms of employment, and productivity is assumed to be constant, which gives rise to the simple identity in the Appendix. The structure of the equation for mainly public employment is similar to those for manufacturing and the other private sector, although in this case constant returns have not been imposed.

Average hours in manufacturing (*see Appendix* (*7.7*))

The maintained hypothesis is equation (7). In this case additional lags on hours beyond one quarter did not prove necessary and lags on output greater than three quarters were insignificant. As we suggested above, the initial output term is positive, but subsequent terms are negative and the long-run influence on hours is almost (and certainly insignificantly different from) zero. The equation suggests that hours will tend to fall by 0.3 per cent per annum if output remains constant. This equation also fails to capture the extent to which average hours fell during the recent recession.

In the course of estimation, on an earlier data set, two additional variables were included in this equation. One was the published series for normal hours, but this was insignificant and had the wrong sign. Our theoretical discussion also suggested a case for including lagged values of employment in the hours equation. In fact the value of manufacturing employment lagged one quarter did have the anticipated negative sign, although it was just insignificant. One curious result was that the *change* in employment lagged three quarters had a highly significant ($t > 4$) positive effect on hours, but as there appears to be no theoretical justification for this effect it was not included in the model equation.

References

[1] Beenstock, M. and Warburton, P., 'An aggregative model of the UK labour market', *Oxford Economic Papers*, vol. 34, 1982, pp. 253–75.

[2] Bosworth, D. L., 'Hours of work and employment in UK manufacturing industry: an empirical analysis', Mimeo, University of Loughborough, 1982.

[3] Briscoe, G. and Peel, D., 'The value of inter-related factor demand models for explaining short-term employment behaviour in the UK manufacturing sector', Warwick University Centre for Industrial Economics and Business Research, Paper no. 52, 1974.

[4] Bruno, M. and Sachs, J., 'Input price shocks and the slowdown in economic activity: the case of UK manufacturing', *Review of Economic Studies*, vol. 49, 1982, pp. 679–706.

[5] Challen, D. W. and Hagger, A. J., 'Demand for labour functions: the wrong track?', *Oxford Bulletin of Economics and Statistics*, vol. 44, 1982, pp. 31–57.

[6] Garegnani, P., 'Notes on consumption investment and effective demand', *Cambridge Journal of Economics, 2*(4), December 1978 and *3*(1) March 1979.

[7] Hart, R. and Sharot, T., 'The short-run demand for workers and hours: a recursive model', *Review of Economic Studies, 45*(2), no. 140, June 1978.

[8] Hazledine, T., 'New specifications for employment and hours functions', *Economica,* vol. 45, May 1978.

[9] Hazledine, T., 'Employment functions and the demand for labour in the short run', in Hornstein, Z., Grice, J. and Webb, A. (eds), *The Economics of the Labour Market,* London, *HMSO,* 1981.

[10] Henry, S. G. B., 'Forecasting employment and unemployment' in Hornstein, Z., Grice, J. and Webb, A. (eds), *The Economics of the Labour Market,* London, *HMSO,* 1981.

[11] Henry, S. G. B. and Wren-Lewis, S., 'Employment and expected output', National Institute of Economic and Social Research, Discussion Paper no. 55, 1983.

[12] Henry, S. G. B. and Wren-Lewis, S., 'The aggregate labour market in the UK: some experiments with rational expectations models', forthcoming in Muet, P. and Malgrange, P. (eds), *Contributions to Modern Macroeconomics.*

[13] Morrison, C. J. and Berndt, E. R., 'Short run labour productivity in a dynamic model', *Journal of Econometrics,* vol. 16, 1981, pp. 339–66.

[14] Muellbauer, J. and Winter, D., 'Unemployment, employment and exports in British manufacturing', *European Economic Review,* vol. 13, 1980, pp. 383–409.

[15] Muellbauer, J., 'Are employment decisions based on rational expectations?', Birkbeck College Discussion Paper, No. 74, 1980.

[16] Muellbauer, J. and Mendis, L., 'Employment functions and productivity change: has there been a productivity breakthrough?', Mimeo, Birkbeck College, 1983.

[17] Nadiri, M. and Rosen, S., 'Interrelated factor demand equations', *American Economic Review,* September 1969.

[18] Nickell, S., 'An investigation of the determinants of manufacturing employment in the UK', Centre for Labour Economics Discussion Paper, no. 105, 1981.

[19] O'Brien, P., 'Forecasting models of manufacturing employment: a comparison, Mimeo, National Institute of Economic and Social Research, 1982.

[20] Peterson, W., 'Employment', in Barker, T. S. (ed), *Economic Structure and Policy with applications to the British economy,* London, Chapman and Hall, 1976.

[21] Rosen, H. and Quandt, R., 'Estimation of a disequilibrium aggregate labour market', *Review of Economics and Statistics,* vol. 60(3), August 1978, pp. 371–9.

[22] Roy, A. and Wenban-Smith, G. 'Prospects for productivity growth', Mimeo, National Institute of Economic and Social Research, 1983.

[23] Sargent, T. S., 'Estimation of a dynamic labour demand schedule under rational expectations', *Journal of Political Economy,* vol. 86, 1979, pp. 1009–44.

[24] Solow, R., 'On theories of unemployment', *American Economic Review,* March, 1980.

[25] Symons, J. S. V., 'The demand for labour in British manufacturing', London School of Economics Centre for Labour Economics, Discussion paper no. 91, 1981.

[26] Tinsley, P., 'A variable adjustment model of labour demand', *International Economic Review*, vol. 12, part 3, October 1971.
[27] Wickens, M., 'Towards a theory of the labour market', *Economica,* vol. 41, August 1974.

5 Wages and Prices
S. Hall, S.G.B. Henry and C. Trinder

Wages

We begin with a discussion of some issues of theory and specification, touch briefly on data sources and then describe the derivation of the wage equation in the National Institute model.

Some theoretical considerations

Much of the empirical work on wage equations over the last decade has been based on the expectations-augmented Phillips curve. This theory, on a broad definition, is taken to include any form of wage equation which uses a measure of excess supply of labour (usually but not necessarily unemployment) and expected price inflation. An alternative theory has emphasised bargaining in the labour market. Empirical work then attempts to describe these bargains in terms of actual and planned, or target, real wages. In these bargaining models nominal wage inflation may also depend on expected price inflation over the contract period and indeed on the level of unemployment (because the outcome of the bargain may depend on the state of the aggregate labour market, again measured by unemployment, as was assumed, for example, by Sargan [10]). Evidently the distinction between Phillips curves and bargaining models, such as those just described, is difficult to draw in a hard and fast way. This is, in part, simply a question of nomenclature; some authors clearly have a preference for describing any wage equation as a Phillips curve providing only that unemployment is included as a regressor variable (see, for example, Nickell [9]). We will be suggesting that there is considerable support for wage models which use both the real wage *and* unemployment as regressor variables and the examples reported in this chapter will be of that variety. The theoretical interpretation of the equations offered here is that they are models of bargaining but of bargains which are significantly affected by unemployment.

Expectations-augmented Phillips curves have traditionally been of the form

$$\dot{W} = \alpha(u - u^*) + \beta \dot{P}^e$$

$$\alpha < 0 \quad \text{and} \quad 1 \leqslant \beta > 0. \tag{1}$$

In this equation u^* is defined as the non-inflationary level of unemployment and P^e the expected price level. Hence, if actual unemployment, u, is equal to u^*, providing that price inflation is fully and correctly anticipated and the β coefficient is unity, then u^* is the 'natural' rate of unemployment. The steady state solution for $\dot{W}$ in equation (1) is indeterminate under these conditions and u^* is compatible with any steady-state value for $\dot{W}$ (see, Artis [1]). In other words, the long-run Phillips curve is vertical. If expectations are formed adaptively, that is,

$$\Delta \dot{P}^e = \theta(\dot{P}^e - \dot{P})_{-1}, \quad \theta < 1 \tag{2}$$

then a temporary trade-off between wage inflation and unemployment will exist.

Much empirical work has focussed on the stability of the augmented Phillips curve, particularly on the stability of the negative coefficient on the unemployment term. Evidence accumulated by the mid-1970s was generally adverse (see Henry, Smith and Sawyer [5] for an example of this scepticism). But, as already anticipated above, rapid increases in unemployment and falling rates of wage inflation, especially since 1979, have led to a reappraisal of the evidence, mainly in the context of the bargaining model, an example of which follows.

A simple form of bargaining model with a target for the real wage is (in logs)

$$\dot{W} = \gamma[(W/P)^d - (W/P)]_{-1} + \delta \dot{P}^e + \epsilon Z \tag{3}$$

where W/P is the real wage and the superscript d refers to a desired or target value. Z represents other variables, which are discussed below. The model has been interpreted as an error correction model (ECM), with the response to the real wage level providing *proportional* error correction towards the desired target $(W/P)^d$. If the coefficient on expected price inflation is unity, the equation allows for full *derivative* correction as well. Under this latter condition changes in the rate of inflation, if fully anticipated, would be matched by equal changes in wage inflation, so that real wages could not move away from the real wage target as a result of variation in the rate of inflation.

The problems which have emerged with this model are largely concerned with the determinants of the real wage target. Henry, Smith and Sawyer (*op. cit.*) proxied this with a time trend. This procedure makes the target exogenous and suggests that, unless real wages grow at the rate implied by the trend, wage inflationary pressures must persist. Whether this is a realistic property of the equation or not is not easily decided. The real wage equation with $(W/P)^d$ proxied by a trend is consistent with trend real wage growth. On the other hand, it may well be unsatisfactory to model targets using a time-trend alone implying that these targets do not adapt in any way to the evolution of the economy. A behavioural model which linked wage targets to economic variables would be more plausible. Henry [3] reports some success with a moving average target of the form $\Sigma_i^H (W/P)_{t-(i+1)}$ which suggests an evolving target based on actual real wage experience (see also Wadhwani [11] for a more elaborate version of this idea). Whilst such an evolving target would introduce considerable inertia into the hypothesised wage setting procedure, it is not as extreme in its behavioural assumptions as is the autonomous real wage movement implied by the use of a time-trend.

Another important issue in the real wage model is whether targets are gross or net of tax and other employee deductions. Sargan [10] uses gross real wages. Henry, Smith and Sawyer [5] use a net figure and also base the target on average earnings rather than on wage rates. Real net earnings, which approximates real take-home pay, lends itself to a bargaining interpretation which emphasises the employees' claims rather than the employers' offers. In the results below we discuss the evidence for a gross rather than a net measure for the target. This can be tested by including the retentions ratio (RR) as an additional variable in the regression. All the examples will use earnings rather than wage rates as a regressor variable.

As already indicated, recent evidence of wage inflation and unemployment movements has increased the interest in hybrid models based on both real wages and unemployment. These are most often given a bargaining interpretation. (For a full account the reader is referred to the paper by Nickell, *op. cit.*, which gives, to our knowledge, the only satisfactory model of wage determination based on postulated union behaviour.) These equations are of the form

$$\dot{W} = \lambda_1 [(W/P)^d - (W/P)]_{-1} + \lambda_2 \dot{P}^e + \lambda_3 f(u) \tag{4}$$

One interpretation of the presence of unemployment in such models is that proposed originally by Sargan (*op. cit.*), that is, that fluctuations in the excess supply of labour exert a moderating influence on the wage claims. The steady-state properties of such an equation are revealing. Evidently if $\dot{W} = g_1$, $\dot{P}^e = \dot{P} = g_2$ then if $(W/P)^d = \gamma t$, the wage equation becomes, $g_1 = -\lambda_1 (W/P)^* + \lambda_1 \gamma t + \lambda_2 g_2 + \lambda_3 f(u)^*$, where * indicates steady-state values, or $(W/P)^* = (\lambda_2 g_2 - g_1)\lambda_1 + \gamma t + \lambda_3/\lambda_1 f(u)^* = \gamma_0 + \gamma_1 t + \gamma_2 f(u)^*$ which particular solution defines a steady-state relationship between unemployment and real wages.

Two radically different approaches to modelling earnings have been reported recently. These are the London Business School model emphasising the demand price of labour and the model given by Minford and Brech, which is based on an equilibrium model of the labour market.

The London Business School model of wages in the manufacturing sector provides an interesting alternative specification to that indicated in equation (4) above. The dependent variable relates to nominal earnings in manufacturing, inclusive of employers' contributions and the National Insurance Surcharge (LBS [6]). The steady-state equation implied by the model is a relationship between real earnings (deflated by wholesale prices), productivity and direct and indirect tax rates. The model is couched in terms of the demand side, emphasising the product wage as the outcome of the wage setting procedure, unlike the bargaining models described above which place more emphasis on the supply side.

The Minford and Brech [7] model of wage rates appears very similar in general specification to equation (4), and is (in logs) $\dot{W} = \alpha_1 P^e + \alpha_2 Q^e + \alpha_3 (W/P)_{-1} + \alpha_4 (\text{var } P) + \alpha_5 (\text{var } Q)$. The superscript $()^e$ refers to an expected variable and the authors use the unrestricted reduced form of a simplified macroeconomic model to provide predictions for price and output, which then enter the wage equation above as data. Except for the variance terms, this equation will be difficult to distinguish empirically from (4) if, as seems likely, expected demand pressure Q^e is correlated with unemployment. The authors interpret it as an equilibrium model, however, and for that reason impose the coefficient on expected price inflation at unity (so that real wages fully correct for changes in expected price inflation). Real wages are described as continuously at their natural rate, apart from random disturbances, which, in accordance with the rational expectations hypothesis, must be uncorrelated. This natural rate is partly determined by the variances of unanticipated inflation and output, since large variances could increase the likelihood of misperception about real and nominal magnitudes.

Later in this chapter equations of the form given by (4) are reported. In those results a forecasting rule is used to generate price expectations. The final part of this section, therefore, is devoted to a brief review of hypotheses about expectation formation, a topic which has remained at the centre of the debate over the determinants of wage inflation.

Much of the early work on wage equations used the adaptive expectations hypothesis when deriving expectations-augmented Phillips curves. The objections to this hypothesis are by now well known: it is mechanical and, when inflation changes, it is non optimal when viewed as a forecasting rule. Higher order time-series models for generating price expectations could reduce some of these deficiencies. Most attention now seems devoted to Muth-rational formation of expectations. In its weakest sense, the rational expectations hypothesis (REH) assumes that the agent uses efficiently all the information available to him to form expectations.

Thus, in general, we may write the wage equation in the form $\dot{W}_t = f(\ldots(P_{t+1}^e | \Omega_t))$ where Ω represents the information set available to agents in period t. The simplest operational form for this hypothesis is to assume that agents use a time-series model for prices and predictions from such a model may than be used to proxy expectations. This is often referred to as the weak form of the REH, and is used in the examples reported below. Like some of the other partial treatments of the REH mentioned below, this procedure may be consistent, although it is clearly not efficient. To implement a more elaborate form of the REH, the agent is assumed to make unbiassed predictions of price inflation using a complete macroeconomic model. This means one must substitute the expected value $E(P)$ for P^e, where $E(P)$ is derived from the restricted reduced form of the whole macroeconomic model. But the macroeconomic model must include the equation for wages that is being estimated. This procedure, therefore, results in a closed form for the wage equation dependent on non-linear functions of model parameters and also on the parameters of the (time-series) model used for projecting exogenous processes (see Wallis [13]). Estimating the wage equation subject to these restrictions would be efficient and the model would also be rational. In practice, however, this implementation is computationally very difficult, since P and W are part of a large interdependent macroeconomic model and the restricted reduced form of this is itself extremely complicated. Because of these difficulties a more simplified model of the macroeconomy may be used to capture the broad features of the complete macroeconomic model (Henry and Ormerod [4] may be interpreted in this way), or an unrestricted reduced form explaining prices in terms of a few exogenous processes may be used.

The definition of wages

Wage data can be derived either from the published wage rates index or from the total of wages and salaries recorded in the national accounts. The variable used in the National Institute model is of the latter kind and is calculated as follows: *WAGERATE = AVEARN/AVHMF, AVEARN = (W + S)/EMP*. Equations appear in the model for *WAGERATE, AVHMF* (average hours in manufacturing, which proxy actual hours worked in the whole economy) and for sub-categories of total employment (*EMP*).

The variable *WAGERATE* is not without its own problems. In particular, its use suggests that the only influence on wage drift is changes in average hours worked, which is clearly an over simplification. The use of the official index of basic wage rates, however, would be even less satisfactory. The coverage of the official index is restricted in that it relates only to the national collective agreements of minimum wage

Chart 5.1   Money wages, real wages and unemployment, 1960–82.

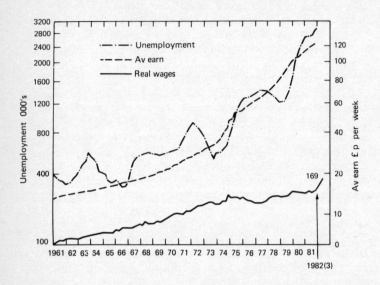

Source: Economic Trends.

ratès for *manual* workers and so does not take account of changes in wages rates determined by local negotiations or the wage settlements of non-manual workers. Moreover, the official index is to be discontinued after December 1983. A comparison of the *WAGERATE* series defined above and official wage rate series since 1962 shows that movements are sometimes very different. For example, the *WAGERATE* series rose much more rapidly than the official index at the end of the period. It was 8.5 per cent higher in 1982(III) than in 1981(III) compared with an increase of 6.1 per cent in the official index over the same period. It is now generally accepted that the official wage rate index no longer accurately serves the function for which it was intended. Estimates by the National Institute, designed to remove the known deficiencies of the official index as a measure of wage settlements, suggest that a more accurate measure of settlements in the 1981–2 round would be 7½ per cent, which is actually closer to the *WAGERATE* index based on national accounts data, than it is to the official index.

The wage equation in the National Institute model
The wage equation in the National Institute model is based on a specification similar to that of equation (4) above. Estimation over the period 1963(IV) to 1981(IV) by autoregressive least squares (autoregressive coefficient = $-0.579(4.6)$) produced the following coefficients:

$$\Delta \ln WAGERATE = -0.04194 + 0.31361 \ \Delta \ln WAGERATE_{-1}$$
$$(1.0) \qquad (2.5)$$
$$+ 0.32647 \ \Delta \ln CPI_{-1} - 0.11325 \ \ln RE_{-2}$$
$$(1.8) \qquad\qquad (2.4)$$
$$- 0.15459 \ \Delta \ln RR_{-1} - 0.66021 \ UPC_{-1}$$
$$(1.7) \qquad\qquad (4.1)$$
$$- 0.01104 \ DUMMY + 0.00151 \ TIME$$
$$(2.8) \qquad\qquad (4.5)$$

$$SEE = 0.01626, \chi_1^2(8) = 4.9.$$

In this equation the variables are defined as:

WAGERATE	Average wage rate
CPI	Consumer price index
RE	Real earnings $= AVEARN/CPI$
RR	Retention ratio $=$ $1 - (NIC - EC + TXPER)/WS - K$
UPC	Rate of unemployment $=$ $UNEMP/(UNEMP + EMP)$
DUMMY	Incomes policy dummy, 1 in 75(III)–78(III), 0 elsewhere.

Whilst this equation is well determined and has plausible signs on its estimated coefficients, it nonetheless has some rather worrying features. Firstly the equation is estimated with a highly significant first order error model. The selection of a model with both systematic and error dynamics may be acceptable for representation of the data, but if it is possible to identify a model with (presumably) different systematic dynamics, regression variables and functional form, which has approximate white noise error, this would generally be preferred to the example above, interpreting systematic error as evidence of misspecification. Secondly, the implied steady-state relationships in the estimated equation are implausible. Ignoring for simplicity all differential terms and the dummy variable, this static relationship between real earnings, time and the rate of unemployment is $\ln RE = -5.827 \ UPC + 0.0132 \ TIME$.

The implications of this equation were thought implausible. Firstly the coefficient on the time trend suggests growth in desired real earnings *ceteris paribus* of 5.4 per cent per annum, which is hard to believe if targets are in any way based on experience. Secondly, the partial effect of changes in unemployment on real earnings growth is very large, indicating that a 1 per cent increase in unemployment would reduce real earnings by almost 6 per cent in the steady-state. Chart 5.1 suggests that fluctuations in unemployment have not typically been associated with fluctuations in real wages on anything like this scale.

In the light of these objections to this form of the wage equation an alternative was devised, based on a fairly radical re-specification of the version just reported. We decided to impose steady-state growth in the real earnings path at the historically given average rate of 2.46 per cent per annum. Instead of relying on a single term in price inflation we introduced a new variable reflecting the weakly rational hypothesis into the formation of price expectations. This meant fitting an autoregressive $(AR(4))$ model for $\Delta \ln P$ and using the predictions from this equation as the expected rate of price inflation.

Other simplifications were adopted in the light of experiments with this restricted form for the wage equation. The most important of these was the omission of the retentions ratio and the dummy variable for the 1975−8 incomes policy. Neither of these variables proved to be significant. Perhaps the poor quality of the econometric results which include the incomes policy dummy is due to a misspecification in treating incomes policy as a exogenous influence on wages. The decision to introduce an incomes policy and the terms of such a policy will depend on inflation objectives and on the behaviour of inflation itself. This suggests that the policy should be specified as part of a system incorporating a structural wage equation and an incomes policy reaction equation (see Wallis [12] on this point, and Desai, Keil and Wadhawani [2] for an example). However, not all researchers have the same experience here. For an example of wage equations with well determined incomes policy effects, see LBS [6].

Finally, a number of experiments were conducted to investigate cyclical correction to the wage rate variable being used as the dependent variable in these equations. These involved a cyclical correction to the dependent variable using $W/(H\bar{N} + (1 + \alpha)(H - H\bar{N}))$ (where $H\bar{N}$ is normal hours, H actual hours worked, and α is the overtime premium), but they failed to remove the problem of serial correlation in the errors. Consequently, a measure of actual hours was entered as a regressor variable, in an unrestricted form, and the influence of this variable on *WAGERATE* was left to the data to determine.

The equation used in the model, which was developed in the light of these developments, may be found in the Appendix (8.1). The response of real earnings in the long run to a 1 per cent increase in unemployment in this equation is about 1½ to 2 per cent.

Prices

The domestic price variables discussed in this section are the consumer price index (*CPI*) and the wholesale price of manufactured goods (*PWMF*). There is also in the National Institute model an equation linking the retail price index (*RPI*) to the *CPI*. Trade prices are discussed in chapter 3. We consider first the specification used for price equations and then present some empirical results.

Theory

The equations used in most macroeconomic models assume that prices are determined as a constant mark-up on unit costs. In the simple linear case they take the form

$$P' = WL + MT + CP' \tag{1}$$

where the price per unit (P') excludes, for the moment, indirect tax. The other variables are wages (W), labour input (L), the price of imported materials (M), imported materials (T) and the constant mark-up (C). All variables are expressed per unit of output. Charges for capital services are not explicitly included in (1). By implication they are met out of the mark-up. Rearranging (1) gives $P' = (1 - C)^{-1}(WL + MF)$ for the level of prices and

$$\dot{P} = a_1\dot{W} + a_1\dot{L} + a_2\dot{M} \tag{2}$$

for the rate of change where a_1 is the share of labour cost in the value of output (that is, WL/P) and a_2 is the share of imports cost, MT/P. There is no explicit recognition of the effects of technical change on prices in this equation, but one way in which these will be introduced is through the growth of labour productivity.

Equation (2) implies a similar effect on prices from variations in output per head whether these are trend growth or cyclical fluctuations. Since inputs are measured per unit of output, $\dot{L}$ is equal to the percentage change in labour input per unit of output. Hence this may be replaced by (the negative of) the proportional change in output per head ($\dot{q}$), that is,

$$\dot{P}' = a_1\dot{w} + a_2\dot{m} - a_1\dot{q} \tag{3}$$

which simply emphasises the property in (1) that changes in wage costs and productivity (or more precisely in output per head) are assumed to have an equal effect on prices. Equations similar to (3), which are estimated *without* the constraint that the coefficients on wage costs and productivity be the same, often produce relatively small effects for productivity. (See, for example, the wholesale price equation in National Institute interim model IV equation (10.2).) This finding supports the argument advanced by Neild [8], that firms plan their prices on a normal cost basis and do not respond to short-run variations in output per head. Trend productivity effects can nevertheless be introduced into the price equation by using a wage cost variable of the form $W/(1 + \rho)^t$ where ρ is the productivity trend. Neild, for example, provided estimated versions of price equations using an extraneous estimate of the trend movement in output per head (approximately 2.5 per cent per annum) and also a direct estimate of trend productivity derived from the price equation itself using the linear approximation $W/(1 + \rho)^t \cong W(1 - t)$ for the wage variable.

A further influence on price changes comes from changes in indirect taxes. In the additive case (since indirect taxes are largely *ad valorem*) we can write prices as $P = P'(1 + t)$ where t is a measure of indirect tax per unit.

Although it is a simple case to analyse, the assumption of a constant mark-up may not be valid. For example, margins may alter with variations in demand or capital productivity. Chart 5.2 shows prices, costs and margins over the period 1962(I) to 1982(IV). It is drawn to show the approximate contribution of the component costs to prices. The residual element reflects movements in margins. These were particularly noticeable in 1971–2, 1974–6 and 1980–1.

The discussion so far has concentrated on simple additive models for prices. The prices model used in the National Institute model is specified in logs and has quite complex dynamics, so that it is more difficult to calculate cost contributions to prices. In dynamic models of this kind actual margins will commonly vary with the rate of inflation.

The type of equation described here is similar to those employed in most macroeconomic models. The Treasury model, for example, has a set of price equations which, though disaggregated on a different basis to that in the National Institute model, are also based on a mark-up theory of pricing. They use trend wage costs rather than actual wage costs and do not incorporate any direct effect from demand. In similar vein, though less restricted than the equations we report, the recent version of the LBS model uses a dynamic equation between prices, unit labour costs, unit costs of materials and a separate, transitory, effect from labour productivity.

The price equations in the National Institute model

For the consumer price index (*CPI*) a general dynamic model was postulated of the form $\theta_1(L)\, \Delta \ln CPI = \theta_2(L)\Delta Z + \theta_3(L) \ln(CPI/Z)$ where Z is a set of explanatory variables, including both labour and import costs. The effects of change in factor prices and productivity have been combined by using unit cost indices. Thus for labour cost the unit cost index is defined as $LAC = (WS + EC + NIS)/OGDP$, and for unit import costs, $MC = M/OGDP$. In these definitions, *WS* is total

Chart 5.2 Contributions to the change in consumer prices, 1962–82.

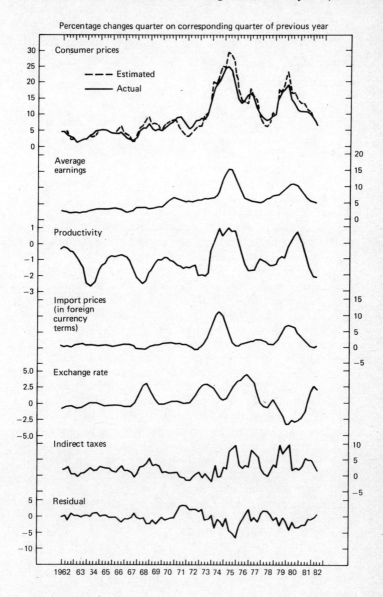

Source: Economic Trends, Financial Statistics and NIESR calculations.

wages and salaries, *EC* is employers' contributions, *NIS* the national insurance surcharge, *OGDP* the output measure of gross domestic product and *M* is the current value of imports of goods and services. An output variable also appears in *Z* to capture demand effects; output of manufactures is used. Finally, an allowance for indirect taxes is made, using the aggregate variable (*TRCE*), which is equal to the average rate of tax on consumers' expenditure.

The equation used in the model for the CPI (see Appendix (10.1)) was estimated by instrumental variables. Instruments for *MC* are lagged values of *LAC, TRCE*, world prices and world trade. This equation is fairly well specified and has approximately white noise error. Its long-run steady-state solution is $CPI = k_1 (LAC)^{0.59} (MC)^{0.308} (TRCE)^{0.103}$ which is approximately homogeneous (implying that prices will change in proportion to total costs). The coefficients correspond quite well to independent estimates of input—output weights.

This equation also attributes a significant short-run effect on prices to a change in demand (proxied by manufacturing output). This is one channel (but not the most significant one in the macroeconomic model as a whole) by which expansion in demand tends to produce increased inflation. In this equation the effect is estimated as *transitory*, since the demand variable enters as a first-difference.

In both the consumer and wholesale price equation, costs are measured in unit value terms. Productivity does not appear as a separate variable in either equation and the use of this form for the determination of prices implies that changes in costs and changes in productivity are constrained to have the same effect on prices in absolute terms. This feature is important in affecting the simulation properties of the complete model since it implies that growth in output which does not add immediately to employment will *reduce* prices. The single equation regression results for this version of these price equations were distinctly better than alternatives using factor prices and productivity as separate variables.

Since the equation has a complex dynamic form, its short-run responses to changes in costs are not obvious. Below, we show the impulse response weights for the equation following a unit change in import cost (*MC*), labour cost (*LAC*) and output (*OMF*).

Within a matter of two years the change in the CPI is very close to its long-run value and the transitory effects from output have died away.

The specification adopted for the wholesale price of manufactures is similar, in general, to the equation for the CPI above. It is a dynamic equation related to the unit value indices already described. The estimated equation (see Appendix (10.3)) is fairly good in terms of its fit and error statistics. Its long-run solution is $PWMF = k_2 (LAC)^{0.72} (MC)^{0.42}$. Short-run dynamic responses obtained from the impulse response weights of the equations are also shown below.

Change in ln*CPI*

Period	Change in *MC*	Change in *LAC*	Change in *OMF*
1	0.047	0	0
2	0.125	0.156	0
3	0.189	0.302	0
4	0.224	0.497	0
5	0.238	0.529	0.085
6	0.246	0.522	0.080
7	0.257	0.499	0.057
8	0.270	0.512	0.021
9	0.280	0.536	0.009
10	0.288	0.559	0.009
30	0.308	0.588	0

Change in ln*PWMF*

Period	Unit change in *LAC*	Unit change in *MC*
1	0	0
2	0.080	0.062
3	0.313	0.133
4	0.421	0.261
5	0.451	0.353
6	0.450	0.369
7	0.389	0.343
8	0.401	0.319
9	0.443	0.322
10	0.482	0.345
30	0.573	0.422

As with the CPI equation, this shows a fairly smooth approach to its long-run value following step changes in exogenous variables. Again, the bulk of the adjustment is completed quickly.

The retail price equation in the model is an estimated relationship linking the RPI to the CPI. It also incorporates lagged effects from the price of new housing and the mortgage rate as regressor variables (see Appendix (10.2)).

References

[1] Artis, M., 'Incomes policies: some rationales' in Fallick, P. and Elliott, R. (eds), *Incomes Policies, Inflation and Relative Pay,* London, Allen and Unwin 1981.

[2] Desai, M., Keil, M. and Wadhwani, S., 'Incomes policy in a political business cycle environment', *London School of Economics, mimeo,* 1982.

[3] Henry, S. G. B. and Omerod, P., 'Incomes policy and aggregate pay', in Fallick, and Elliott, *op. cit.*

[4] Henry, S. G. B. and Ormerod, P., 'Incomes policy and wage inflation: empirical evidence for the UK 1961–1977', *National Institute Economic Review*, no. 85, August 1979.

[5] Henry, S. G. B., Sawyer, M. C. and Smith, P., 'Models of Inflation in the UK: an evaluation', *National Institue Economic Review*, no. 77, August 1976.

[6] *London Business School Quarterly Model of the UK economy*, 1982.

[7] Minford, P. and Brech, M., 'The wage equation and rational expectations', University of Liverpool *Working Paper no.* 7901, 1979.

[8] Neild, R., *Pricing and employment in the trade cycle*, NIESR Occasional Paper no. XXI, Cambridge University Press, 1963.

[9] Nickell, S., 'A bargaining model of the Phillips curve', *Discussion paper no.* 130, Centre for Labour Economics, LSE, 1982.

[10] Sargan, D., 'Wages and prices in the UK: a study in econometric methodology', in Hart, P. *et al, Econometric Analysis for National Economic Planning*, London, Butterworth, 1964.

[11] Wadhwani, S., 'Wage inflation in the UK', Centre for Labour Economics, LSE, *Discussion paper* no. 132, 1982.

[12] Wallis, K., 'Wages, prices and incomes policies: some comments', *Economica*, August 1971.

[13] Wallis, K., 'Econometric implications of the rational expectations hypothesis', *Econometrica*, vol. 48, no. 1, January 1980.

6   The Exchange Rate
S. Hall

The exchange rate is something of a misnomer as there are in fact many
bilateral exchange rates. In order to simplify the situation it has become
common practice to concentrate on a single trade-weighted or 'effective'
exchange rate index. This index reflects the movements of eighteen
bilateral exchange rates weighted to reflect the importance of each
currency to the determination of the United Kingdom trade balance.
The National Institute model focuses on the determination of the effective exchange rate rather than on any of the individual bilateral rates.
This allows us to simplify considerably the analytical work of modelling
the exchange rate, as we need only divide the world into two parts, the
United Kingdom and the rest of the world. If we were to model a bilateral
rate, such as the sterling–dollar rate, it would be necessary to consider
three sets of variables, those relating to the United Kingdom, to the
United States and to the rest of the world. The effective exchange rate
index which we use is published quarterly by the CSO in *Economic Trends.*

Chart 6.1 shows the movements in both the nominal and real effective
exchange rate since the formal abandonment of fixed exchange rates on
23 June 1972. The real exchange rate is the nominal rate adjusted for
domestic and world inflation (world and domestic wholesale prices have
been used for this purpose). Between 1972 and 1976 the nominal rate
fell almost continuously; it then remained fairly stable until the end of
1978, when it began to rise quite steeply, reaching a peak in the first
quarter of 1981. A fall occurred through 1981 and the exchange rate
then stabilised around 90 (1975 = 100) until the end of 1982 when a
further fall occurred. The real effective exchange rate also reflects
movements in relative inflation. During 1972 and 1973 the real rate
fell closely in line with the nominal rate. During 1974 and 1975, however, the real rate rose steadily; there was then a sharp drop in 1976,
followed by a steady rise until the start of 1981. There has been an
overall fall of about 45 per cent in the nominal rate over the period
covered by Chart 6.1, while the real rate has risen by 14 per cent.

A simple model of exchange rate determination
The exchange rate is a price which moves so as to clear the foreign

Chart 6.1   The real and nominal effective exchange rate, 1972–82

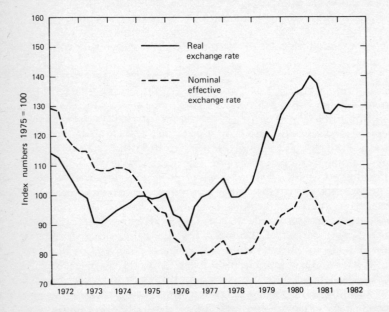

Source: Economic Trends and NIESR calculations.

exchange markets. The market can be subdivided into two fairly distinct sectors, the current account and the capital account. The market clearing condition is therefore that any excess of demand on one account must be equal to an excess of supply on the other. This can be stated quite simply as

$$CURB = -\Delta A \tag{1}$$

where *CURB* is the current account balance and ΔA is the capital account balance. This ignores intervention and official financing and this assumption will be maintained throughout the chapter.

Both the current and capital account balances are functions of many variables including the exchange rate. The exchange rate is believed to have a particularly powerful and quick effect on the capital account through the actions of many professional market agents. In the very short term the influence of the exchange rate on the current balance works only through trade prices and not through any price effects on the volumes of exports or imports. The work reported here has made no allowance for any exchange rate effect on the current balance but has rather concentrated on the asset markets and the capital account. The determination of the capital account can be described the following way

$$\Delta A = f(r, E, \Omega) \tag{2}$$

where r is the differential between the domestic nominal interest rate and an appropriate world rate, E is the nominal exchange rate and Ω is a vector of terms which affect the expected exchange rate such as oil prices, government policy, inflation rates or expected movements in the current account balance. The possibility that the terms in $f(\ldots)$ may appear as differences as well as, or instead of, levels is discussed below. Then we can derive an expression for the exchange rate itself by using (1) to arrive at (3), where the terms in $g(\ldots)$ may include either differences or summations as well as levels.

$$E = g(CURB, r, \Omega) \tag{3}$$

The current balance is determined endogenously within the complete macroeconomic model. The form of interest rate and expectation effects in this equation will depend on the type of behaviour which is assumed for asset markets. It is helpful, therefore, to consider some of the main approaches which might be adopted to explain the behaviour of international capital flows.

The early work of Flemming [2] and Mundell [6] set exchange rate determination within a fairly simple open economy model with the conventional IS-LM framework. The exchange rate was seen to move so as to bring about equilibrium on the combined current and capital accounts of the balance of payments. If domestic interest rates were to be raised, for example, investment, and consequently output, would fall. Imports, seen as an increasing function of output, would also fall and a current account surplus would result. At the same time higher domestic interest rates would cause an increased flow of funds into the country, causing a surplus on the capital account. Both effects would work to drive up the exchange rate until equilibrium was restored. Perhaps the distinguishing feature of this view of exchange rate determination is that the interest rate affects the flow of funds on the capital account permanently, rather than having an effect on the stock of internationally traded assets. More recently Dornbusch [1] concentrated on the concept of stock equilibria for foreign and domestic assets. So a change in the domestic interest rate will lead to a change in equilibrium stock levels and only have a temporary effect on flows.

The difference between these two approaches may be formalised. In the Flemming-Mundell view it is the flow of funds in the capital market which is affected by the existence of a differential between domestic and foreign interest rates. If we denote the total stock of domestic assets by A_t then the flow of funds on the capital account may be defined as ΔA_t, if we ignore the possibility of the domestic creation of net assets. So the functional relationship proposed by the Flemming-Mundell view is strictly

$$\Delta A_t = f(r_t, E_t, \Omega_t) \tag{4}$$

where r_t is the interest rate differential. For any given r_t the equilibrium asset stock is undefined. If $f(\ldots)$ is positive, then the domestic asset stock will tend towards infinity; if it is negative, it will go to minus infinity and if it is zero, assets will be unchanged at an arbitrary level.

The stock equilibrium approach would imply a different formulation; it is the equilibrium stock level itself (A_t^*) which would be a function of the interest rate differential, $A_t^* = g(r_t, E_t, \Omega_t)$. Now the flow between equilibrium levels will be

$$\Delta A_t^* \cong g(\Delta r_t, \Delta E_t, \Delta \Omega_t) \tag{5}$$

Here the flow is a function of the change in the interest rate differential and the long-run behaviour of the stock of assets is now defined. When this type of model is implemented in econometric work explaining the balance on the capital account it is, therefore, usually characterised by a term in the change in the interest rate differential (Δr_t). This, however, has an important implication which is not often explicitly stated. For Δr_t to be the relevant dependent variable we must assume that the stock equilibrium is reached within a single data period. That is to say, if quarterly data are being used, then stock equilibrium must be attained within one quarter. There are, however, many reasons why such stocks might take much longer than this to reach their full equilibrium; for example, many assets are committed for a set period and, even if these can be realised prematurely, there are likely to be both costs and delays. Also, asset managers are unlikely to realise less liquid assets until they are sure that the interest rate differential is going to persist. So, while the stocks of very liquid assets might move into equilibrium quickly, as we consider progressively less liquid assets the speed of stock adjustment will be progressively slower.

Perhaps the simplest assumption to make, in order to formulate this idea, is that asset stocks follow a partial adjustment process. That is, if the equilibrium asset stock is $A_t^* = f(\ldots)$, then at any point in time the actual asset stock will be $A_t = \lambda A_t^* + (1 - \lambda)A_{t-1} = \lambda f(r_t) + (1 - \lambda)A_{t-1}$. The flow of assets will be $\Delta A_t = \lambda f(\ldots) - \lambda A_{t-1}$. The relevant pattern of interest rate effects which will finally enter the exchange rate equation is not at all obvious. The initial effect should be positive but the lag structure may be either short or long and the individual terms are of an indeterminate sign.

The interest rate differential is not, of course, the only factor to be considered here; the other crucial factor is the expected movement of the exchange rate itself. Exchange rate expectations are both elusive and vitally important in the determination of the exchange rate (see Kohlhagen [5] and Ormerod [7]). It is possible to divide expectations factors into two broad sets: those which are directly related to a measureable economic variable such as world prices or the value of North Sea oil, and factors which are not so easily measured, such as the political climate or market sentiment. No attempt can be made to model the second set of factors but the first set can be included by making allowances for the dollar value of North Sea oil reserves and by allowing for the effect on expectations of changes in relative domestic and world prices by using real rather than nominal interest rates.

Equation (3) is generally assumed to be homogeneous of degree zero in prices in the long run. This means that an increase in domestic prices, other things being equal, will eventually produce a proportionate fall in the nominal exchange rate but leave the real rate unaffected. If we assume some lag in this relationship the expected change in the exchange rate will be related to the present (or recent) divergence between domestic and foreign inflation rates. This being so, the use of the real interest rate differential, rather than the nominal interest rate differential, in equation (2) will incorporate the effect of expected changes in the exchange rate insofar as they are due to changes in relative prices. Other expectations effects will need to be incorporated separately.

We can now state a general equation which is based on equation (3) but which may be used as the basis for estimating an econometric relationship. Because of the definitional link between the real and nominal exchange rate, we may express that equation in either real or nominal terms. From a formal point of view it makes little difference but it was felt that it was better to have the real exchange rate as the dependent variable since this would remove the long-term trend caused by the relative movement of world and domestic prices. It may also be the case that the monetary authorities have been more concerned with long-term movements in the real than in the nominal rate and the nature of their behaviour will be shown to be important later in the chapter.

We can therefore redefine equation (3) in terms of the *real* exchange rate (R_t) and the *real* interest rate differential (i_t). After differencing we then derive the equation:

$$\Delta R_t = f\left(\sum_{i=0}^{n} q_i i_{t-i}, \sum_{i=0}^{n} b_i CURB_{t-i}, \sum_{i=0}^{n} c_i \Delta \frac{P_{t-i}}{P_{t-i}^d}, \sum_{i=0}^{n} d_i \Omega_{t-i}\right) \quad (6)$$

where the long-run effects of the variables on the right-hand side may, or may not, be zero.

An econometric equation can now be estimated on the basis of the general equation (6). The following equation was estimated by OLS for the change in the real effective exchange rate:

$$\Delta R_t = \underset{(0.7)}{0.25 i_t} + \underset{(1.2)}{0.49 i_{t-1}} - \underset{(0.26)}{0.11 i_{t-2}} + \underset{(2.5)}{0.56 CURB_t} - \underset{(0.27)}{0.08 CURB_{t-1}}$$

$$- \underset{(1.0)}{0.28 CURB_{t-2}} + \underset{(1.96)}{171.1 OR_t} - \underset{(1.9)}{176.9 OR_{t-1}} - \underset{(1.15)}{84 DRP_t}$$

$$+ \underset{(0.6)}{54.7 DRP_{t-1}} - \underset{(1.4)}{132.8 DRP_{t-2}} + \underset{(1.7)}{113.3 DRP_{t-3}}$$

DW $= 1.98$, $R^2 = 0.66$, t-statistics in parentheses, where OR is the real dollar value of North Sea oil reserves and DRP is the relative movement of domestic and world prices.

For the empirical work a number of decisions had to be made regarding the specific data to be used. The exchange rate used was the sterling effective exchange rate. The interest rates which were used were the three-month United Kingdom Treasury bill rate and the Euro-dollar rate. The price indices used were wholesale prices. The value of oil reserves was defined as discovered oil reserves valued at the dollar export price of North Sea oil. Both this and the current balance were deflated by the United Kingdom wholesale price index.

This equation fits the data reasonably well, the current balance terms are correctly signed and at least the first term is significant. The effect of the value of oil stocks is also correctly signed and reasonably significant with a long-run effect very close to zero. The effect of a change in relative prices is not very significant and the four terms sum to a number not significantly different from zero. The interest rate effects have very low t-statistics although the initial effect has the correct sign. In general the t-statistics are very unsatisfactory. This is particularly true in the case of the interest rate effects which we might expect to have been particularly powerful and significant.

This is not an unusual result, indeed the most unusual feature of this equation is that the use of the real interest rate differential as opposed to the nominal differential has allowed a positive initial effect to be observed. Hacche and Townend [4] have produced a number of examples which illustrate the robustness of a *perverse* interest rate effect in exchange rate equations. This empirical result is well known although it apparently contradicts both theory and the prevailing views of dealers in the foreign exchange markets themselves. Following the arguments presented by Hacche and Townend, the most likely cause of this result would seem to be bias resulting from interaction between this equation and the systematic behaviour of the monetary authorities. It seems that the authorities try to set domestic interest rates so as to moderate changes in the exchange rate. This 'leaning into the wind' was a widely recognised part of the authorities' behaviour from 1972 to 1979. This simply means that the authorities wanted a stable exchange rate, so if the exchange rate rose they would reduce domestic interest rates to moderate any further rise in it and, if it fell, they would increase domestic interest rates to stabilise it. The resulting correlation between the exchange rate and the interest rate differential will therefore be negative even though the structural parameter on interest rates in an exchange rate equation reflecting market forces is stable and positive. Hacche and Townend have attempted to cope with this problem by using an instrumental variable technique but they found that this met with little success; either the coefficient remained negative or it became insignificant. The method proposed here for dealing with this problem is slightly different to that used by Hacche and Townend. Instead of simply using an instrumental variable technique, a specific reaction function has been estimated over the period 1972(I)–1979(II). This has then been substituted into the exchange rate equation, which can then be estimated by a technique which avoids the risk of bias. This equation has then been estimated over the full period 1972(I)–1981(IV). This approach not only removes the risk of bias but also makes use of information about the likely form of the authorities' reaction function, and of the belief that it operated over only part of the period.

The estimation procedure in outline

The procedure begins with two structural equations. The equation for the change in the real exchange rate is:

$$R_t = R_{t-1} + \alpha i_t + (BX) \tag{7}$$

where X and B are two suitably dimensioned vectors of exogenous variables and their coefficients.

The equation for the reaction function is:

$$i_t = \gamma \Delta R_t + (\phi Z_t) \tag{8}$$

where again Z and ϕ are vectors of exogenous variables and their coefficients.

The procedure begins by estimating (8), using an instrumental variables technique as ΔR_t is endogenous. With these parameter estimates for γ and ϕ, (8) is substituted into (7) to give

$$R_t = R_{t-1} + \alpha [\gamma \Delta R_t + (\phi Z_t)] + (BX_t) \tag{9}$$

This equation now embodies the reaction function, but a direct estimate would still be biased so it must be rearranged in order to bring the current R_t term to the left-hand side. This yields equation (10):

$$R_t = \frac{R_{t-1}}{1 - \alpha\gamma} + \alpha\left[\frac{\gamma R_{t-1}}{1 - \alpha\gamma} + \frac{(\phi Z_t)}{1 - \alpha\gamma}\right] + \frac{(BX_t)}{1 - \alpha\gamma} \qquad (10)$$

If the reaction function was believed to operate over the whole period it would be possible to estimate this equation. But on the supposition that after the second quarter of 1979 the government ceased to use the interest rate to control the exchange rate and used it instead to control £M3, this would not be a correct procedure. It is necessary, therefore, to make a further adjustment in order to allow for this. When the reaction function is not operating, over the period 1979(II)–1981(IV), the appropriate equation to estimate is simply the structural equation (7). When the reaction function is operating, the appropriate equation is (10). These two equations must be transformed so that a single set of structural parameter estimates can be achieved over the whole period. This can be done by transforming the variables on the right-hand side of the estimated equation in the following way.

Define $\qquad A_t = \begin{cases} 1/1 - \alpha\gamma & t = 1972(\text{I})-1979(\text{II}) \\ 1 & t = 1979(\text{III})-1981(\text{IV}) \end{cases}$

then define $\quad \bar{R}_{t-1} = R_{t-1}A_t \qquad\qquad\qquad (11a)$

$$\bar{X}_t = X_t A \qquad\qquad\qquad (11b)$$

and finally define a new variable

$$\bar{\Gamma}_t = \begin{cases} \dfrac{\gamma R_{t-1}}{1 - \alpha\gamma} + \left(\dfrac{\phi Z_t}{1 - \alpha\gamma}\right) & t = 1972(\text{I})-1979(\text{II}) \\ i_t & t = 1979(\text{III})-1981(\text{IV}) \end{cases} \qquad (11c)$$

The equation for estimation using the whole data set may then be expressed as

$$R_t = \bar{R}_{t-1} + \alpha\bar{\Gamma}_t + (B\bar{X}_t) \qquad (12)$$

For the period up to 1979(II) this equation will contain the reaction function as part of the transformed variables, after this period the equation is simply the structural equation (7). In order to carry out the transformation, (11a), (11b) and (11c), to the data set an estimate of α is necessary. This means that the equation cannot simply be estimated in a single operation. We must know one of the estimated coefficients before estimation of the rest is possible. This problem has been dealt with by using an iterative estimation process; that is to say a value for α was chosen initially, the data were transformed and equation (12) was estimated. This produced a new estimate of α as one of the parameters of equation (12); this estimate was then used to re-transform the data and equation (12) was re-estimated. This process continued until the α used to transform the data was the same as the α produced in the subsequent estimation.

Empirical results

A restricted and an unrestricted version of the exchange rate equation were estimated. The version with no restrictions was (t-statistics in parenthesis):

$$R_t = R_{t-1} + 0.34\bar{\Gamma}_t + 0.52CURB_t - 0.39CURB_{t-2} - 85DRP_t$$
$$\quad\quad (6.08) \quad\quad (2.2) \quad\quad\quad (1.7) \quad\quad\quad\quad (1.0)$$

$$+ 50DRP_{t-1} - 117DRP_{t-2} + 102DRP_{t-3} + 172OR_t - 175OR_{t-1}$$
$$\quad (0.5) \quad\quad (1.3) \quad\quad\quad (1.4) \quad\quad\quad (1.96) \quad\quad (1.85)$$

$R^2 = 0.67.$ $\hspace{6cm}$ (13)

Γ is defined above (11c), *CURB* is the current balance deflated by the wholesale price index. *DRP* is the ratio of world wholesale prices to domestic wholesale prices. *OR* is the value of the stock of North Sea oil deflated by the wholesale price index. As the actual stock of oil is relatively constant over the period, this variable fluctuates mainly because of changes in the price of oil. The relative price terms are included in the equation so that, in the short run, the real exchange rate may be affected by changes in absolute price levels. If this was not allowed for it would imply that the nominal exchange rate could adjust instantaneously to any change in domestic or world prices. These terms allow this adjustment to take place over four quarters.

The version with simplifying restrictions of this equation is given below.

$$R_t = R_{t-1} + 0.348\bar{\Gamma}_t + 0.51(CURB - CURB_{t-2}) - 50.8(DRP_t - DRP_{t-1})$$
$$\quad\quad (12.6) \quad\quad (3.2) \quad\quad\quad\quad\quad\quad (0.8)$$

$$- 116.0(DRP_{t-2} - DRP_{t-3}) + 161(OR_t - OR_{t-1}) \hspace{2cm} (14)$$
$$\quad (2.0) \quad\quad\quad\quad\quad\quad (2.2)$$

$R^2 = 0.66$; CHI SQ(16) = 16.2 (for random correlogram); LM(8) = 5.16; DW = 1.9.

The initial α which was used to transform the data in this estimate was 0.35; there is no sign of autocorrelation in the error terms and the coefficients in the equation have the expected signs and generally satisfactory t-statistics. This equation has been estimated over the full data set available so as to achieve the best possible fit and definition of the structural equation. This, of course, precludes the use of structural stability tests in the usual way. However, in order to gain some idea of how stable this equation actually is, the equation was re-estimated without using the last eight observations. In fact, the resulting equation was very similar to that reported above; no parameters changed sign, although the smaller data set produced lower t-statistics. The parameter stability statistics for this exercise were: CHOW test $(8,21) = 0.53$ and CHI SQ(8) $= 5.9$, which are satisfactory.

The final equation presented above contains only the current interest rate effect although the earlier theoretical discussion suggested that a series of lagged interest rate effects might be observed with the expectation that the long-run coefficient might well be zero. Lagged interest terms were tried, but they typically had very low t-statistics and a positive sign. Two lagged values of i were included in the above restricted equation. There was virtually no change in any of the reported parameters, the parameter estimates for the first and second lag were 0.05 and 0.29 respectively, with t-statistics of 0.1 and 0.5.

A number of variations in data were tried during the development of this equation: the United States Treasury bill rate was used instead of the Euro-dollar rate; the performance of this equation was almost identical to that presented above. A weighted average of the United States Treasury bill rate and the German three-month loan rate was also tried; this equation also performed satisfactorily, although it had no claim to preference on statistical grounds over the other two. The version using the Euro-dollar rate was chosen for inclusion in the model, partly on the grounds that the Euro-dollar rate is free from direct controls and so may act as a good indicator of general movements in world interest rates.

One experiment which did not prove successful was to apply the same model and estimation technique to the sterling—dollar rate. This failed to produce sensible results. The reason seems to be that the reaction function itself did not work for the sterling—dollar rate. It seems that the authorities were reacting to movements in the effective exchange rate and not the dollar rate.

The equation finally chosen for inclusion in the model was the restricted version given above. It is possible to use this equation to evaluate the relative importance of the various factors influencing the exchange rate over the last ten years. Table 6.1 shows the effective exchange rate and the effects on it of four principle factors identified in the estimated equation. The second column is simply the ratio of world to domestic wholesale prices. This clearly shows the downward trend in this ratio caused by our relatively faster inflation rate. The third column shows predicted movement in the effective nominal exchange rate in each quarter as a result of changes in the current balance. The fourth column gives the predicted movement which was due to the

Table 6.1 The effective exchange rate and its determinants, 1972(I)–1982(III)

	Effective exchange rate	Relative price ratio	Current balance effect	Real interest rate effect	Oil stocks effect
1972	129.0	1.13	1.26	− 0.15	1.56
	128.3	1.13	1.62	− 0.19	− 0.18
	120.6	1.11	− 2.07	− 0.26	− 0.18
	117.2	1.11	− 1.31	− 0.98	− 0.40
1973	115.1	1.13	− 1.10	0.38	0.90
	115.1	1.17	− 1.20	0.67	0.27
	108.2	1.19	− 0.43	− 0.96	0.85
	107.0	1.17	− 2.35	0.36	1.40
1974	107.7	1.16	− 3.24	0.61	7.19
	109.3	1.14	− 3.00	0.34	− 0.37
	108.9	1.13	0.17	0.66	− 0.63
	107.1	1.10	0.24	− 0.55	− 0.43
1975	105.1	1.05	2.43	− 0.92	4.30
	101.8	1.01	3.48	− 0.44	− 0.62
	97.5	0.98	− 0.55	0.17	− 0.92
	95.1	0.96	1.08	0.90	− 0.59
1976	94.0	0.93	3.38	0.11	− 0.87
	86.3	0.92	− 0.72	0.71	− 0.77
	84.1	0.91	− 2.11	1.01	0.96
	78.1	0.88	0.15	1.61	− 1.00
1977	80.8	0.84	0.38	0.14	0.32
	80.6	0.81	− 0.16	− 0.34	− 0.15
	80.8	0.80	1.93	− 0.49	− 0.35
	82.6	0.80	2.11	− 0.38	− 0.17
1978	84.8	0.81	− 1.34	− 0.63	− 0.12
	79.9	0.80	0.35	0.27	− 0.32
	80.6	0.80	0.82	0.62	0.13
	80.6	0.80	0.32	0.68	− 0.19
1979	82.4	0.79	− 1.84	0.43	0.33
	87.0	0.78	− 1.31	0.27	0.87
	91.3	0.75	1.44	− 0.40	1.59
	88.5	0.75	− 0.63	0.48	0.54
1980	93.0	0.73	0.59	− 0.28	1.47
	94.5	0.72	0.55	1.10	1.44
	96.7	0.72	1.54	0.54	0.46
	100.2	0.72	3.37	− 0.47	− 0.59
1981	101.8	0.71	2.43	− 0.54	0.23
	97.8	0.71	0.29	− 1.17	− 0.73
	90.6	0.71	− 3.73	− 1.40	− 0.68
	89.7	0.70	− 0.94	− 0.10	0.34
1982	91.2	0.70	0.78	− 0.76	− 0.76
	90.3	0.70	− 0.98	− 0.90	− 1.18
	91.5	0.71	0.37	− 0.52	0.33

real interest rate differential. The final column shows the estimated effects of changes in the value of oil stocks in each quarter.

The real interest rate differential has a permanent effect on the rate of change of the real exchange rate. 1 per cent on the real interest rate differential will cause a rise of 0.35 in the real exchange rate every quarter for as long as the differential persists. A change in either the current balance or the value of oil stocks will affect the level of the real exchange rate permanently but will have no permanent effect on the rate of growth of the real exchange rate. A change in relative prices will have only transitory effects on both the level and the rate of growth of the real exchange rate; there will be no long-term effect on either.

References

[1] Dornbusch, R., 'Monetary policy under exchange rate flexibility', in *Managed Exchange Rate Flexibility: the recent experience,* Federal Reserve Bank of Boston, Conference Series no. 20, 1978.

[2] Flemming, J. M., 'Domestic financial policies under fixed and floating exchange rates', IMF Staff Papers, 1962.

[3] Frankel, J. A., 'Tests of rational expectations in the forward exchange markets', *Southern Economic Journal,* no. 46, April 1980.

[4] Hacche, G. and Townend, J., 'Exchange rates and monetary policy: modelling sterling's effective exchange rate 1972–80', *Oxford Economic Papers, 33,* July 1981 Supplement.

[5] Kohlhagen, S. W., The behaviour of foreign exchange markets – a critical survey of the empirical literature, New York University Monograph Series in Finance and Economics, 1978.

[6] Mundell, R. A., 'Capital mobility and stabilisation policy under fixed and flexible exchange rates', in American Economic Association, *Readings in international economics,* London, Allen and Unwin, 1968.

[7] Ormerod, P., 'The forward exchange rate for sterling and the efficiency of expectations', National Institute of Economic and Social Research, *Discussion Paper no.* 31, 1978.

7 North Sea Oil
S. Hall

Oil was first discovered in the North Sea in 1969 (the Montrose field) and the first major oil field was found in 1970 (the Forties). Offshore oil production began in 1975 in the Forties and Argyll fields although total production was only 1.1 million tonnes. The forecast for production in 1983 is 110 million tonnes. This dramatic rise, spanning only seven years, has been a major factor in our economic performance in recent years (see [1], [2], [3] and [4]). North Sea oil now accounts for over 5 per cent of our gross domestic product and the direct contribution of oil to the current balance is of the order of £10 billion. Table 7.1 summarises the rapid rise in oil production and the corresponding rise in total government tax revenues.

Table 7.1   Oil production and tax revenues

	Oil production		Tax revenues	Average
	mn tonnes	£ bn	£ bn	tax rate, %
1976/7	16.6	0.9	0.1	9
1977/8	41.4	2.4	0.2	8
1978/9	59.6	3.2	0.5	16
1979/80	79.6	6.8	2.3	34
1980/1	81.4	9.5	3.8	40
1981/2	90.5	12.7	6.4	50
1982/3[a]	105.0	14.6	7.7	53
1983/4[b]	110.0	15.0	9.1	61

Source: *Economic Trends* and NIESR estimates.
[a] Estimate
[b] Forecast

Oil production increased very rapidly from 1976/7 to 1979/80, but the rate of increase then slowed down and it is generally believed that the level of production will reach a peak of around 110 million tonnes a year in 1983. This level of production may be sustained for some years, or it may decline, depending largely on the amount of new development and exploration which is undertaken in the near future. The value of oil production rises at an almost constant rate in table 7.1 despite the reduction in the rate of increase of production. This is due to the large rises in the price of oil which occurred in 1979 and 1980. Government tax revenues follow a similar pattern to the rise in the value of oil production but the actual path is delayed approximately three years by the capital expenditure allowances which form part of the tax structure.

The National Institute model contains three equations which make North Sea oil taxes and company profits endogenous. This chapter outlines the reasoning behind these equations and describes their use in actual forecasting.

The first part of the chapter gives a brief description of the tax system itself and outlines a detailed computer model of the North Sea. This model is used to produce a base forecast of oil revenues and company profits on an initial set of assumptions about North Sea oil prices, the United Kingdom dollar exchange rate, oil production and various tax rates. As this base forecast must be carried out before the full macroeconomic model forecast can be produced, it is unlikely that all these assumptions will be consistent with the final forecast values. This is particularly true of the exchange rate which is endogenous to the full macroeconomic model. The second section outlines the derivation of the three oil equations in the macroeconomic model which adjust the base forecast of oil revenues and profits to make it consistent with the forecast of other variables.

Modelling the tax system

Revenue accrues to the government from the North Sea oil sector through five distinct channels. These are royalties, petroleum revenue tax (PRT), advanced petroleum revenue tax (APRT), corporation tax and the profits of nationalised companies trading in the North Sea. This produces a highly complex tax structure which is further complicated by a broad range of allowances and delays in payments. A brief account of the current tax system is given below and a more detailed account of the development of this system may be found in Motamen and Strange [5].

The Continental Shelf Act (1964) established the royalty system of taxation. Royalties are charged at 12½ per cent of the value of oil production. There are no allowances against this tax and liability is calculated on the basis of the value of production over six-month periods. These periods start on 1 July and 1 January. The definition of the value of oil production has changed; for discoveries under the first four licensing rounds it is defined as the well-head value, but for subsequent discoveries it is defined to be the actual landed value of the oil. The well-head value may be considerably below the landed value as it makes allowance for the cost of bringing the oil ashore. This means that most of the oil fields actually pay less than the full 12½ per cent royalty rate on the landed value of the oil.

Petroleum revenue tax was introduced by the Oil Taxation Act of 1975. This tax has undergone a large number of changes since its introduction, which will not be detailed here. Since 1 January, 1983, PRT is assessed at 75 per cent of total revenue after the deduction of royalties, APRT, operating costs and a complex range of allowances which include past capital and new exploration expenditure. In effect, therefore, this is a tax on profits. The payments are again based on six-month chargeable periods although from 1 July, 1983, the bulk of PRT is to be collected monthly. This tax is further complicated by the advance payment of future PRT liabilities. This is not the same as APRT.

Advanced petroleum revenue tax was introduced in the March 1980 budget in order to replace supplementary petroleum duty. Both taxes are charged at a rate of 20 per cent of the gross value of oil production after an initial oil allowance. APRT is considered as pre-payment of actual PRT and so subsequent PRT liabilities are reduced. Supplementary petroleum duty was treated instead as an allowance against PRT payments. The final payments of supplementary petroleum duty were made in July 1983. APRT is calculated on a six-month chargeable period but again actual payments are made monthly. The March 1983 budget proposed to phase out this tax over a period of years. The rate of APRT was reduced to 15 per cent from 1 July, 1983 and it is further proposed to reduce it to 10 per cent on 1 January, 1985, to reduce it to 5 per cent on 1 January, 1986 and to abolish it from 1 January, 1987.

Corporation tax on oil company profits operates in much the same way as Standard Corporation tax. It is charged at 52 per cent of profits after allowing for royalties, PRT and APRT. It differs from normal corporation tax in that there is a 'ring fence' around oil companies' North Sea activities. This means that losses incurred outside the North Sea may not be offset against North Sea profits in the calculation of corporation tax. The ring fence does, however, allow companies to offset the cost of new exploration and development within the North Sea against their corporation tax liability from other North Sea fields.

The purpose of the North Sea oil (NSO) model is to provide forecast values for three of the exogenous inputs to the National Institute macroeconomic model. The NSO model has therefore been tailored to produce output which is compatible with the required inputs to the macroeconomic model. These inputs are royalties, direct taxes and oil company profits. Royalties are identical to tax royalties, discussed above. Direct taxes are defined as the sum of corporation tax, PRT and

APRT (or supplementary petroleum duty). The macroeconomic model is a quarterly model so the NSO model produces quarterly estimates of these three variables in nominal terms on an actual payment basis. The NSO model works on a field by field basis covering all 26 of the fields which are currently in production or under development. The exogenous variables in the calculation of tax revenues for each field are the production profile of the field, the dollar price of oil, the exchange rate and the profile of capital expenditure for the field. The price of oil will in fact vary for each field as the quality of the oil varies. The NSO model does not allow for this, so the overall price used is the average price of United Kingdom crude oil exports. As oil exports are currently 60 per cent of total production this figure should be a good approximation to the average price of North Sea oil as a whole. Figures for oil production and capital expenditure are estimated on the basis of data from a number of sources including the Department of Energy and company estimates.

Once the model has calculated the field by field tax payments these are aggregated to produce total tax payments on a quarterly basis. The model is not able to cope exactly with the lags which occur between the accrual of a tax liability and its eventual payment. These lags can often be both long and unpredictable. This is particularly true of corporation tax. The model therefore imposes appropriate average lags on each of the four taxes and then smooths out the quarterly path of the total tax yield. Total North Sea oil company profits are then calculated using the aggregate figures for total oil revenue, operating expenditure, capital investment and taxation.

Assessing the accuracy of a model of this type is difficult. An econometric model comes complete with an accompanying set of statistics which allow the informed reader to assess its overall fit and performance. This is obviously not possible here but in order to give some idea of the overall accuracy of the model we can compare its estimates of past tax revenues with actual data. However, it must be borne in mind that the model does not distinguish the past from the future. That is to say it does not have an estimation period over the past for which it necessarily fits well. Furthermore the past is actually far more difficult to model than the future, as it contains the rapid rise in North Sea oil production from 1976–81 which produced a similarly rapid rise in tax revenues. Having made these qualifications, table 7.2 compares the official figures for total tax revenues with the model estimates.

The model tracks the official figures closely. There is a largely offsetting error in the two years 1978–9 and 1979–80 where the first year was overestimated and the second underestimated. This is due to an underestimation of the lag which occurred in payments in 1978–9,

Table 7.2   A comparison of total actual North Sea tax revenues with the NSO model estimates

£ million

	Official figure	NSO Model estimate
1977–8	238	335
1978–9	562	1,054
1979–80	2,329	2,055
1980–1	3,891	3,972
1981–2	6,430	6,528

Source: Official figures are from the Department of Energy, Development of oil and gas resources of the UK 1982.

causing part of the actual 1979–80 revenues to be put back into the earlier year. Given the very sharp rise which was occurring in tax revenues at the time, the NSO model seems to be performing reasonably well. The official total tax yield over the period covered by table 7.1 is £13,450 million, the NSO model generates an estimate of £13,944, an error overall of less than 4 per cent.

The relationship between the NSO model and the National Institute macroeconomic model

We have two large models which are linked simultaneously in only a very few areas. In principle, we should load the whole North Sea model into the macroeconomic model and solve the two models together. This would be expensive. But because the links between the two models are sparse we can exploit this in the following way. We can describe the links between the models by the following diagram.

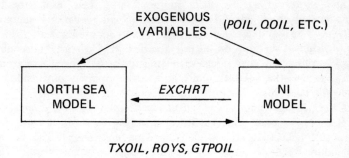

There are two principal exogenous variables which the models have in common, *POIL, QOIL,* the price of oil and oil production. The North Sea model cannot be solved until the dollar exchange rate (*EXCHRT*) is supplied by the macroeconomic model. The macroeconomic model cannot be solved until the oil tax and company profits (*TXOIL, ROYS, GTPOIL*) are provided by the North Sea model.

If, however, we could derive a simple equation for *TXOIL, ROYS, GTPOIL* these could be incorporated in the macroeconomic model, which could then be solved on its own in a consistent fashion. As mentioned above, the North Sea model is a highly complex one which could not be exactly presented as a single equation. However, we may take a Taylor series expansion around a base forecast for the North Sea and present this as a single equation for each of the three variables.

There are two forms which the Taylor expansion might take. The first is the simple linear form; it is also possible to formulate it in percentage terms by defining the variables as logs. It then becomes $TXOIL = TXOIL^1(1 + f'[EXCHRT - EXCHRT^1/EXCHRT^1])$.

The choice of these two forms depends on whether we consider $f()$ to be more nearly linear or log-linear. In the case of the North Sea model it is very nearly log-linear, so the second formulation has been chosen.

The next problem is the calculation of the derivatives $f'(.)$. This cannot be done exactly, but the derivatives may be found numerically by solving the model for a base set of exogenous variables and then changing one of these variables for only one quarter. The model is then resolved and the difference between the base solution and the new solution divided by the change in the variable will be a discrete approximation to the derivative. Because the tax model is fairly complex, a change in one quarter's exogenous variable may affect the tax revenue for many quarters. The derivatives must therefore be calculated for all future periods until they tend to zero.

This process is repeated for each of the exogenous variables to the North Sea model which might vary when the macroeconomic model is used either in a forecast or in simulations. This results in three equations which are added to the macroeconomic model and which will produce close approximations to the full North Sea model.

The derivatives will only need re-calculating every two or three years, assuming no major change in the tax structure. The base forecast, which is the point around which the approximation is made, will probably need to be redone only once a year, unless there is some very large change in one of the exogenous variables.

It is possible, using the first three equations set out in the Appendix (15.1), (15.2), (15.3), to calculate the long-run elasticities of oil taxes and company profits with respect to changes in dollar oil prices, the

Table 7.3 The long run elasticities of direct taxes, royalties and company profits

	Dollar price of oil	Dollar exchange rate	Oil production	PRT rate	Corporation tax rate
Direct taxes	1.4	−1.3	1.4	0.2	0.2
Royalties	1.0	−1.0	1.0	−	−
Company profits	1.0	−0.9	1.0	−	−

Source: NIESR estimates

dollar exchange rate, oil production and some of the more important tax parameters. Table 7.3 illustrates this point.

This suggests that a 10 per cent increase in the dollar price of oil will produce a 14 per cent rise in direct tax revenue, a 10 per cent increase in royalties and a 10 per cent increase in company profits. It must be remembered that the short-run effect will be different.

References

[1] Atkinson, F., Brooks, S. and Hall, S., 'The economic effects of North Sea oil', *National Institute Economic Review,* no. 104, May, 1983.

[2] Bank of England, 'North Sea Oil and Gas: a challenge for the future', *Bank of England Quarterly Bulletin,* vol. 22, 1982.

[3] Brooks, S., 'The economic implications of North Sea oil', National Institute of Economic and Social Research, *Discussion Paper no.* 38, 1981.

[4] Byatt, I., Hartley, N., Lomax, R., Powell, S. and Spencer, P., 'North Sea oil and Structural adjustment', HM Treasury *Working Paper,* no. 22, 1982.

[5] Motamen, H. and Strange, R., 'The structure of the UK oil taxation system', Imperial College *Discussion Paper,* no. 82/2.

8   The Monetary Sector
K. Cuthbertson

The monetary aggregates most often referred to by commentators in the United Kingdom and used in setting policy targets are the 'broad' money aggregate *£M*3 (consisting of notes and coin plus sterling sight and interest bearing deposits, including wholesale deposits) and the 'narrow' aggregate *M*1 (consisting of notes and coin and sterling sight deposits). Both aggregates consist mainly of sterling deposits held in United Kingdom banks by United Kingdom (non-bank) residents. Movements in *£M*3 are closely correlated with changes in bank lending (see chart 8.1). In recent years particularly, the growth of *£M*3 has often been negatively correlated with changes in *M*1.

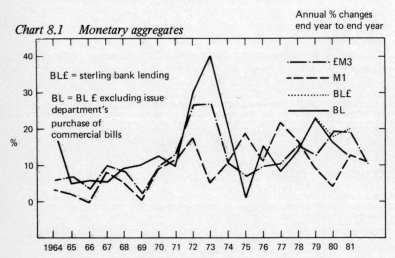

Chart 8.1   Monetary aggregates

Annual % changes end year to end year

BL£ = sterling bank lending

BL = BL £ excluding issue department's purchase of commercial bills

——·—— £M3
—— —— M1
·············· BL£
———— BL

Source: Bank of England Quarterly Bulletin.

In the National Institute model the monetary linkages operate through changes in financial aggregates (for example, expenditure on consumer durables is influenced by the change in personal sector liquid assets) and changes in interest rates. Interest rates have direct effects on expenditure (for example, on consumer durables, stockbuilding and housing investment) as well as indirect effects through the exchange rate.

Early attempts to establish the importance of money in this country concentrated on the search for a stable demand for money function depending on a small number of variables, usually output, interest rates and, more recently, wealth (see Laidler [18] and for recent United Kingdom evidence, Hendry [15] and Grice and Bennett [14]). In general, the evidence suggests that the demand for the narrow monetary aggregate (*M*1) may well be stable but that the demand for the broad aggregates (*M*3 and £*M*3) is unstable. A different approach, using reduced form equations (see, for example, Goodhart and Crockett [13] and Matthews and Ormerod [20]) yielded estimates of money and fiscal multipliers. Studies of the portfolio behaviour of particular institutions such as the commercial banks, discount houses and building societies and insurance companies provided additional evidence on the behaviour of financial markets, but until the late 1970s there was no complete working model of the United Kingdom monetary sector.[1]

This chapter begins with a discussion of some theoretical issues. A detailed discussion of the National Institute asset demand functions follows, relating them to other empirical work; the chapter ends with a look at the equations for interest rates.

Theory and specification

The theory of asset demand distinguishes three motives for holding financial assets: transactions, precautionary and speculative.[2] A transactions model recognises the importance of relative yields but emphasises the relation of different assets (bank deposits for example) to current transactions. In a speculative model, wealth, W, is introduced as a scale variable and expected holding-period yields, including expected capital gains, R^e, provide the other determinants of demand. A precautionary model has the *variance* of transactions and relative yields as arguments. In equilibrium the demand for the ith asset (in a choice set of N assets) may be written (in linear form) as

$$A_i^* = f_i(R_i^e, W, Z) = b_{0i} + \Sigma_j^N b_{ij}R_j^e + c_iW + d_iZ \tag{1}$$

where Z is a vector of additional variables (for example a transactions or risk variable, see Smith and Brainard [30]). The form of equation (1) is so general that practical application must involve some restriction or simplification. The notion of separability in investment decisions is often invoked to limit the number of assets included in the vector of asset returns R^e considered relevant and the coverage of the wealth variable (for example, to exclude from it the value of physical wealth such as owner-occupied houses). The rational desires hypothesis assumes that the total value of desired asset stocks must equal actual wealth (that is, $\Sigma_i^N A_i^* = W$); this imposes cross equation restrictions (that is, $\Sigma_i^N b_{0i} = \Sigma_i^N b_{ij} = \Sigma_i^N d_i = 0$ and $\Sigma_i^N c_i = 1$).

Particular care must be taken in the specification of the expected returns and several approaches have been tried. Expected holding-period yields may be assumed to be unitary (that is, expected gains are assumed to be zero and R^e is therefore simply the running yield); alternatively, expected yields may be estimated using autoregressive expectations (McCallum [21]) or weakly rational predictors. Ideally, one should pay particular attention to the possible impact of policy changes on expectations to avoid the Lucas [19] critique.

Adjustment to equilibrium is often assumed to involve minimisation of the (quadratic) costs of being out of equilibrium $(A^* - A)$ and the costs of change $(A - A(-1))$ subject to the rational desires hypothesis (see Christofedes [4]). This results in interdependent asset adjustments which, for the ith asset, are of the form

$$\Delta A_i = \Sigma_j^N \theta_{ij}(A_j^* - A_j(-1)) = \Sigma_{j \neq k}^N \theta'_{ij}(A_j^* - A_j(-1)) + h_i \Delta W \quad (2)$$

Substitution of the determinants of A_i^* in (2) does not in general allow identification of the structural parameters (except when *all* N equations are estimated). Simple partial adjustment (that is, $\theta_{ij} = 0, i \neq j$) is highly restrictive and forces the speed of adjustment to be determined by one parameter rather than the whole matrix of parameters θ_{ij} and frequently results, in practice, in implausibly slow lagged responses.

Full understanding of financial markets requires one to distinguish the behaviour of supply and demand. Identification in simultaneous equation systems can be based on parameter restrictions (particularly exclusion restrictions) or on the assumption that markets do not clear continuously (see Spencer and Mowl [32] and Smith and Brainard [30]). Neither approach is entirely satisfactory. If identification is not possible, the best one can do is to estimate a reduced form for the market in question with the dependent variable (the asset stock) related to the exogenous determinants of both the supply and demand curves. The supply side of financial markets is not developed in the National Institute model, so an implicit assumption of perfectly elastic supply would have to be made in order to identify the estimated equations as demand functions. Further discussion on this point is in Cuthbertson [7].

The theory of asset demand described here provides some restrictions on the form of asset demand functions which might guide empirical work, but the inter-relations suggested are very complex and the requirements for data (on expectations in particular) are formidable. It is perhaps not surprising, therefore, that in most econometric models the asset demand equations can only be interpreted as broadly consistent with the theoretical approach outlined above. The lags, for example, are usually determined empirically and must be understood as a convolution of adjustment, recognition and expectation lags. In this the National Institute model is no exception. The adjustment lags have been estimated starting with a general (autoregressive distributed) structure, followed by reparameterisation to produce a simpler form which might be interpreted as a decision rule used by asset-holders (see Davidson *et al* [10] and Henry and Richard [16]).

The monetary sector of the National Institute model (*see Appendix (14.7) and (14.8)*)

The monetary sector of the model has its origins in Savage [29] and most of the asset demand equations have remained broadly unchanged in structure. The model concentrates on the determination of £M3. Fitting a single equation for this aggregate did not seem the most promising approach, whether it was to be interpreted as a structural equation or a reduced form.[3] We also rejected the view that the United Kingdom banking system could be modelled using a reserve ratio approach (see Goodhart [12]) and used as our starting point the following identities:

$$PSBR = \Delta CUR + \Delta G + \Delta BLPUB + \text{other exogenous items} \quad (3)$$

$$\Delta £M3 = \Delta BLPUB + \Delta BLIC + \Delta BLOP + \text{other exogenous items} \,(4)$$

The first identity expresses the fact that the PSBR may be financed by issuing currency (ΔCUR) selling government debt to the non-bank private sector (ΔG) or by borrowing from the banking sector ($\Delta BLPUB$). The PSBR is given from the income—expenditure side of the model. The demand for currency and the demand for government debt are separately modelled, while bank lending to the public sector (in the form of bankers' balances, Treasury bills and other government debt) is treated as the residual source of public sector finance (and the residual of equation (3)). The second identity shows how the change in £M3 can be built up from the asset side of the commercial banks' balance sheet. Separate equations exist for bank lending to industrial and commercial companies (*BLIC*) and to persons (excluding loans for house purchase (*BLOP*)). The asset demand equations in the model, including the demand for government debt, depend on interest rates. In a model with this structure it is the response of government debt sales and of bank lending to interest rate changes which provides the mechanism for control of £M3 by means of market forces rather than direct controls.

Currency and M1

Currency held by the non-bank private sector is assumed, not unreasonably, to be demand determined. The transactions variable used in the equation is real consumers' expenditure and a time trend picks up secular changes in the uses of cash to make payments. These two influences dominate any possible yield effects (that is, effects of interest rates and inflation) which were found to be statistically insignificant.

The equation for narrow money ($M1$) is similar (the scale variable being GDP at market prices) but in this case the opportunity cost of holding money, (as measured by a representative short rate, the local authority three-month rate) was found to be a significant influence on demand.

Statistically, the performance of both the currency and the $M1$ equations is satisfactory. Both standard errors are about 2 per cent of the outstanding stock and the autocorrelation statistics show no sign of dynamic misspecification (see Appendix). The testing down and reparameterisation of the equations into growth rates and equilibrium or ratio terms is in accord with the error correction view of dynamic disequilibrium behaviour (see Hendry and von Ungern Sternberg [17]) and involved a trade-off between the degree of fit and the plausibility of step response and long-run solutions.

Both equations describe adjustment towards an equilibrium defined in terms of a stock rather than a flow, and both have unit long-run expenditure elasticities. For any *constant* real (or nominal) growth in expenditure the asset—expenditure ratios remain constant. The time trend indicates a fall of about 3 per cent per annum in currency holdings due to changes in the payments mechanism. The equilibrium asset—expenditure ratios depend negatively on the growth in real expenditure, partly because of the lagged response of the asset stocks to step changes in real expenditure. This is not an altogether plausible long-run result and may be due to the fact that the limited data set provides a rather ill-determined point estimate (see Currie [5]). The own interest rate semi-elasticity of $M1$ with respect to the local authority three-month rate (RLA) is about eight.

The equation for $M1$ has an imposed instantaneous unit price elasticity (the demand for money responds immediately in proportion to changes in the price level). Hendry [15], using a similar formulation, imposes only long-run price level homogeneity and (although the price terms cannot be readily interpreted as an expected inflation effect) short-run homogeneity is clearly rejected by his data set. Grice *et al* [14], who include gross financial wealth as a determinant of the demand for $M1$, also reject instantaneous price level homogeneity but obtain much smaller interest rate and expenditure effects.

The demand for gilts[4]

The flow demand for gilts, by persons, pension and life assurance funds and other financial intermediaries, ΔG, is assumed to depend on (a proxy for) the change in gross financial wealth of this composite sector, ΔW, and a set of yields including the expected capital gain on gilts, CG. Expected capital gains are not assumed to be zero because of the existence of risk aversion, because the market is not atomistic on the demand side and because supply depends on intervention by the government broker.

Experimentation with variables representing returns to property (house prices) and expected gains on equity, using McCallum [21] weakly rational predictors and the *ex post* return, proved unsuccessful. The equity yield gave a negative coefficient but this became insignificant when instrumental variable estimation was used.

The expected relative yield on gilts, R^e, is defined as $(CG + R - RLA)$, where R is the running yield on 2½ per cent consols and RLA is the local authority three-month rate. It was generated using a McCallum [21] weakly rational predictor. The following equation was found for R^e:

$$R^e = \underset{(2.3)}{-58} + \underset{(3.7)}{10.3R_{-1}} + \underset{(0.9)}{2.0RLA_{-1}} - \underset{(1.6)}{4.0REU} + \underset{(1.6)}{0.75REU_{-1}}$$

$$- \underset{(2.4)}{6.6REU_{-3}} + \underset{(2.2)}{2.0\dot{E}_{-1}} + \underset{(1.2)}{0.8\dot{E}_{-5}} \tag{5}$$

$7201 - 8102 \ R^2 = 0.42$; SEE $= 22$; DW $= 2.4$

where $REU =$ Eurodollar three-month rate, $\dot{E} =$ annual percentage change in the effective exchange rate. The positive coefficient on R_{-1} probably reflects the authorities' behaviour over the period of estimation which sometimes involved engineering expectations of a capital gain by raising long rates abruptly by a large amount. (This was referred to as the 'Grand Old Duke of York' strategy.) The positive coefficient on RLA_{-1} indicates some delay in the response of long rates to short rates, perhaps because of smoothing by the authorities. The negative influence of the Eurodollar rate may reflect a policy designed to stabilise the exchange rate or it may represent international financial asset arbitrage. Similar arguments apply to the exchange rate terms.

Using the predictions from the above equation to generate $\hat{R}^e$ and instruments for the current period change in gross wealth, W, we obtained the following gilts equation:

$$\Delta\ln(G/P) = \underset{(3.4)}{0.015} + \underset{(3.1)}{1.24\Delta\ln(W/P)} + \underset{(1.6)}{0.00043\hat{R}^e} - \underset{(1.5)}{0.158\ln(G/Y)_{-1}} \tag{6}$$

1972(III)–1981(II) SEE $= 0.021$; DW $= 2.4$; $Z_1(5) = 4.8$; LM(8) $= 9.8$

where Y is personal disposable income and Z_1 is a Chi-squared statistic indicating the independence of instruments and errors. The equation has white noise residuals and performs reasonably well within sample and out of sample (forecasts over 10 quarters from 1978(IV) give a Chow statistic $F(10, 18) = 0.1$ and a post sample Chi-squared statistic, $Z_2(10) = 1.2$).

The least satisfactory feature of this equation is the equilibrium term (G/Y). Inclusion of the preferred form (G/W) produced results which were not acceptable. (Spencer [31] found similar problems.) The underlying difficulty may be one of measurement and valuation, both of the stock of gilts held by the private sector and of the sector's financial wealth. For the results reported here stock data were derived from cumulated flows and estimates of revaluations.

Bank lending to industrial and commercial companies (*see Appendix* (*14.5*))

There are a large number of studies of *aggregate* bank lending for the United Kingdom based loosely on a transactions approach (see Melitz and Sterdyniak [23]) but little empirical work has been done for the United Kingdom on disaggregated bank lending equations (see Cuthbertson and Foster [9] for a survey). The existence of unused overdraft facilities and the intense competition between banks to maintain customer loyalty (of large firms) leads one to believe that bank lending to companies may be demand determined.

In the National Institute model the (stock) demand for (real) bank lending (QBL) to industrial and commercial companies (ICC) is determined by the level of transactions (proxied by GDP), a vector of interest rates, the borrowing requirement of the company sector and a dummy variable to pick up the effects of Competition and Credit Control, CCC.[5]

The borrowing requirement (which is on a payments basis) picks up the impact of short-run financial flows on lending. The local authority three-month rate, RLA, and the bank lending rate, RBL, are included to proxy the relative cost of financing a given borrowing requirement by running down liquid assets or by bank borrowing. The $RLA-RBL$ differential also measures the arbitrage return to round tripping from bank advances into short-term assets when $RLA-RBL$ is positive (as happened particularly in the 1973–4 period). Other studies (see HM Treasury [36] and Moore and Threadgold [28]) measure the return to round tripping as $RT = \max(0, RLA-RBL)$ but inclusion of this variable as well as $(RLA-RBL)$ indicated the empirical superiority of the latter. (Sprenkel and Miller [34] give additional theoretical reasons for the use of *RLA—RBL* rather than *RT* in the context of a precautionary demand model.)

The inclusion of the Eurodollar rate (*REU*) may either measure the (relative) cost of sterling as against foreign currency bank borrowing or the cost of borrowing in the Eurosterling market. Alternative (weighted) foreign rates gave similar results to the Eurodollar rate. Use of the forward premium or the expected exchange rate, as proxied by the actual future rate, together with the Eurodollar rate, proved unsuccessful. This result may suggest that expectations are unitary (that is, expected exchange rate changes are zero) or that switching only takes place between the domestic and Eurosterling market.

The zero-one dummy variable for the introduction of *CCC* attempts to pick up the change in quality factors (collateral, payback period etc.) on the demand side, after the introduction of *CCC*. As will be seen below it has a powerful influence on lending. Experiments with alternative *CCC* effects (for example, zero effect, short-run effect only) indicate that the parameters of the equation are highly sensitive to the form of dummy variable used.

The specification search for this equation was carried out on seasonally unadjusted data and the preferred equation then transferred to seasonally adjusted data. (Using seasonally adjusted data the *CCC* effect is increased and the relative domestic interest rate effect is substantially reduced relative to the results using unadjusted data.) A general autoregressive distributed lag equation formed the unrestricted specification and the resulting equation (with data acceptable restrictions) has a long-run dynamic equilibrium solution of the form:

$$\left(\frac{QBL}{Y}\right) = A - 0.61g_y^4 - 0.025RBL + 0.021(RLA - RBL)$$

$$+ 0.012REU + 0.30CCC + 0.011RB \tag{7}$$

where *QBL* = real stock of bank lending to *ICC, Y* = real GDP, *RBL* = real borrowing requirement, $g_y^4 = \Delta \ln Y$, *A* is a constant.

The semi-elasticities of the stock of lending with respect to *RBL*, (*RLA—RBL*) and *REU* are 2.5, 2.1 and 1.2 respectively. The nominal borrowing requirement has a current period marginal effect on bank lending of about 0.35, indicating that changes in bank lending account for about 35 per cent of the financing of the current period borrowing requirement. The equation has a long-run real output elasticity of unity and *CCC* adds 30 per cent to the stock of lending. There is a small negative effect of the rate of growth of output on the lending to output ratio.

The results indicate that control of bank lending (and hence *£M*3) depends crucially on the behaviour of *relative* interest rates. An increase in short rates initiated by a rise in RLA could (especially in the short run) lead to a perverse response of bank lending and $£M3$, particularly if the rise in United Kingdom short rates is accompanied by an increase in foreign rates. An increase in the company sector borrowing requirement has a positive effect on bank lending. This suggests that a recession, partticularly one induced by high interest rates, is likely to increase bank lending (in part because interest debiting increases the borrowing requirement).

The equation (see Appendix) has reasonable statistical properties: a standard error of 1.9 per cent and no sign of dynamic misspecification as evidenced by the autocorrelation statistics. Additional variables tested in the equation, without success, are long-term interest rates, price expectations and the variance of output. Relaxation of the instantaneous unit price level restriction in the estimated equation suggested that such a restriction is inappropriate; however, relaxation of the restriction rendered a number of other variables insignificant and produced marked autocorrelation in the residuals. The equation predicts reasonably well outside the sample period of estimation (see Cuthbertson [8]).

The Treasury [36] model listing for bank lending to ICC is very similar to the National Institute model but has $RT = \max(0, RLA - RBL)$ in place of $(RLA - RBL)$ and also includes a term in the expected exchange rate which has a much smaller coefficient than that on the foreign interest rate. No test statistics for the Treasury equation are given but an evaluation of the equation may be found in Cuthbertson [8].

The Bank of England eschew the transactions approach to bank lending to ICC and relate the *increase* in nominal lending to the increase in a set of nominal costs variables (wages, imports, taxes and stockbuilding), the RT variable and a real own-interest rate variable. Although the equation has no CCC variable some of the CCC effect is picked up by the RT variable which has a *permanent* effect on the stock of lending.

Bank lending to persons (*see Appendix* (*14.4*))

In the 1960s and the first half of the 1970s personal sector bank advances were frequently subject to direct controls and less formal moral suasion by the authorities. Attempts to model this market in disequilibrium by Spencer and Mowl [32] initially proved successful but this equation in the Treasury model has now been replaced by a conventional demand equation including personal disposable income, wealth, prices, stockbuilding (of unincorporated businesses) and the own interest rate as determinants. It is not surprising that a relationship appropriate to a period of direct control should have broken down completely now that lending is market determined and growing very rapidly.

Personal sector bank lending (excluding lending for house purchase) in the National Institute model is determined by real personal disposable income, Y (a transactions variable), the net acquisition of financial assets of the personal sector, *DFAPER*, which is a proxy for financial wealth, a temporary *CCC* dummy variable and the own rate of interest *RBL*.

Starting from a general distributed lag equation we are able to accept the restriction of a unit real income elasticity, but interest rate effects on the stock of lending are found to be rather poorly determined statistically, with the interest rate semi-elasticity rather small at ½ per cent. Although the equation passes the autocorrelation diagnostic tests, its within-sample standard error is rather large at 4.3 per cent of the stock of lending.

Interest rate equations (*see Appendix* (*14.15*))

The monetary authorities are able to determine short-term interest directly by operations in the money markets. We do not attempt to model this behaviour so the short-term interest rates are treated as exogenous. Other interest rates are influenced by short-term rates but not controlled directly. To complete the monetary sector of the model we need equations to determine long-term interest rates and the rate applied to bank lending.

The long-term rate (that is, the yield on 2½ per cent consols) is determined by a term structure equation. In the absence of transactions costs and of a premium for risk, the yield on an N period bond R_t^N would be equated to a series of one period yields r_t. Equating expected terminal wealth for £1 invested in the two securities gives:

$$(1 + R_t^N)^N = (1 + r_t)(1 + {}_tr_{t+1}^e)(1 + {}_tr_{t+2}^e) \ldots (1 + {}_tr_{t+N-1}^e) \quad (8)$$

where ${}_tr_{t+j}^e$ is the short rate expected to rule in $t + j$ with the expectation being formed at time, t.

Taking logarithms and using the approximation $\ln(1 + x) \cong x, |x| < 1$ we obtain

$$R_t^N = \frac{1}{N}(r_t + {}_tr_{t+1}^e + {}_tr_{t+2}^e + \ldots + {}_tr_{t+N-1}^e) \quad (9)$$

Equation (9) embodies the pure expectations hypothesis (Meiselman [22]) since there is no risk premium. The preferred habitat hypothesis (Modigliani and Sutch [27]) takes a more agnostic view about riskiness, the overriding requirement here being that bonds which mature at dates close together should be close substitutes and have similar risk premia. According to the liquidity preference hypothesis, equation (9) has a risk premium added which is likely to increase as N increases. A possible reason for this is that future short rates may be expected to move broadly with future inflation so that the *real* return on a series of short-term investment will be fairly risk-free, whereas for a long-term bond the expected *real* return depends on the expectation of inflation over all future periods and is therefore subject to great uncertainty.

The National Institute term structure equation is consistent with the pure expectations hypothesis. Following Modigliani and Schiller [26] we model expectations about future nominal yields by assuming separate forecasting rules for real yields and for inflation. Both rules are adaptive and based on the experience of the recent past. The equation is expressed in terms of first differences: $\Delta R^N = a_0 + \Sigma_0^5 b_i \Delta RTB_{-1} + \Sigma_{i=0}^6 c_i \Delta \dot{P}_{-i}$ where R^N is the yield on 2½ per cent consols, RTB is the Treasury Bill rate and $\dot{P}$ is the (quarterly) rate of inflation in the *CPI*.

The estimated equation has a reasonably within-sample fit ($\bar{R}^2 = 0.46$) and the Almon lag profiles give a long-run weight of 0.77 to RTB and 0.39 to $\dot{P}$.

Bank lending rate (*see Appendix* (*14.12*))
This linking equation merely assumes that the bank lending rate RBL reacts, with fixed mark-up, to changes in the certificate of deposit rate, CDR. The lags are short, about 50 per cent of any change in the CDR rate is reflected in RBL in the current quarter and a unit long-run effect is accepted by the data. The possible influence of the Supplementary Special Deposits scheme on this relationship is not modelled.

Notes
[1] Spencer and Mowl [32], Savage [29] and the Bank of England [1] provide examples of early United Kingdom monetary models.

[2] The transactions model originates with Baumol [2] and its relevance to large firms is critically discussed in Sprenkel [33]. The speculative model is presented in Tobin [35]. The precautionary model is to be found in Miller and Orr [25] and Sprenkel and Miller [34] and a survey of these models is to be found in Laidler [18]. Friedman's [11] 'general utility' approach to the demand for assets covers elements of all three models.

[3] We rejected a direct pseudo-reduced form equation linking the *PSBR* and *£M*3 on theoretical (see Middleton *et al* [24]) and on empirical grounds (see Cuthbertson *et al* [6]), although such an approach has been used by the London Business School (see Beenstock and Longbottom [3]).

[4] The equation described here is an updated version of that used in producing the model simulations reported in chapter 10 below but (probably) involves only minor changes in the model properties.

[5]Acceptance credits held outside the banking system during the period of the imposition of the Supplementary Special Deposits Scheme in 1978–80 and the Issue Department's large holdings of commercial bills after 1978 are counted as part of 'bank lending' and included in the dependent variable in the estimation of the equation.

References

[1] Bank of England, 'Bank of England model of the UK economy', Bank of England Discussion paper no. 5, September 1979.

[2] Baumol, W. J., 'The transactions demand for cash: an inventory theoretic approach', *Quarterly Journal of Economics*, vol. 66, November 1952.

[3] Beenstock, M. and Longbottom, A., 'The money supply and the PSBR', *Economic Outlook*, vol. 4, no. 9, June 1980.

[4] Christofides, L. N., 'Quadratic costs and multi-asset partial adjustment equations', *Applied Economics*, vol. 8, no. 4, 1976.

[5] Currie, D., 'Some long-run features of dynamic time-series models', *Economic Journal*, September 1981.

[6] Cuthbertson, K., Henry, S. G. B., Mayes, D. and Savage, D., 'The money supply and the PSBR', *National Institute Economic Review*, no. 94, November 1980.

[7] Cuthbertson, K., 'A comparative study of bank lending: theoretical survey and preliminary empirical results', National Institute of Economic and Social Research. mimeo. March 1982.

[8] Cuthbertson, K., 'Bank lending to ICC: some variants on the HM Treasury equation', National Institute of Economic and Social Research, mimeo, March 1983.

[9] Cuthbertson, K. and Foster, N., 'Bank lending to industrial and commercial companies in three models of the UK economy', *National Institute Economic Review*, no. 102, November 1982.

[10] Davidson, J. E. H., Hendry, D. F., Srba, F. and Yeo, S., 'Econometric modelling of the aggregate time series relationship between consumers' expenditure and income in the UK', *Economic Journal*, vol. 88, no. 4, 1978.

[11] Friedman, M. 'The quantity theory of money: a restatement', in Friedman, M. (ed), *Studies in the Quantity Theory of Money*, University of Chicago Press, 1956.

[12] Goodhart, C. A. E., *Money Information and Uncertainty*, London, Macmillan, 1975.

[13] Goodhart, C. and Crockett, A. D., 'The importance of money (Appendix I)', *Bank of England Quarterly Bulletin*, 10(3), June 1970.

[14] Grice, J. and Bennett, A., 'The demand for sterling M3 and other aggregates in the UK', Government Economic Service Working Paper no. 45, August 1981.

[15] Hendry, D. F., 'Predictive accuracy and econometric modelling in macro-economics: the transactions demand', in Ormerod, P. A. (ed), *Economic Modelling*, London, Heinemann, 1979.

[16] Hendry, D. F. and Richard, J. F., 'The econometric analysis of economic time series', *Journal of Econometrics*, vol. 20, 1982.

[17] Hendry, D. and von Ungern Sternberg, T., 'Liquidity and inflation effects on consumers' expenditure', forthcoming in Deaton, A. (ed), *Essays in the Theory and Measurement of Consumers' Behaviour.*

[18] Laidler, D. E. W., *The Demand for Money: Theories and Evidence* (2nd ed), New York, Dun-Donnelly, 1977.

[19] Lucas, R. E. Jr., 'Econometric policy evaluation: a critique', in Brunner, K. and Meltzer, H. H. (eds), *The Phillips Curve and Labour Markets,* Supplement to the *Journal of Monetary Economics,* 1976.

[20] Matthews, K. G. P. and Ormerod, P. A., 'St. Louis models of the UK economy', *National Institute Economic Review,* no. 84, May 1978.

[21] McCallum, B. J., 'Rational expectations and the natural rate hypothesis: some evidence for the UK', *Manchester School,* vol. 43, March 1975.

[22] Meiselman, D., *The Term Structure of Interest Rates,* Oxford, Clarendon Press, 1962.

[23] Melitz, J. and Sterdyniak, H., 'An econometric study of the British monetary system, *Economic Journal,* June 1979.

[24] Middleton, P., Mowl, C., Riley, C. and Odling Smee, J., 'Monetary targets and the public sector borrowing requirement' in Wood, G. and Griffiths, B. (eds), *Monetary Targets,* London, Macmillan, 1981.

[25] Miller, M. and Orr, D., 'A model of the demand for money by firms', *Quarterly Journal of Economics,* August 1966.

[26] Modigliani, F. and Schiller, R. J., 'Inflation, rational expectations and the term structure of interest rates, *Economica,* vol. 60, no. 157, February 1973.

[27] Modigliani, F. and Sutch, R., 'Innovations in interest rate policy', *American Economic Review Papers and Proceedings,* vol. 56, 1966.

[28] Moore, B. J. and Threadgold, A. R., 'Bank lending and the money supply', Bank of England Discussion paper no. 10, July 1980.

[29] Savage, D., 'The monetary sector of the NIESR model: preliminary results', National Institute of Economic and Social Research Discussion paper no. 23, 1978.

[30] Smith, S. G. and Brainard, W., 'The value of a priori information in estimating a financial model', *Journal of Finance,* vol. XXXI, no. 5, December 1976.

[31] Spencer, P., 'A model of the demand for British government stocks by non-bank residents 1967–77', *Economic Journal,* vol. 91, no. 364, December 1981.

[32] Spencer, P. D. and Mowl, C., 'A financial sector for the Treasury model', Government Economic Service Working Paper no. 17, December 1978.

[33] Sprenkel, C. M., 'Large economic units, banks and the transactions demand for money', *Quarterly Journal of Economics,* August 1966.

[34] Sprenkel, C. M. and Miller, M. H., 'The precautionary demand for narrow and broad money', *Economica,* vol, 47, no. 188, November 1980.

[35] Tobin, J., 'Liquidity preference as behaviour towards risk', *Review of Economic Studies,* vol. 25, February 1958.

[36] HM Treasury, Macroeconomic Model Technical Manual, HM Treasury, December 1982.

PART TWO: FORECASTING AND SIMULATION

9 The Use of the Model for Forecasting
D. Savage

In contrast to the voluminous literature on the specification and estimation of econometric models, comparatively little has been written on the use of models for forecasting.[1] There is probably widespread ignorance, even among academic economists, as to how bodies like the National Institute make forecasts. Popular conceptions of forecasting with an econometric model stretch from the naive view that it is simply a matter of mechanically turning the handle, to the cynical view that forecasters so impose their prior notions on the model that its role is reduced to that of an elaborate adding machine which ensures that the National Accounting identies are respected.

Since 1959, nearly every issue of the *Economic Review,* published in February, May, August and November, has contained a general survey of the economic situation and an assessment of short-term prospects. For many years the latter has taken the form of a quarterly forecast looking eighteen months to two years into the future. Once a year, usually in the November issue, the *Review* also contains a medium-term assessment, looking five years ahead. In recent years this has been prepared using the same model of the economy as we use for the short-term forecast.

The most comprehensive account of the National Institute's forecasting methods, together with an account of the version of the model in use at that time, was published in Surrey [8]. This account is now considerably out of date. The size of the model has expanded enormously since 1971, a development which reflects both greater disaggregation of the relationships used and the fact that relationships have been included for variables that were previously either treated as exogenous or ignored entirely. The role of the model in the forecast has expanded as a result, and the proportion of the work done off model has declined.

Although forecasts have been published in the quarterly *Review* since 1959, an econometric model of the whole economy has only been an integral part of the exercise since August 1969. Before this, forecasts were prepared following what might be described as a trial and error procedure.[2] Starting from quantitative assumptions for a number of basic variables, values of other variables were derived within an income—expenditure framework by means of estimated relationships, accounting identities or rules of thumb. If the results obtained were untenable, alterations were made to remove the offending features. This might lead to other contradictions, after which new changes were made, and so on until all the requirements of internal consistency were met.

To be more specific, the point of departure was to put down some tentative figures for the main expenditure components of output. From these were derived income and, from income, expenditure. The question then was whether the derived expenditure figures, especially consumers' expenditure, squared with those on which the initial estimate of output was based. If not, some new intermediate figures were tried. After several rounds of iteration, a final reconciliation was achieved by touching up the figures by hand.

The advantages of solving simultaneously a system of equations in the form of a complete model of the economy are fairly obvious. In the first place, the sheer computational effort required to solve even a very simple system of simultaneous equations by a manual trial-and-error method is very considerable; the solution of a large non-linear system would be quite unfeasible. Also, the use of a formal model has the great advantage of making the assumptions underlying the relationships between economic variables explicit, whereas the assumptions underlying a forecast reached by informal methods tend to be less transparent.

Forecasting with an econometric model does not imply rigid adherence to a particular set of equations, since it is possible to programme a model in a way which allows the forecaster to incorporate judgemental adjustments. The way in which an econometric model is used for forecasting may be set out formally as follows. For each endogenous variable (Y), there is a behavioural relationship of the following form: $Y = f(X, Z,) + u$ where X is the vector of endogenous explanatory variables, that is, variables for which solution values are generated elsewhere in the model; Z is the vector of exogenous explanatory variables, that is, variables which are unaffected by other variables in the model; u is the error term. The forecasting problem consists of selecting future values of Z and u, with $u = 0$ one possibility.

Before describing in more detail the procedures by which we prepare our forecast of the United Kingdom economy each quarter, it is useful to list the main steps:

1) The partial information we have to hand about the immediate past is used to estimate values in the most recent quarter for variables on which complete data are not yet available. The attempt to get a fix on the current situation, the base from which the forecast is made, is an important first step in the forecasting exercise.

2) Projections are made for exogenous variables, the most important of which are public expenditure on goods and services, which is taken to be set by the government as a policy decision, and variables such as world trade which are taken to be independent of events in this country.

3) Using the latest data, residuals[3] for the recent past are obtained for the structural form of each behavioural equation in the model. A more or less mechanical extrapolation of these residuals is combined through the model with the projections of exogenous variables to obtain a base run. The base run is, loosely speaking,[4] what the model would predict for a given set of exogenous variables in the absence of judgemental intervention.

4) The base is adjusted to remove features which are thought inconsistent with external sources of evidence or which are judged to lack credibility.

The preparation of a forecast takes about two to three weeks. The actual operation of the model involves only two or three people, but they draw on information and advice provided by a much larger team. The succeeding sections of this chapter describe, in turn, each of the consecutive stages in the preparation of the forecast. A final section describes the way in which we monitor our performance through repeated checking of the accuracy of our forecasts.

Estimating the immediate past

Before the model can be run, it is necessary to bring the data files as up to date as possible. Official estimates of the National Accounts are only available after a substantial time lag, so that when we make our February forecast, for example, we only have complete National Accounts for the first three quarters of the previous year. We update the National Accounts by one quarter ourselves, making use of the fragmentary information we have to hand.

Our estimate of GDP, at constant prices, is based largely on the index of industrial production, which we know for two months of the quarter. The expenditure components for which we have the firmest information are consumers' expenditure and net trade. For the former we usually have the CSO's first provisional estimate. For the latter, we have volume indices for exports and imports of goods from the trade figures but no official information on services. An estimate of fixed investment is pieced together from a variety of sources, including housing completions, engineering orders and orders for new construction work. We have no concrete information on general government current spending on goods and services but this does not usually fluctuate much from one quarter to the next. Usually, the biggest problem is to decide what has happened to stockbuilding, changes in which are (arithmetically) the most important source of quarterly fluctuations in GDP. The CBI survey provides some guide to stock changes in manufacturing. But we usually derive stockbuilding by residual as that necessary to reconcile what we know about GDP, from industrial production, with what we know about the other expenditure components.

We know less about incomes than we do about expenditures. Our estimate of wages and salaries, the largest component of income GDP, is based on the index of average earnings, which is available for two months of the quarter, and employment in index of production industries. We have no direct information on the other income components. We are better informed about prices. The retail price index is a good guide to the consumer price index of the National Accounts and export and import prices (for goods) are available from the trade figures.

Exogenous variables

The exogenous assumptions underlying our forecasts fall into two main categories, those about variables which are believed to be directly under the control of domestic policy and those about developments in the rest of the world, which are of critical importance to an open economy like Britain.

Our forecasts are usually prepared on the assumption of unchanged fiscal policy. In accordance with accepted convention, this is taken to mean no changes, other than those which may have been already announced, in tax rates or allowances or in social security benefit rates, apart from indexation. Public spending on goods and services is treated as wholly exogenous and is projected by interpreting official statements of spending intentions. It is possible that some expenditure programmes are sensitive to the economic climate, for example, there may be an accelerator linkage between nationalised industry investment and economic activity and the rate of progress on building works may be affected by tight supply conditions in the construction industry. But to the extent to which such effects are taken into account, it is done judgementally, off model.

The most comprehensive source of information on public expenditure plans is the Public Expenditure White Paper, which in recent years has been published at the time of the Budget in the early Spring or just before it. The projections in the White Paper are not in the form which we require for the forecast. They are for financial years only and are based on different definitions from those of the National Accounts. There is also an element of judgement in the treatment of two unallocated items of expenditure; the contingency reserve and the provision for shortfall.[5]

The biggest problem, however, is that White Papers do not contain figures on a price base similar to the constant price statistics in the National Accounts. Until 1982, expenditure plans were expressed in constant, survey prices (broadly the prices of around the end of the previous calendar year). After 1976–7 the government sought to control the level of public spending in nominal as well as in real terms through cash limits, the implication being that the volume of public spending on goods and services would tend to be reduced if the increase in the price of goods purchased by the government exceeded the rate of increase assumed in fixing the cash limits.

The 1982 White Paper was the first to show public expenditure plans in cash (current price) terms rather than in constant survey prices. Since the inflation assumptions underlying the projections were known, it was possible to form some rough idea of the planned path for spending in real terms. The projection of expenditure volumes under the new system involves similar sorts of judgements to those encountered under the old. Thus, if we think a contradiction is likely to develop between the cash plans and the prospective levels of public sector pay settlements, we have to assess whether this will cut into the volume of current spending on goods and services, or whether overspending on current goods and services will occur, at the expense of other forms of spending or of the contingency reserve.

Our assessment of the prospects for the world economy is a substantial exercise in its own right, meriting a chapter of its own in the *Economic Review*. A large part of the work is in the nature of an intelligence gathering exercise, since we rely heavily on forecasts for the other industrial countries made within those countries, often by institutions similar to ours. Given limited resources, it would hardly be reasonable for us to take a wholly independent view of the prospects for the United States, for example. Nevertheless, own-country forecasts are not accepted without qualification; they are subjected to critical scrutiny, updated if they fail to take into account the latest statistics and adjusted if they are based on assumptions (for example, about oil prices or economic policy) that are different from our own. For most countries there are a number of competing forecasts and a judgement has to be made between them.

Forecasts for the large industrial countries are combined with broader brush projections for the smaller countries, developing countries and centrally planned economies, to form an aggregate picture of the prospects for world trade. Within our model of the domestic economy, world trade is a major exogenous determinant of export volumes and hence of output and the balance of payments. From inflation forecasts for the larger industrial countries and from a judgemental assessment of the prospects for commodity prices, forecasts are derived (in terms of foreign currency) for the export prices of our foreign competitors and for United Kingdom import prices. Inflation in other countries works to the advantage of export volumes and import substitutes by improving their price and cost competitiveness, but to the disadvantage of the balance of payments, in the short term at least, by worsening the terms of trade. The rate of increase in import prices (in foreign currency terms) is a major exogenous determinant of domestic inflation.

The base run

When the updating of the data base is complete, single equation residuals are calculated for the recent past (the last three or four years, which is as far back as data revisions normally extend). We look for any unusually large residuals, which may be attributable to data errors or to special factors such as strikes, and for any systematic pattern in the residuals. (For the latter purpose our model solution programme contains a subroutine which calculates the mean and variance of residuals and tests for autocorrelation.)

An equation which fitted the data well during estimation may develop residuals that are large and non-random through failure to forecast well outside its period of estimation. But large revisions to official data for the past can cause systematic over or underprediction even within the original estimation period. In these circumstances, the results obtained from simulating the model over the future with zero residuals would inevitably contain absurdities; step increases would be generated for variables where equations had been underpredicting and step falls for variables whose equations had been overpredicting. In order to obtain a useful base run the model has to be realigned in some way. This is done by extrapolating residuals into the future at their average level over the recent past (the last four quarters or so). This effectively changes the constant term of each behavioural equation, shifting each function up or down.[6] At this stage, no other, more subjective, adjustments are made to the model, other than allowance, where possible, for known special factors.

Judgemental adjustments

The base run is likely to lack credibility in some respects. In the first place, the generated values of some variables may be inconsistent with other, quite independent, sources of evidence. Direct information about likely future movements of various components of private investment is afforded by leading indicators such as investment intentions data, construction and engineering orders and housing starts. Generally, the usefulness of leading indicators for forecasting diminishes as the forecast horizon extends further into the future. Our forecasts of manufacturing investment often rely heavily on the intentions data for the current year, but place greater weight on the equation for the following year when the intentions data are less dependable. In situations in which an econometric relationship and a relevant leading indicator give contradictory readings we have no formal procedures for reconciling the two sets of evidence: the weight attached to the results of the equation tends to depend on considerations such as its performance over the recent past. Greater weight is sometimes attached to intentions data when there are felt to be distinctive factors affecting the outlook, a sharp squeeze on company profits and cash flow for example, which are not adequately captured by the equation.

Although we normally treat average earnings as endogenous throughout the forecast period for the purpose of the base run, our assessment of the short-term prospects for wages and earnings relies mainly on detailed monitoring of recent settlements and outstanding claims. Just as leading indicators of fixed investment are only useful for forecasting a relatively short period ahead, so current claims and settlements are only a guide to wages and earnings in the current wage round; forecasts further into the future have to rely either on judgement or on an econometric wage equation.

In addition to the incorporation of objective external information into the forecast, residual adjustments of a more subjective kind are sometimes made. If equations are required to forecast in an environment very different from that of their estimation period, we may feel it necessary to apply judgement to the results. For example, if Corporation Tax were abolished, there is little doubt that forecasts based solely on our model, which contains few direct linkages between company income, dividends, investment and stockbuilding, would go badly astray. In such a situation we would not mechanically turn the handle; true we may be forced to guess to some extent, but the results would probably be closer to the outcome than a purely model-generated forecast. We also look at new forecasts in the light of what we said on previous occasions, checking that the changes we have made are reasonable, given new information, changes to the model and conscious changes of mind with respect to judgemental adjustments.

Assessing forecasts

The National Institute has made a practice of reporting and analysing its forecasting performance. Every year in the February or May *Economic Review* a post mortem is conducted into the previous year's forecasts. In addition, a number of special studies have looked at the Institute's track record in forecasting key economic variables.[7] The difficulties inherent in such post mortems are well known. The actual course of events cannot be stated with very great precision; estimates of national income and expenditure are subject to large and frequent revisions. Another difficulty is that, since the Institute's forecasts are based on the assumption of no change in government policy, ideally one would wish to correct for the effects of policy changes so as to put both forecast and actual on the same basis. But, of course, exact estimates of the effects of policy changes are not possible. Notwithstanding these problems, the monitoring of forecasting performance is a valuable exercise. It gives users a guide to the margin of error surrounding economic forecasts. Post mortems are also useful to the forecasters themselves. By identifying the most important sources of error they are a guide to where further development work is required most.

Table 9.1 gives a simple summary of errors in our one-year ahead through-the-year forecasts of GDP and inflation, distinguishing between the accuracy achieved on average during the period of relative stability up to 1973, and the accuracy achieved thereafter. During the earlier period the average absolute error in GDP forecasts was about 1¼ per cent. Since 1974 it has risen to a little over 1½ per cent. The average error, which is fairly close to zero before 1974, is positive for the later period, indicating some systematic tendency towards over-prediction. For inflation, the average absolute errors are about 2 per cent before 1974 and 3 per cent since. The large negative errors indicate a well-defined downward bias in the forecasts.

Table 9.1   Average forecast errors[a]

	Change in real GDP		Change in consumer prices	
	Average error	Average absolute error	Average error	Average absolute error
1959–73	−0.23	1.31	−2.04[b]	2.04[b]
1974–82	0.98	1.58	−1.82	2.91
1959–82	0.23	1.41	−1.94[c]	2.45[c]

Source: NIESR calculations.
[a]Our forecasts published in February issues of the *Review* compared with the latest estimate of the outturns. [b]1964–73. [c]1964–82.

Most assessments of forecasting performance are of this kind: they have simply compared published forecasts with the actual outcome. Since the Institute, in common with most other forecasters using econometric models, does not use without qualification the predictions generated by the model, such studies are not adequate as tests of the predictive performance of econometric models. It is not clear whether errors in a published forecast are the consequence of errors in the model predictions or in the residual adjustments which have been imposed or errors in the projection of exogenous variables.

Work at the Institute has attempted to disentangle the roles of model and forecaster by quantifying the effects of the different factors which give rise to observed forecasting errors. The basic framework can be illustrated by the following very simple one-equation one-identity model:

$$C = \alpha + BY_t + u \tag{1}$$

$$Y = C + Z \tag{2}$$

where C and Y are endogenous variables, Z is an exogenous variable, u is the error in the model prediction of C.

Let u^* be the judgemental residual adjustment to equation 1.

The error in the forecast of $C(\delta C)$ can (given the linearity of the model) be decomposed into that part which is due to error in the projection of $Z(\delta Z)$, that part which is due to the error in the model prediction and the effect of the residual adjustment to equation (1):

$$\delta C = \frac{B}{1-B} \delta Z + \frac{1}{1-B} u + \frac{1}{1-B} u^* \tag{3}$$

If u and u^* are of opposite signs, the residual adjustment will have tended to offset the model error and the forecast will have been improved. If they are of the same sign, the residual adjustment will have reinforced the model error.

Notes

[1] There has, for example, been no recent account of the methods adopted by the Treasury for making official economic forecasts. An early account of the methods used by the National Institute, now of historical interest only, is Neild and Shirley [5]; more recent accounts include Surrey [8], Worswick [11] and Surrey and Ormerod [9].

[2] See Neild and Shirley, *op. cit.*

[3] These are 'one-step ahead' and 'single equation'; that is to say, they are generated using actual values of all the explanatory variables including lagged dependent variables.

[4] 'Loosely speaking' because the selection of a mechanical rule to project residuals is necessarily somewhat arbitrary.

[5] The principle behind the contingency reserve is that it provides a margin within which additions can be made to estimated expenditure because of unforeseen circumstances. A judgement has to be made as to the extent to which the contingency reserve will be drawn upon and how the resulting additions to expenditure will be allocated across the different expenditure categories. Shortfall, on the other hand, allows for a systematic tendency in practice for actual public expenditure to fall short of planned expenditure. The allocation of shortfall presents less of a problem since it is known to apply mainly to the nationalised industry investment programme.

[6] It might be argued that residual drift and data revisions would be better handled by re-estimating the model each quarter on the latest statistics. However, even if regular re-estimation of an unchanged specification succeeded in making the model fit the recent past, it might well produce changes in parameters that were unacceptable *a priori*.

[7] For example, Kennedy [3], Ash and Smyth [1], Worswick [11], Osborn [6] and Savage [7].

[8] Teal and Osborn [10], Brooks and Cuthbertson [2] and NIESR [4].

References

[1] Ash, J. C. K. and Smyth, D. J., *Forecasting the United Kingdom Economy*, Farnborough, Saxon House and Lexington, Mass., D.C. Heath, 1973.

[2] Brooks, S. and Cuthbertson, K., 'Econometric models and econometric forecasts', National Institute of Economic and Social Research, *Discussion Paper* no. 41, February 1981.

[3] Kennedy, M. C., 'How well does the National Institute forecast?' in *National Institute Economic Review*, No. 50, November 1969.

[4] National Institute of Economic and Social Research, 'Assessing economic models and economic forecasts' in *National Institute Economic Review*, no. 95, February 1981.

[5] Neild, R. R. and Shirley, E. A., 'Economic Review: an assessment of forecasts, 1959–60' in *National Institute Economic Review*, no. 15, May 1961.

[6] Osborn, D. R., 'National Institute gross output forecasts: a comparison with US performance' in *National Institute Economic Review*, no. 88, May 1979.

[7] Savage, D., 'The assessment of the National Institute's forecasts of GDP, 1959–82', *National Institute Economic Review*, no. 105, August 1983.

[8] Surrey, M. J. C., *The analysis and forecasting of the British economy*, NIESR Occasional Paper XXV, Cambridge University Press, 1971.

[9] Surrey, M. J. C. and Ormerod, P. A., 'Formal and informal aspects of forecasting with an econometric model' in *National Institute Economic Review*, no. 81, August 1977.

[10] Teal, F. and Osborn, D. R., 'An assessment and comparison of two NIESR econometric model forecasts' in *National Institute Economic Review*, no. 88, May 1979.

[11] Worswick, G. D. N., 'National Institute Experience with Econometric Models' in Renton, G. A. (ed), *Modelling the Economy*, Heinemann Educational Books, 1975.

10 Simulation Exercises with the Complete Model
S. Brooks and S.G.B. Henry

Simulation exercises are one method of exploring the properties of large-scale non-linear models. These exercises reveal properties of the system as a whole which may help in the process of model selection. For any given model they also represent an end use, contributing, we hope, to understanding the macroeconomy and, in particular, its response to policy changes.

A simulation exercise begins with a base run of a model over a period of several years with given exogenous variables. A change is then introduced into one or more exogenous variables, for example, to an external variable like world trade, or a policy variable like the rate of income tax. The model is again solved dynamically over the same period. The resulting changes to endogenous variables relative to the base run are calculated. These changes are estimates of the consequences of the change in the exogenous variable.

The use of such simulations rests on the assumption that the structure and coefficients of the model would be unchanged by the substitution of different values for the variables treated as exogenous. This assumption is a strong one if the simulation involves substantial and systematic differences in the behaviour of exogenous variables and especially the behaviour of policy makers. Whether any valid policy conclusions can be drawn in this way has been questioned, especially by Lucas [1] in his seminal discussion of policy analysis. His objection concerns the problem of identifying system dynamics separately from the dynamics introduced by agents' expectations. Policy changes, and especially changes in policy rules, will change the way that expectations are formed and hence change the behaviour of the economy. Some recognition of this problem is involved in the treatment of announcement effects in published simulations of the Treasury model (see HM Treasury [3], p. 138). The simulations reported here, however, are based on the coefficients of the model as estimated, with no adjustments for special effects on expectations (unless one included the adjustment made to the VAT simulation reported below).

Further qualifications of a more routine nature are also relevant here.

Firstly, the assumptions made in defining simulations have to be carefully noted. Each of the following fiscal simulations, for example, is conducted by changing a policy variable and assuming a floating exchange rate and fixed interest rates. Alternative assumptions are sometimes made. Minford [2], for example, assumes that a (long-run) rule for balanced finance holds at all times when changing central government expenditures. This is defined as financing deficits by equal changes in bond issues and changes in the money supply. On the other hand, some simulations of increases in central government expenditure, reported by the Treasury, assume that monetary targets are achieved by varying interest rates, while others are conducted subject to the achievement of a fixed PSBR–GDP ratio (HM Treasury [3], pp. 139 and 147). Secondly, the simulations below measure the deviations produced by shocks to the model from a base run over the period 1977–81. Because the model is non-linear, the simulation results will depend on the historical values of the exogenous variables over that period. Comparisons between non-linear models simulated over different historical periods must be treated with some caution, since the differences between the simulations of different models will be compounded with differences in the time period chosen.

The simulations

Each of the simulations reported below is based on the period 1977–81 (except for some of the monetary policy runs, as explained below). Each simulation assumes indexation of the tax system. This includes the indexation of personal tax allowances in the second quarter of each year in line with inflation over the previous calendar year and the indexation of specific excise duties in the same way. (Certain items of government revenue are not indexed and are treated as exogenous variables; among these are local authority rates and general government subsidies on expenditure.)

(i) *An increase in current public expenditure of £2 billion (at 1981 prices); Table 10.1*

The change in policy assumption for this simulation is an increase in current expenditure on goods and services which is assumed to be spent on increasing employment in the public sector. Procurement is assumed unchanged. The direct effect on imports is, therefore, zero, but as private sector expenditures increase in subsequent periods, imports begin to increase as well. Total employment increases fairly rapidly at first and the amount of the increase by the end of the period is about 300,000 or 1½ per cent. This matches the increase in output which is also approximately 1½ per cent higher after five years.

Table 10.1   *Increase in government current spending worth £2 billion (1981 prices)*

Per cent[a]

Quarter	Y	C	I	ΔS	X	M	P	W	ER	CB	PSBR	EMP
1	0.9	−0.0	0.0	3	0.0	0.1	0.2	0.0	−0.0	−7	156	0.4
2	1.2	0.8	0.0	9	0.0	0.6	−0.4	2.2	−0.3	−90	134	0.6
3	1.1	0.5	0.1	12	0.1	0.5	−0.3	0.5	−0.5	−89	178	0.6
4	1.3	0.7	0.1	39	0.1	0.8	−0.4	1.3	−1.0	−144	174	0.7
6	1.3	0.8	0.3	18	0.2	0.9	0.4	1.9	−0.9	−115	156	0.8
8	1.4	1.0	0.3	23	0.4	1.0	0.5	2.5	−1.9	−173	182	1.0
12	1.5	1.0	0.0	15	0.6	0.8	1.0	3.1	−2.9	−204	266	1.2
16	1.4	1.1	−0.2	−3	0.6	0.8	2.1	3.9	−3.2	−59	346	1.3
20	1.5	1.2	−0.2	5	0.7	0.8	2.5	4.4	−4.6	−174	542	1.5

KEY TO TABLES 10.1–10.8

W	= average earnings	Y	= GDP at factor cost
ER	= sterling effective exchange rate	C	= consumers' expenditure
CB	= current balance	I	= fixed investment
£M3	= money supply, £M3 definition	ΔS	= stockbuilding
M1	= money supply, M1 definition	X	= exports
PSBR	= public sector borrowing requirement	M	= imports
EMP	= employment, UK total	P	= consumer price index

[a]Except for Δs (£m 1975 prices) and PSBR and CB (£m current prices).

The change in private sector output is accounted for by changes in consumption induced by the initial expenditure increase and investment and stockbuilding changes produced by changes in output. The increase in imports, already alluded to, naturally dampens growth in output but exports also increase as the nominal exchange rate falls, so the net trade offset to the increase in output is fairly small. The nominal exchange rate falls, initially because of the effect of worsening trade on the current balance. Thereafter, the adverse movement in domestic, relative to foreign, prices further compounds the depreciation (nominal interest differentials are unchanged in this simulation). One consequence of this is that competitiveness, the ratio of United Kingdom exporters' prices to competitors' export prices, improves by 1 per cent through the period. The other consequence is that the rate of domestic inflation rises by ½ per cent over the period as a whole and the price *level* is 2½ per cent higher by the end of five years. Wage inflation also increases and by the end of the period is ½ per cent faster than it was in the base run. Two effects are compounded here: firstly, the effect of increased price inflation on wage inflation, although there are lags in this adjustment and, secondly, the effect of a lower level of unemployment. (Changes in unemployment in the model are 90 per cent of the employment change.) The level of real wages increases throughout the simulation however, so that they end at a value almost 2 per cent higher than in the base run.

The effect of the policy change on the level of output is virtually flat over the last two years of the simulation. The main explanation for this is the fading of the accelerator effects on stockbuilding and investment. An additional factor arises from the influence of increasing price inflation on consumption, operating through the inflation-loss term in the consumption function in the model.

(ii) *An income tax cut equivalent to £2 billion (1981 prices); Table 10.2*
This simulation shows the effects of another fiscal change maintained throughout the five year period. It is an income tax cut equivalent to an additional tax yield of £2 billion in 1981 prices. The effects of this stimulus for output and prices are, as expected, smaller than in the previous case, since the first period effects of the present simulation are produced by changes in personal sector spending as real disposable incomes rise. The output, employment, wage and price effects are about one half those in the previous simulation, although, apart from the first period, the effects are produced by the same mechanisms as were described above.

Table 10.2   Reduction in personal taxation worth £2 billion (1981 prices)

Per cen

Quarter	Y	C	I	ΔS	X	M	P	W	ER	CB	PSBR	EM
1	0.2	0.5	0.0	1	0.0	0.3	0.2	0.0	−0.2	−44	262	0.0
2	0.4	0.9	0.0	4	0.0	0.5	−0.2	0.3	−0.5	−95	257	0.1
3	0.4	0.9	0.1	23	0.1	0.7	−0.2	0.2	−0.8	−121	260	0.2
4	0.5	0.9	0.3	24	0.2	0.8	−0.2	0.2	−1.0	−133	258	0.2
6	0.5	0.9	0.4	10	0.3	0.8	0.4	0.6	−1.2	−121	265	0.3
8	0.6	1.1	0.5	16	0.4	0.9	0.3	1.1	−1.7	−153	271	0.3
12	0.6	1.1	0.2	9	0.5	0.8	0.6	1.5	−2.3	−172	341	0.4
16	0.6	1.2	0.1	−4	0.5	0.8	1.4	2.1	−2.3	−65	397	0.5
20	0.7	1.3	0.2	2	0.5	0.8	1.6	2.4	−3.3	−161	566	0.6

One point worth emphasising here concerns the possibility of direct effects of income tax changes on wage bargains. Chapter 5 above discusses our assessment of the evidence for the inclusion of such an effect in wage equations. In spite of strong *a priori* grounds for including such a variable, the poor empirical results for this variable in a wage equation lead us to omit it from the wage equation. Others include such an effect. The income tax simulation reported by the Treasury (HM Treasury *op. cit*), for example, include this direct tax effect. If we made a special adjustment for this factor to our simulation it would imply lower earnings movements, *ceteris paribus,* in the early part of the simulation.

(iii) *A reduction in VAT worth £2 billion (1981 prices); Table 10.3*
To produce this simulation, the existing parameters for indirect taxes in the price equation of the model have been overwritten. That equation suggests a relatively slow effect of taxes on prices whilst experience suggests that tax changes announced as policy measures are normally passed on into prices almost at once. The assumption used for this simulation is that 90 per cent of the tax effect is shifted onto prices in the first quarter. The initial effect of the change in tax is to decrease prices by 1.2 per cent, thus producing an immediate stimulus to expenditures by increasing disposable incomes. Furthermore, because of the dependence of wage settlements on lagged prices, the fall in prices produces a downward wage–price movement. The effect on wages is partly offset by increases in employment, although the scale of these changes in the labour market is not very substantial, particularly in the early years of the simulation.

Table 10.3   *Reduction in VAT worth £2 billion (1981 prices)*

Per cent[a]

Quarter	Y	C	I	ΔS	X	M	P	W	ER	CB	PSBR	EMP
1	0.2	0.5	0.0	1	0.0	0.3	−1.2	0.0	−0.2	−57	273	0.1
2	0.2	0.4	0.1	4	0.1	0.3	−1.2	−0.4	−0.5	−77	290	0.1
3	0.2	0.4	0.1	22	0.2	0.4	−1.3	−0.8	−0.5	−82	289	0.1
4	0.3	0.5	0.3	6	0.3	0.5	−1.4	−1.0	−0.4	−78	283	0.1
6	0.4	0.6	0.4	10	0.4	0.6	−1.7	−1.2	−0.3	−82	258	0.2
8	0.5	0.7	0.6	10	0.5	0.7	−1.9	−1.4	−0.1	−97	260	0.3
12	0.5	0.8	0.6	7	0.4	0.8	−2.1	−1.5	0.3	−106	262	0.4
16	0.6	1.0	0.6	3	0.4	1.0	−2.3	−1.5	0.7	−129	316	0.4
20	0.5	1.0	0.6	0	0.3	0.9	−2.3	−1.5	0.8	−161	392	0.5

For the first two years the exchange rate is lowered by the tax change; thereafter it is raised. The first of the mechanisms at work here is a relative price change (the ratio of domestic to foreign prices falls). The long-run effect of this is to move the exchange rate up (because of the long-run property built into the exchange rate equation that purchasing power parity is maintained despite changes in domestic prices). There is, however, downward pressure from the worsening current balance, which at first moves the exchange rate in the opposite direction. In the trade accounts, although exports are aided marginally by the initial fall in the exchange rate, the net effect on the trade balance is adverse as increased expenditures draw in imports. Finally, the exchange rate rises because of the longer-run effect of relative prices and the increase in domestic *real* interest rates assuming no change in *nominal* interest rates (see Chapter 6 for an account of the exchange rate equation).

(iv) *A cut in the National Insurance surcharge (NIS) worth £2 billion (at 1981 prices); Table 10.4*

Changes in the NIS, or indeed, changes in any direct element of labour cost, will have two distinct effects on the economy. The first is a change in the demand for labour. The second is the effect of reduced labour cost on prices and thence on the level of real disposable incomes. Chapter 5 above describes the possibility that labour costs influence employment at any given level of output. That discussion concluded that the evidence is not persuasive and in the equation used in the model employment depends on lagged output alone. Thus the effect of a change in the NIS in our model works principally through the effect on prices. As in the VAT simulation, the effect of the policy change increases real disposable income, which in turn produces direct and indirect increases in expenditure. The effects on output are slower and weaker than in the previous simulation because the tax change is not passed on so quickly. For this reason the rise in the PSBR is larger than in any of the earlier simulations, since the decreased receipts from the policy change are not offset to the same extent by increases in receipts as activity rises.

Downward pressure on wages evolves initially through a lower rate of inflation but is also sustained as long as real earnings are higher than they otherwise would be. Again, the increase in activity is muted, so there is

Table 10.4   Reduction in national insurance surcharge worth £2 billion (1981 prices)

Per cent[a]

Quarter	Y	C	I	ΔS	X	M	P	W	ER	CB	PSBR	EMP
1	0.1	0.3	0.0	1	0.0	0.1	−0.6	0.0	−0.1	−29	295	0.0
2	0.1	0.3	0.0	2	0.1	0.2	−0.7	−0.2	−0.2	−40	310	0.0
3	0.1	0.3	0.1	11	0.1	0.3	−0.9	−0.5	0.0	−36	315	0.1
4	0.2	0.4	0.1	4	0.1	0.3	−1.1	−0.5	0.2	−38	323	0.1
6	0.3	0.5	0.2	7	0.2	0.4	−1.4	−1.0	0.4	−46	322	0.1
8	0.3	0.6	0.4	5	0.2	0.5	−1.6	−1.3	0.8	−53	327	0.2
12	0.3	0.7	0.3	4	0.1	0.6	−2.0	−1.6	1.3	−59	367	0.2
16	0.4	0.9	0.3	3	0.1	0.7	−2.3	−1.7	1.8	−114	436	0.3
20	0.4	1.0	0.3	0	0.0	0.7	−2.6	−1.9	2.2	−132	520	0.4

not much influence from changes in unemployment on wage inflation. The exchange rate appreciates because of the relative price effect discussed in the previous section.

(v) *A devaluation of 10 per cent; Table 10.5*

In this simulation we assume that the exchange rate is 10 per cent below the base run figure throughout the simulation period. This should not be understood as a policy change (produced, for example, by a change in domestic interest rate) but rather as the result of a change in confidence. The first effect is that sterling import prices rise and export prices in foreign currency fall. Output increases slowly, because the improvement in competitiveness helps exports and reduces imports. Because the price elasticity is low and lagged, the increase in exports builds up slowly. Moreover, imports fall initially but then the increase in activity swamps the price effect and they grow over the first two years, to fall again as the change to output tapers off. The increase in output is 1 per cent after two years; thereafter it remains virtually constant.

Table 10.5   10 per cent step devaluation in the exchange rate

Per cent[a]

Quarter	Y	C	I	ΔS	X	M	P	W	ER	CB	EMP
1	0.4	−0.2	−0.0	2	0.8	−0.9	0.6	0.0	−	−666	0.1
2	0.3	−0.2	−0.1	6	1.5	0.0	1.0	0.8	−	−629	0.1
3	0.2	−0.3	−0.2	4	1.9	0.6	1.7	0.8	−	−504	0.1
4	0.4	−0.3	−0.4	18	2.4	0.6	2.1	1.5	−	−358	0.2
6	0.9	−0.1	−0.5	30	3.2	0.2	3.1	3.3	−	−114	0.4
8	1.0	0.0	−0.5	35	3.3	0.3	3.6	4.4	−	−53	0.5
12	1.2	0.2	−0.1	11	2.5	−0.6	4.3	5.9	−	−35	0.8
16	1.0	0.2	−0.1	−9	2.2	−0.7	5.5	6.7	−	232	0.9
20	0.9	0.3	−0.3	1	1.9	−0.4	5.7	6.9	−	149	0.9

The price and wage effects show a familiar pattern. Prices rise initially because of the effect of the devaluation on sterling import costs. Wages rise, after a lag, because of the increase in prices and the increase in the level of employment. Real wages fall because nominal wages respond to price changes with a lag. By the middle of the second year, however, the real wage decline ends and from that point onwards real wages grow, reflecting the effects of declining unemployment. Export competitiveness in manufacturing initially improves by 8 per cent: exporters increase their sterling prices by only 2 per cent following the 10 per cent change in the sterling equivalent of competitors' prices. However, this gain in competitiveness is steadily eroded as United Kingdom costs increase because of the higher level of import prices and the higher level of wages. By the end of five years only about 2 per cent of the original 8 per cent remains.

(vi) *A reduction in United Kingdom short-term interest rates of 2 per cent; Table 10.6*

This simulation illustrates the properties of the model, but it is not clear whether it represents a realistic policy option. The interest rate differential between domestic and foreign rates is changed throughout the simulation period. Since the change in the exchange rate according to the model depends, *inter alia,* on the *level* of this differential, the lower levels of the domestic interest rate produce a falling exchange rate throughout. This may not be plausible for a long period since either capital flows or else a reaction by the domestic monetary authorities (directed at stabilising the exchange rate) would sooner or later tend to equalise the differential. The longer-term results of this simulation may not, therefore, be considered reliable or relevant. Only the first two years are shown in table 10.6.

Table 10.6   2 per cent fall in UK short-term interest rates

Per c

Quarter	Y	C	I	ΔS	X	M	P	W	ER	CB	£M3	MI
1	−0.0	−0.1	0.1	−0	0.1	−0.1	0.2	−0.0	−0.9	−44	0.2	1.6
2	0.1	0.0	0.3	1	0.2	−0.1	−0.0	0.1	−2.0	−128	0.6	1.0
3	0.2	−0.0	0.4	−1	0.4	−0.0	0.0	0.2	−3.3	−181	1.2	2.5
4	0.3	0.0	0.4	9	0.7	0.2	0.2	0.2	−4.5	−239	1.4	3.5
6	0.8	0.1	0.4	92	1.5	0.5	1.4	1.1	−8.0	−434	3.4	5.9
8	1.1	0.3	0.5	96	2.6	0.9	2.3	2.4	−11.9	−611	6.5	7.9

Consumer spending is raised by a combination of interest rate and real balance effects. Monetary effects on investment are confined to the housing component, which is stimulated both by the lower cost of mortgage finance and its easier availability in the interim before building society borrowing rates adjust to other short-term rates. There is also a substantial interest rate effect on stockbuilding.

The direct effects on domestic expenditure are reinforced by the effects of the exchange rate depreciation on net trade. After two years output is higher by a little over 1 per cent. Consumer prices are higher by about 2½ per cent.

(vii) *A 2 per cent reduction in both United Kingdom and United States short-term interest rates: Table 10.7*

As this simulation maintains the historical interest rate differential unchanged, there is no direct effect on the exchange rate. In this simulation, therefore, attention centres on the domestic consequences of the change in domestic interest rates. These affect durable consumption, housing investment and stockbuilding. After two years output has increased by ½ per cent because of the decrease in real interest rates and the further multiplier and accelerator effects on consumption, stockbuilding and investment. The increases in activity worsen the trade balance and the exchange rate falls in response, noticeably by the end of the period. The increase in prices is quite small, although the inflationary impact of this simulation is evidently building up towards the end of the period with the changes in the exchange rate just noted.

Table 10.7   *2 per cent fall in UK and US short-term interest rates*   *Per cent[a]*

Quarter	Y	C	I	ΔS	X	M	P	W	ER	CB	£M3	MI	EMP
1	−0.0	−0.1	0.1	−0	−0.0	−0.1	0.2	−0.0	0.1	13	0.1	1.8	−0.0
2	0.1	0.0	0.3	0	−0.0	0.0	−0.2	0.1	0.1	1	0.2	1.3	0.0
3	0.1	0.0	0.4	−2	−0.0	0.0	−0.3	0.0	0.1	−4	0.2	2.8	0.0
4	0.2	0.2	0.5	6	0.0	0.1	−0.4	−0.1	−0.0	−24	−0.2	3.6	0.1
6	0.4	0.2	0.6	84	0.0	0.5	0.0	0.2	−0.2	−72	0.2	5.7	0.2
8	0.5	0.5	0.8	78	0.1	0.7	−0.2	0.4	−0.7	−126	1.3	6.9	0.3
12	0.6	0.5	0.8	60	0.3	0.6	−0.1	0.6	−1.1	−135	3.3	9.9	0.4
16	0.5	0.4	0.7	32	0.3	0.5	0.6	1.1	−0.9	−36	4.2	12.6	0.4
20	0.4	0.3	0.5	23	0.2	0.3	0.6	1.1	−1.4	−53	5.9	13.7	0.4

(viii) *An increase in world trade of 1 per cent per annum; Table 10.8*

This simulation illustrates the effects of a change in the external environment, rather than in policy. (No changes are made to world *prices*.) The increase in activity is initiated through the trade balance. With the improvement in the net trade balance, sterling appreciates. Although employment rises, this is not sufficient to overcome the effects of the higher exchange rate, so that by the end of the simulation period, inflation is virtually unchanged from base. The effect on output, however, is small because of the high import propensity associated with export demand (see Chapter 6) we have already described. By the end of the period output has increased, but by only 0.1 per cent.

Table 10.8 · 1 per cent increase in world trade · *Per cent*[a]

Quarter	Y	C	I	ΔS	X	M	P	W	ER	CB	£M3	M1	PSBR	EMP
1	0.0	−0.1	0.0	1	0.5	0.2	0.2	−0.0	0.2	44	−0.1	0.2	−21	0.0
2	0.1	0.1	0.0	4	0.6	0.4	−0.2	0.1	0.3	40	−0.1	−0.0	−14	0.0
3	0.2	0.2	0.0	2	0.5	0.4	−0.3	−0.0	0.3	31	−0.1	−0.1	−5	0.0
4	0.2	0.2	0.0	12	0.6	0.5	−0.4	−0.1	0.2	19	−0.1	−0.2	−1	0.1
6	0.1	0.0	0.1	2	0.5	0.4	0.1	−0.1	0.4	53	−0.3	0.1	−36	0.1
8	0.2	0.2	0.1	4	0.5	0.4	−0.3	0.1	0.3	23	−0.5	−0.1	−23	0.1
12	0.2	0.2	0.0	−5	0.5	0.4	−0.5	−0.2	0.1	9	−0.5	−0.2	−7	0.1
16	0.1	0.2	−0.0	−8	0.6	0.4	−0.1	−0.0	0.3	48	−0.8	−0.0	−69	0.1
20	0.1	0.2	−0.0	−1	0.6	0.4	−0.3	−0.2	0.2	32	−0.8	−0.1	−27	0.1

Some comparisons

Strictly, comparisons between simulations on different models present many problems of interpretation, in particular they should use the same policy assumptions (for example, for the determinants of interest rates) and be carried out over the same time period. With these qualifications in mind, it is still of interest to observe the main features which emerge from different models conducting similar simulation experiments. This is the spirit in which the following comparisons between two simulations of the National Institute and the Treasury model are made. These are simulations of a change in central government spending on goods and services and of a change in direct taxation. The simulation of a change in central government spending reported by the Treasury is on the basis of unchanged nominal interest rates (see HM Treasury [3], p. 145 and associated table), as is the one reported by the National Institute (table 10.1 above). The Treasury simulation of a change in direct taxation does not assume fixed nominal interest rates however.

(a) *An increase in government spending; Table 10.9*

The simulations reported by HM Treasury [3] and earlier in this chapter differ in certain respects. These are, firstly, that the simulation of the National Institute model assumes an annual increase of £2 billion in 1981 prices. This is equivalent to an injection of 0.96 per cent of GDP in 1977 and of 0.89 per cent of GDP by 1981. The Treasury assumes a constant stimulus of 0.5 per cent of GDP. Secondly, the initial expenditure increase is allocated equally between procurement and employment in the Treasury simulation. The National Institute simulation assumes the expenditure is all directed at increasing employment.

In spite of these differences, the comparison of the effects produced in the models is interesting. The obvious feature is the similarity of the results. For an injection almost twice as large, the output effects in the

Table 10.9   Increase in central government expenditure on goods and services of 0.5 per cent of GDP for HM Treasury, for National Institute see text

Change from base	Real GDP % HMT	Real GDP % NI	Inflation % HMT	Inflation % NI	Unemploy- ment '000s HMT	Unemploy- ment '000s NI	Exchange rate % HMT	Exchange rate % NI	PSBR £m HMT	PSBR £m NI
Year 1	0.7	1.3	0.2		−80	−157	−1.5	−1.0	850	642
Year 2	0.8	1.4	0.5	0.8	−110	−211	−1.7	−1.9	800	676
Year 3	0.8	1.5	0.7	0.5	−120	−251	−2.7	−2.9	600	1064
Year 4	0.5	1.4	1.1	1.1	−95	−270	−2.8	−3.2	500	1384

National Institute simulation are approximately twice as large also, except for the last year when the output effects in the Treasury simulation slacken markedly (see table 10.9 above). This crowding out is partly produced by the effect of higher inflation on the company sector, producing falls in disposable income of that sector and leading to cuts in company spending on stocks, employment and dividends ([3], p. 137). Otherwise the rough translation of the size of changes on the real side appears to hold. There is a reduction in unemployment after three years of 120,000 and 251,000 for the Treasury and the National Institute respectively.

The nominal side presents a slightly more complex comparison. In the simulations the exchange rate depreciates by roughly equal amounts, in spite of the differences in the size of the assumed stimuli to aggregate spending and the Treasury exchange rate equation is evidently the more responsive. At the end of four years the Treasury calculates that the exchange rate depreciates by 2.8 per cent, whereas the National Institute gives 3.2 per cent depreciation. In spite of this, the inflation effects are comparable between the two simulations, with the National Institute being 1.1 per cent in year 4, just equal to the Treasury figure. This difference illustrates the more powerful effect for unemployment in the Treasury wage model than that estimated by the National Institute.

(b) *An income tax simulation; Table 10.10*

A similar comparison may be made between the two income tax simulations. Figures produced by the Treasury are for an income tax increase and, assuming linearity of the model with respect to the policy change, we may reverse the sign for comparison. The size of the implied stimulus is 0.5 per cent of GDP for the Treasury and, for the National Institute simulation, an income tax change giving a yield of approximately

Table 10.10   Increase in income tax of 0.5 per cent of GDP for HM Treasury, for National Institute an income tax decrease, see text for details

Change from base	Real GDP %		Inflation %		Unemploy- ment '000s		Exchange rate %		PSBR £m	
	HMT	NI	HMT	NI	HMT	NI	HMT	NI	HMT	NI
Year 1	−0.2	0.5	0.0	−	10	−42	−0.4	−1.0	−1050	1037
Year 2	−0.3	0.6	0.2	0.5	30	−74	−0.5	−1.7	−1200	1072
Year 3	−0.3	0.6	0.0	0.3	35	−98	−0.8	−2.3	−1200	1364
Year 4	−0.2	0.6	−0.4	0.8	30	−113	−1.3	−2.3	−1200	1588

(−) 0.9 per cent of GDP in 1977. One important difference between these simulations is that the Treasury assumes a constant money supply and the level of nominal interest rates increases by 1.1 per cent over the period in their simulation. In the National Institute simulation nominal interests rates are held constant.

There are some close similarities between the simulations. Output increases by roughly equivalent amounts, although the increases slacken by the fourth year in the Treasury simulation.

Inflation effects differ between the two models, however. There are two major reasons for this difference. First, the assumption about interest rates: the Treasury assumption of higher interest rates tends to increase the exchange rate, which in turn holds down prices. Second, the Treasury wage model includes an effect of changes in the average level of direct taxes (the retention ratio). Decreases in average direct taxes increase the retention ratio and tend, *ceteris paribus*, to produce lower nominal wage claims. The National Institute model does not have this effect. Inflation, therefore, is much slower to build up in the Treasury simulation, although the effects on the two models after four years are quite similar.

References

[1] Lucas, R., 'Econometric policy evaluation: a critique', in Brunner, K. and Meltzer, A. (eds), *The Phillips Curve and Labour Markets, Supplement to the Journal of Monetary Economics*, 1976.

[2] Minford, P., 'The nature and purpose of UK macroeconomic models', *The Three Banks Review*, no. 125, March, 1980.

[3] HM Treasury, Macroeconomic Model Technical Manual, 1982.

11 A Tracking Exercise
S. Brooks and S.G.B. Henry

There are a variety of exercises which can be conducted to show the properties of a complete large-scale econometric model. Knowledge of complete model properties may be seen either as an aid to model selection given *a priori* views about the behaviour of economic systems, or conversely as an aid to understanding the economy, given a valid model. In the previous chapter we described some simulation exercises using the whole model. In this chapter we describe a different kind of exercise, that of using the model to track historical data for a recent period.

In any tracking exercise model predictions are compared with actual outturns. Actual data is used for all the exogenous variables. The model could be solved equation by equation using actual data for all independent variables in every equation even when they are endogenous to the model as a whole. The discrepancies shown by that kind of exercise are called single equation residuals (SERs). In a full model tracking exercise of the kind reported here, the predictions from the model are used to calculate the values of all endogenous variables and the model is solved simultaneously. The resulting tracking errors then reflect the properties and the goodness of fit of the whole model. A *static* exercise of this kind uses actual data for lagged values of endogenous variables; a *dynamic* exercise of the kind reported here uses model predictions for lagged values and solves the model over successive time periods (starting from given initial conditions).

Within-sample tracking exercises should be distinguished from similar exercises conducted on data outside the period of estimation. If the fit outside the estimation period were markedly worse than the fit inside it, that could be, for a complete model as for a single equation, a symptom of mis-specification. But tracking within the estimation period can also be informative, especially tracking at the end of the estimation period, immediately prior to that which the model will be used to forecast.

A general methodological question arises about the role of dynamic tracking exercises in model selection. It has been argued that the preferred form of individual equations should be arrived at by sequential testing from a general dynamic specification of the equation, simplified by means of data-based restrictions of the general equation. Extensions of this methodology to simultaneous systems can be made in principle, where potential biases in parameter estimates are avoided by the use of appropriate simultaneous estimators. According to this line of argument, within-sample dynamic tracking runs reveal the properties of the selected model (equation or set of equations) and should *not* serve to guide the modeller in respecifications in the light of these dynamic properties. This is perhaps too purist a line for practical application. Many applied economists might feel justified in revising their model structure in the light of information on its dynamic tracking performance, which might alert them to possible dynamic instability undetected at the single equation stage.

The larger the set of exogenous variables in models of comparable size, the more likely it is that the model will track well in an *ex post* mode. This remark assumes that models are otherwise broadly similar and emphasises the fact that in *ex post* situations exogenous variables are usually replaced by their actual values. Similarly, a model which specifies lags by means of a long series of lagged independent variables might fit better in the early stages of a tracking run than one which used a single lagged dependent variable. This illustrates the general difficulty of using goodness of fit in tracking as a criterion for model selection.

In the next section, a tracking run for the period 1977(I) to 1981(IV) is reported. This length of period was chosen because five years was considered to be sufficient to reveal the inherent dynamics of the model as applicable to most of its uses. Also, this particular time period was used since the sharp fall in output experienced in 1980 was thought to provide a stringent test of the tracking performance of the model. It is well known that certain years are particularly difficult to track using an econometric model. The consequences for prices of the appreciation of sterling in 1979, or the substantial fall in employment in 1980–1, could well provide an example. Even a model which provided a fairly good fit over the whole data period may not fit well in untypical sub-periods. Its predictions might well substantially differ from actuals when initialised in 1980, for example, if the average lags built into the model did not imply such rapid adjustment of prices or volumes as occurred in that period.

A general point might be made about the base-dependency of dynamic exercises. The solution of any set of difference equations may be written $Y_t = Y^* + k_0 \lambda^t$ where, provided the roots of the system are less than unity in absolute value $(|\lambda| < 1) Y_t$ will converge to its long-run value Y^* asymptotically. For exercises on a relatively short data set, where the dynamic system is not heavily dampened, the behaviour of Y_t will depend largely on initial conditions, here represented by the set of constants k_0.

Tracking with the National Institute model

The role of adjustments

Most econometric models are subjected to residual adjustment of various sorts when used for constructing a forecast. Apart from additive residual changes as suggested by the analysis of individual equations' recent errors (SERs), other qualitative information and judgement may be used as extraneous input into the forecasting process. In tracking, ideally the model would not be subjected to judgemental interventions of this sort. However, for many models tracking exercises can be conducted only by intervening to some degree in the mechanical solution. The study by Britton and Whittaker [1], for example, reporting the tracking performance of the Treasury model, uses solutions which incorporate a large number of residual adjustments and uses actual rather than predicted values for some endogenous variables (see Britton and Whittaker [1], p. 2). Minford [4], in an apparent application of the rational expectations hypothesis to a small macroeconomic model of the United Kingdom, constrains the movement of certain endogenous variables in using the model in dynamic mode. These boundary conditions are imposed to ensure that what the author describes as the 'absurd' solution values delivered by the model otherwise do not occur (see Minford [4], p. 38).

Even when intervention is unavoidable it is important in tracking runs that the model is used in as neutral a fashion as possible, since the convolution of residual changes and other interventions in the solution mean that the model properties as such, the identification of which is the purpose of the exercise, are obscured. However, it must also be recognised that there may be a need to make mechanical adjustments to the model, since a particular equation may have been estimated on a now distant sample, there may be an estimated error model as part of the behavioural equation (errors in measurement could induce MA error for example), or a common factor restriction could be upheld as a data-preferred simplification, as in Hendry and Mizon [3], or the tracking run may be initialised at a period when there are substantial residuals in certain equations which nonetheless fit quite well over the whole sample period.

In the tracking run reported below we have made a mechanical adjustment to some equations in the light of the errors produced by the equations. The model solution package used at the National Institute has the facility for computing a number of alternate models for the residuals. These are (1) no adjustment, (2) a constant average adjustment, (3) an autoregressive adjustment of order 1, that is, $U_t = c_0 + c_1 U_{t-1}$ and (4) a second order autoregressive adjustment, $U_t = c_0 + c_1 U_{t-1} + c_2 U_{t-2}$ (see Osborn and Teal [5] for a discussion of some versions of these). However, in this exercise, we have restricted the possible choices to options (1) and (2), that is, either no residual is imposed or a residual equal to the average single equation error over the period is used.

Each of these rules may be estimated for the period over which the tracking exercise is to be run. The best rule can then be selected by comparing the goodness of fit of each of the error models.

We have selected for residual adjustment only those equations where the average residual differed significantly from zero at the 10 per cent level of significance. The use of this rule generates about twenty candidates for adjustment and these variables are listed at the foot of table 11.1. Many of them are variables which we consider to be predicted by rule rather than by an estimated behavioural equation; the two most important exceptions are *QMMF* (imports of manufactured goods) and *EFFRAT* (the effective exchange rate).

Apart from the use of the residual rule mentioned above, the tracking exercise is intervention free. All endogenous variables are predicted as part of the solution and none set at their actual value. (In this we differ, for example, as explained above, from the study by Britton and Whittaker with the Treasury model.) Table 11.1 records for each of the main variables the actual value, the model's prediction and the percentage prediction error.

Commentary on the results
In commenting on the main features of the tracking exercise, the emphasis is on what new information the exercise reveals, as distinct from information about the properties of the model which is known already from study of SERs. The tracking run reveals the interactions between the main equations of the model over time, which it would be impossible to establish in quantitative terms without solving the whole system. Two themes provide the focus for the rest of our comments; the behaviour of GDP and the interactions between wages, prices and the exchange rate. These two aspects are not independent of each other, of course, since wages and prices affect the level of personal disposable income and since inflation affects the real level of financial assets and hence both consumption and output. Moreover, there are linkages between the exchange rate, the trade balance and the level of output.

The tracking of GDP is moderately good overall. By the end of the five year period, there is an overprediction of 4–5 per cent, which is of a size comparable with that reported in the tracking exercise of the Treasury model (see Britton and Whittaker *op. cit.*). However, the components of aggregate expenditure show offsetting errors in their movements. We can consider the main components in detail. It is widely recognised that the arithmetic cause of the sharp fall in output in 1980 was substantial destocking. Our model of stockbuilding is a distributed lag (that is, a backward looking) model. Like other models based on a distributed lag equation, our stockbuilding equations fail to predict the substantial falls actually recorded in 1980–1, although they do predict the turning point. The failure to capture this very sharp movement actually recorded in stockbuilding is perhaps the inevitable consequence of the specification used. There are other factors in the model as a whole which tend to produce overpredictions in GDP over most of the period. The most obvious example is the effect of the underprediction of the exchange rate on net trade through most of the period. Predicted exports are higher than actual by a relatively constant amount, because of this underprediction of the exchange rate. This contributes to the underprediction of imports too, though this is not the only reason for this discrepancy; the problems of deriving an adequate explanation of the movements in imports over 1979–80 are well documented (see Brooks and Cuthbertson [2]). These errors tend to produce overprediction of output but they are offset by a regular tendency to underpredict consumption (except initially and in the last quarter) and investment (except for the final year). The net result is that GDP tends to be under predicted until 1980 when the overprediction of stockbuilding, in particular, produces a change to overprediction of GDP for the last two years of the exercise.

We have already noted the underprediction of the exchange rate. This is partly due to the overpredictions of prices for most of the period, although this argument is in part circular since there is a feedback from the lower exchange rate to prices. The other major influence on prices is earnings. Earnings tend to be overpredicted for the first half of the tracking run, in spite of predicted employment being lower than actual (and consequently unemployment being overpredicted). What this part of the results does reveal is the strength of the real wage and lagged inflation effects in the wage equation, with only weak effects being exerted by higher levels of unemployment. The conjuncture of these factors, that is the tendency to overpredict earnings and prices plus the underprediction of employment, implies a relatively correct prediction of average real wage but an underprediction of total employment income. Hence there is an underprediction of aggregate disposable income, which is the proximate cause of the underprediction in consumption.

Table 11.1   Tracking performance of Model 6^a

(i)   *Exports of Goods and Services, £m, 1975 prices*

		predicted	actual	percentage residual			predicted	actual	percentage residual
1977	I	7732.1	7722.0	−0.1	1979	III	8542.7	8373.0	−2.0
	II	7323.9	7885.0	0.8		IV	8598.4	8421.0	−2.1
	III	7926.1	8161.0	2.9	1980	I	8644.9	8509.0	−1.6
	IV	8017.5	7826.0	−2.4		II	8461.4	8316.0	−1.7
1978	I	8042.7	7912.0	−1.7		III	8298.5	8116.0	−2.2
	II	8239.0	7987.0	−3.2		IV	8327.4	8116.0	−2.6
	III	8241.8	8067.0	−2.2	1981	I	8368.4	7856.0	−6.5
	IV	8394.7	8126.0	−3.3		II	8312.1	8017.0	−3.7
1979	I	8393.2	7380.0	−13.7		III	8347.2	8211.0	−1.7
	III	8495.1	8740.0	2.8		IV	8271.8	8337.0	0.8

(ii)   *Fixed Investment, £m, 1975 prices*

		predicted	actual	percentage residual			predicted	actual	percentage residual
1977	I	4954.8	4882.0	−1.5	1979	III	5117.8	5323.0	3.9
	II	5113.4	5112.0	−0.0		IV	5078.9	5395.0	5.9
	III	5009.6	5035.0	0.5	1980	I	5123.7	5292.0	3.2
	IV	5099.2	5132.0	0.6		II	5019.7	5163.0	2.8
1978	I	5077.6	5268.0	3.6		III	4874.8	5036.0	3.2
	II	5189.2	5343.0	2.9		IV	4887.3	4952.0	1.3
	III	5062.8	5178.0	2.2	1981	I	4758.9	4690.0	−1.5
	IV	4961.5	5056.0	1.9		II	4792.3	4667.0	−2.7
1979	I	4980.7	5091.0	2.2		III	4753.9	4663.0	−2.0
	II	4967.7	5230.0	5.0		IV	4892.6	4754.0	−2.9

(iii)   *Stockbuilding, £m, 1975 prices*

		predicted	actual	residual			predicted	actual	residual
1977	I	513.9	537.0	23.1	1979	III	78.9	542.0	463.1
	II	245.2	457.0	211.8		IV	153.1	284.0	130.9
	III	26.2	10.0	−16.2	1980	I	−70.4	−273.0	−202.6
	IV	−120.2	383.0	503.2		II	−7.8	−22.0	−14.2
1978	I	−3.4	304.0	307.4		III	−49.6	−427.0	−377.4
	II	89.6	276.0	186.4		IV	−50.1	−833.0	−782.9
	III	199.4	253.0	53.6	1981	I	−167.9	−642.0	−474.1
	IV	294.0	313.0	19.0		II	−115.6	−694.0	−578.4
1979	I	283.8	781.0	497.2		III	−76.2	−226.0	−149.8
	II	89.0	175.0	86.0		IV	38.2	−309.0	−347.2

Table 11.1 continued

(iv) Consumers' Expenditure, £m, 1975 prices

		predicted	actual	percentage residual			predicted	actual	percentage residual
1977	I	16025	16001	−0.1	1979	III	16907	17816	5.1
	II	16124	16034	−0.6		IV	16950	18072	6.2
	III	16264	16154	−0.7	1980	I	16980	18120	6.3
	IV	16123	16394	1.7		II	17276	17729	2.6
1978	I	16206	16840	3.8		III	17316	17831	2.9
	II	16560	16884	1.9		IV	17477	17870	2.2
	III	16872	17249	2.2	1981	I	17420	18032	3.4
	IV	16714	17254	3.1		II	17646	17860	1.2
1979	I	16700	17396	4.0		III	17971	17915	−0.3
	II	17291	18315	5.6		IV	18065	17955	−0.6

(v) Consumer Price Index, 1975 = 100

		predicted	actual	percentage residual			predicted	actual	percentage residual
1977	I	127.6	127.6	0.0	1979	III	173.6	168.1	−3.3
	II	133.8	132.1	−1.3		IV	179.2	174.2	−2.9
	III	137.9	135.2	−2.0	1980	I	183.6	181.1	−1.4
	IV	143.8	137.5	−4.5		II	188.0	188.2	0.1
1978	I	146.8	140.6	−4.4		III	191.4	192.5	0.6
	II	151.9	143.6	−5.7		IV	195.2	197.2	1.0
	III	153.6	146.2	−5.1	1981	I	200.8	201.5	0.4
	IV	158.9	149.1	−6.6		II	206.0	208.7	1.3
1979	I	162.0	153.6	−5.5		III	209.1	213.5	2.1
	II	168.1	158.0	−6.4		IV	211.7	218.3	3.0

(vi) Real Personal Disposable Income, £m, 1975 prices

		predicted	actual	percentage residual			predicted	actual	percentage residual
1977	I	18175	17989	−1.0	1979	III	19659	20695	5.0
	II	17886	17548	−1.9		IV	19560	21628	9.6
	III	18491	18059	−2.4	1980	I	19835	21085	5.9
	IV	17836	18753	4.9		II	20175	20865	3.3
1978	I	18278	18730	2.4		III	20396	21402	4.7
	II	18663	19264	3.1		IV	20878	21388	2.4
	III	19575	19955	1.9	1981	I	20769	21204	2.1
	IV	18998	20276	6.3		II	20626	20611	−0.1
1979	I	19310	20593	6.2		III	21369	20660	−3.4
	II	19704	20712	4.9		IV	21448	20455	−4.9

Table 11.1 continued

(vii)   *Employment in UK, thousands*

		predicted	actual	percentage residual			predicted	actual	percentage residual
1977	I	22342	22597	1.1	1979	III	21776	22879	4.8
	II	22276	22606	1.5		IV	21708	22822	4.9
	III	22144	22629	2.1	1980	I	21705	22680	4.3
	IV	22059	22638	2.6		II	21630	22489	3.8
1978	I	21995	22715	3.2		III	21579	22145	2.6
	II	22067	22742	3.0		IV	21539	21767	1.0
	III	21987	22779	3.5	1978	I	21392	21465	0.3
	IV	21946	22886	4.1		II	21324	21171	−0.7
1979	I	21879	22873	4.3		III	21328	20981	−1.7
	II	21878	22900	4.5		IV	21285	20782	−2.4

(viii)   *Sterling Effective Exchange Rate, 1975 = 100*

		predicted	actual	percentage residual			predicted	actual	percentage residual
1977	I	77.5	80.8	4.1	1979	III	78.7	91.3	13.8
	II	74.4	80.6	7.7		IV	80.3	88.5	9.3
	III	73.0	80.8	9.7	1980	I	83.7	93.0	10.0
	IV	72.0	82.6	12.5		II	87.8	94.5	7.1
1978	I	69.0	84.8	18.7		II	90.2	96.7	6.7
	II	70.2	79.9	12.2		IV	90.8	100.2	9.4
	III	72.8	80.6	9.7	1981	I	92.9	101.8	8.7
	IV	71.2	80.6	11.7		II	94.1	97.8	3.8
1979	I	73.4	82.4	10.9		III	93.1	90.6	−2.8
	II	76.1	87.0	12.5		IV	95.8	89.7	−6.8

(ix)   *Current Balance, £m, current prices*

		predicted	actual	residual			predicted	actual	residual
1977	I	−790.7	−326.0	464.7	1979	III	470.8	34.0	−436.8
	II	−1008.9	−396.0	612.9		IV	363.7	−310.0	−673.7
	III	−733.6	333.0	1066.6	1980	I	203.8	68.0	−135.8
	IV	−298.5	348.0	646.5		II	686.7	−39.0	−725.7
1978	I	−1014.6	−143.0	871.6		III	1262.5	943.0	−319.5
	II	649.3	485.0	−164.3		IV	1235.0	1893.0	658.0
	III	101.5	160.0	58.5	1981	I	1969.6	2391.0	421.4
	IV	249.0	516.0	267.0		II	2279.9	1946.0	−333.9
1979	I	703.8	−571.0	−1274.8		III	2208.9	216.0	−1992.9
	II	266.4	−6.0	−272.4		IV	2589.4	1483.0	−1106.4

Table 11.1 continued

(x)   *Gross Domestic Product at Factor Cost, Expenditure Estimates, £m, 1975 prices*

		predicted	actual	percentage residual			predicted	actual	percentage residual
1977	I	24418	24580	0.7	1979	III	25374	26072	2.7
	II	24503	24762	1.0		IV	25411	25991	2.2
	III	24354	24673	1.3	1980	I	25638	25717	0.3
	IV	24458	25225	3.0		II	25535	25443	−0.4
1978	I	24596	25401	3.2		III	25490	25243	−1.0
	II	25407	25636	0.9		IV	25612	25085	−2.1
	III	25166	25518	1.4	1981	I	25346	25143	−0.8
	IV	25250	25729	1.9		II	25455	24722	−3.0
1979	I	25302	25449	0.6		III	25769	24533	−5.0
	II	25628	26199	2.2		IV	25862	24893	−3.9

(xi)   *Average Earnings, pounds per week, current prices*

		predicted	actual	percentage residual			predicted	actual	percentage residual
1977	I	61.12	60.51	−1.0	1979	III	85.92	84.29	−1.9
	II	60.42	61.49	1.7		IV	87.37	88.62	1.4
	III	66.17	62.72	−5.5	1980	I	91.82	92.98	1.2
	IV	65.75	64.84	−1.4		II	95.81	98.20	2.4
1978	I	70.48	66.97	−5.2		III	97.63	103.43	5.6
	II	71.53	70.05	−2.1		IV	102.89	106.39	3.3
	III	77.41	71.76	−7.9	1981	I	105.14	108.47	3.1
	IV	76.18	73.73	−3.3		II	106.29	111.35	4.6
1979	I	79.96	77.10	−3.7		III	113.09	114.79	1.5
	II	82.04	80.32	−2.1		IV	114.82	117.70	2.4

(xii)   *Imports of Goods and Services, £m, 1975 prices*

		predicted	actual	percentage residual			predicted	actual	percentage residual
1977	I	7726.5	7600.0	−1.7	1979	III	8347.4	9031.0	7.6
	II	7776.8	7844.0	0.9		IV	8432.8	9089.0	7.2
	III	7810.9	7667.0	−1.9	1980	I	8184.3	8793.0	6.9
	IV	7636.6	7448.0	−2.5		II	8289.8	8914.0	7.0
1978	I	7756.7	7873.0	1.5		III	8091.2	8360.0	3.2
	II	7654.4	7796.0	1.8		IV	8211.4	8076.0	−1.7
	III	8160.4	8079.0	−1.0	1981	I	8145.1	7688.0	−5.9
	IV	8158.7	8006.0	−1.9		II	8274.2	8261.0	−0.2
1979	I	8096.5	8152.0	0.7		III	8363.9	9243.0	9.5
	II	8245.6	9054.0	8.9		IV	8481.0	8895.0	4.7

[a]Variables for which constant residuals have been selected (see text for details):—

QEXFB	Exports of foods and basic materials
QDKPM	Investment in plant and machinery
QMMF	Imports of mainly manufactured goods
TXNO	Non-oil company corporate income taxes
QAFC	Factor cost adjustment
OMF	Output of manufactures
OMP	Output of the mainly public sector
OPAD	Output of public administration and defence
EMPAD	Employment in public administration and defence
UNEMP	UK unemployment
RPER	Rent, personal sector
NPIPER	Net property income, personal sector
PPAC	Deflator, general government current expenditure
GTPNO	Gross trading profits excluding oil and gas
PNH	Price of new houses
NPIPUB	Net property income, public sector
BLOPERS	Bank lending to persons (excluding house purchasing)
GDKPER	Gross investment, in current prices, personal sector
GDKCO	Gross investment, in current prices, company sector
DETINT	Debt interest
EFFRAT	Effective exchange rate
SACO	Stock appreciation, company sector
SAPER	Stock appreciation, personal sector
PXGMA	Deflator, exports of manufactures, excluding erratics
PXGER	Deflator, exports of manufactures, including erratics

References

[1] Britton, A. and Whittaker, R., 'The tracking performance of the Treasury model', Government Economic Service Working Paper no. 58, 1982.

[2] Brooks, S. and Cuthbertson, K., 'Econometric models and econometric forecasts', National Institute of Economic and Social Research Discussion Paper no. 41, February 1981.

[3] Hendry, D. and Mizon, G., 'Serial correlation as a convenient simplification, not a nuisance: a comment on a study of the demand for money by the Bank of England', *Economic Journal*, vol. 88, September 1978.

[4] Minford, A. P. L., 'A rational expectations model of the UK under fixed and floating exchange rates', in Brunner, K., and Meltzer, A., (eds), *On the State of Macroeconomics*, Amsterdam, North Holland, 1980.

[5] Osborn, D. and Teal, F., 'An assessment and comparison of two NIESR econometric model forecasts', *National Institute Economic Review*, no. 88, May, 1979.

Appendix: Full Listing of National Institute Model 6

This listing sets out the equations in the model in fifteen groups, as follows:

I	Consumption	IX	Taxes
II	Investment	X	Prices
III	Stocks	XI	Exchange rates
IV	Exports	XII	GDP identities and current
V	Imports		price variables
VI	Output	XIII	Financial assets
VII	Employment	XIV	Monetary sector
VIII	Incomes	XV	North Sea oil

The variables in the model are then listed in alphabetical order, indicating their definitions, sources, whether they are exogenous or endogenous and, if they are endogenous, the equation in which they are determined.

Conventions followed in the listing of equations

The prefix ln indicates that the variable is expressed as a natural logarithm and the suffix $_{-1}$, $_{-2}$, etc. indicates the lag attached to the variable (measured in quarters). Δ_K refers to a Kth difference (i.e. $X - X_{-K}$).

The error statistics shown for the estimated equations (where applicable) are:—

R^2	Multiple correlation coefficient
$\bar{R}^2$	Multiple correlation coefficient adjusted for degrees of freedom
SEE	Standard error of the equation
DW	Durbin-Watson statistic
h	Durbin's h-statistic
RHOi	i^{th}-order autoregressive parameter
CHI_1 (n)	Box Pierce test with correlogram of length n
LM(n)	Lagrange Multiplier test; n degrees of freedom

t-statistics are shown in parenthesis beneath the estimated coefficients.

Next is the method of estimation:—

OLS   Ordinary least squares
ALS   Autoregressive least squares
IV   Instrumental variables
GIVE Generalised autoregressive instrumental variables.

Finally, the period over which the equation was estimated, stating the year and quarter and the vintage of the data used, is shown.

The model in outline

The National Institute model can be thought of as explaining the components of the standard national income expenditure and output identities in constant and current prices. GDP is built up from the expenditure side of the accounts with all variables expressed in real (i.e. constant price) terms.

Thus expressing GDP at factor cost

$$QGDP = QTFS + QDS - QM - QAFC \tag{1}$$

where

$$QTFS = QCE + QDK + QEX + \overline{QPAC} \tag{2}$$

QTFS is total final sales
QDS is stockbuilding
QM is imports of goods and services
QAFC is adjustment to factor cost
QCE is consumers' expenditure
QDK is gross fixed investment
QEX is exports of goods and services
and *QPAC* is general government expenditure on goods and services.

All variables are measured quarterly at 1975 prices and seasonally adjusted. A superior rule denotes an exogenous variable.

There are therefore five categories of expenditure to be determined endogenously; *QDS*, *QM*, *QCE*, *QDK* and *QEX*. Of these, consumers' expenditure is the largest and is disaggregated into expenditure on durables and on non-durables. The major determinant of *QCE* is real personal disposable income, *QRDY*, but the inflation loss on personal sector liquid assets also enters into the equations.

Gross fixed investment is determined in a much more complex manner with nine individual components, six of which are exogenous. Investment in the public sector is treated as exogenous as is investment in other areas subject to large measures of government influence or to discontinuities or where a small number of decisions affect the outcome. These industries include iron and steel, petroleum and natural gas and shipping. The three endogenous categories are private dwellings, manufacturing and the remaining parts of the private sector. The last of these, which consists primarily of investment by service industries, is determined by the preexisting capital stock, a distributed lag on consumers' expenditure and a dummy variable.

Investment in private dwellings is determined by the demand for new housing. The equation takes into account relative prices, mortgage costs and the availability of mortgage finance. This entails the development of a small sub-model to explain the dependence of building societies' lending on mortgage rate and other interest rates, which provides a link between monetary policy and real activity. The remaining investment equation, that for manufacturing, is a function of lagged manufacturing output. The dependent variable aggregates over expenditure on the acquisition and expenditure on the leasing of capital items.

The third of the five endogenous components of the expenditure GDP identity, stockbuilding, is divided into three sub-components: manufacturing, distributive trades and a residual. Stockbuilding in manufacturing is determined by a flexible accelerator while stockbuilding by the distributive trades is related to consumers' expenditure and includes a significant role for interest rates.

Leaving aside the adjustment to factor cost, the expenditure identities, (1) and (2), are completed by the explanation of the trade balance. Some categories, such as oil, are treated as exogenous. Both exports and imports are explained by demand functions with activity and relative price variables as the main arguments. An appreciation of the exchange rate improves the current balance in the short run because the volume of trade adjusts more slowly than prices. In the longer run the balance worsens, though not substantially. This demonstrates what is usually known as the *J* curve effect.

The explanation of expenditures in the economy has required the introduction of five groups of further endogenous variables which in turn have to be explained themselves. They are
(i)   incomes
(ii)   output and capacity utilisation
(iii) monetary aggregates and interest rates
(iv)   prices
(v)   the rate of exchange.

Incomes from employment are derived by multiplication of average hours and employment by the wage rate. The wage rate plays a crucial role as it is also a major determinant of prices. Thus, unlike the expenditure side of the model, wages and salaries are determined in nominal not real terms. As the equation is described in detail below (see Section VIII), only a brief outline is given here. Much recent research has concentrated on two factors influencing wage inflation, previous real wage (or earnings) levels and unemployment. The former is a development of the wage inflation model originated by Sargan (1964), whilst the latter is the well publicised Phillips curve. The wage equation in this version of the model incorporates *both* of these factors, reflecting the evidence for steady growth in real wages, coupled with the growing evidence, particularly over the last three years, of a slackening in *nominal* wage inflation due to the considerable growth in unemployment.

The remaining categories of income are also endogenous: rents are related to the previous quarter's GDP at market prices; income from self-employment (after stock appreciation) is related to average earnings of employees and gross trading profits of companies after tax and stock appreciation; property incomes are related to interest rates and each sector's holdings of financial assets; and net profits are determined as the difference between income GDP and the sum of income from employment and income from rent and self employment. Gross profits include in addition stock appreciation. The direct tax model determines income after tax; adding current grants, giving personal sector disposable income.

Having built up GDP from expenditures it is then divided amongst the output sectors of the economy, with implications for productivity, capacity utilisation, employment and unemployment. Sectoral output is determined by a form of input-output matrix and by exogenous information. Employment depends, with a distributed lag, on output and time trends. Unemployment is then determined by changes in the labour force relative to employment, where the labour force is derived exogenously, largely on the basis of Department of Employment estimates.

The financial sector is composed of equations which determine the demand for financial assets and an equation which determines the term structure of interest rates. The net acquisition of financial assets by each sector is determined in the 'income-expenditure' section of the model. The public sector deficit must be financed by borrowing from the other sectors: by sales of debt to the non-bank private sector, by issuing currency, by borrowing from the domestic banking systems, and by borrowing from the overseas sector. Demand equations determine the stock of government debt and currency held by the non-bank private sector. Bank lending to the public sector is a residual item. Equations for bank lending to various sub-categories of the private sector enable £*M*3 to be determined from the assets side of the banking system.

Prices are largely determined by costs. Consumer price inflation for example is a function of changes in import prices, unit wage costs, productivity and taxation on consumers' expenditure, plus a contribution from the change in output, reflecting the pressure of demand. Export prices are influenced both by domestic and world prices reflecting the need to compete in world markets.

The model is completed by the determination of the exchange rate which is expressed in real terms. The main influences are the real interest rate differential, relative prices and the real value of the current balance.

I CONSUMERS' EXPENDITURE

Total consumers' expenditure (QCE) is disaggregated into expenditure on non-durables ($QCND$) and durables ($QDURABLE$). Both categories are modelled by demand equations, where the primary determinant in each case is real personal disposable income. It is also argued that in the case of non-durables, consumers' spending decisions are affected by the desire to maintain a share of their wealth in form of liquid assets. Thus, if the real value of personal sector liquid assets falls relative to real incomes, consumers are posited to try to restore the value of these 'real balances'. Equation (1.1) therefore includes the loss in the real value of personal sector liquid assets, which is defined below (IL).

The demand for durable goods in turn is affected by the availability of credit, here represented by the demand for bank lending ($LPER$) and the real rate of interest. The equation also incorporates three dummy variables to take account of anticipatory purchases at the time of the 1968, 1973 and 1979 Budgets. Since it is argued that the purchases are only a bringing forward and not a net increase, the variables hold the value 1 in the quarter before the Budget and -1 in the next quarter.

(1.1) *Consumption of non-durables*

$$\Delta_4 \ln QCND = -\; 0.0885 \ln (QCND/QRDY)_{-4} \;+\; 0.458\,\Delta_4 \ln QRDY$$
$$\qquad\qquad\quad (5.2) \qquad\qquad\qquad\qquad\qquad (13.9)$$
$$\qquad -\; 0.072\left(\frac{IL + IL_{-1}}{4}\right)$$
$$\qquad\quad (3.4)$$

where $IL = (\Delta_4 \ln CPI_{-4})(QLAP_{-1}/QRDY)_{-4}$
OLS; $R^2 = 0.75$, SEE $= 0.010$, DW $= 1.9$, $CHI_1(8) = 13.1$, LM(4) $= 14.1$
1965(I)–1981(III) (Nov 1982 data).

(1.2) *Real value of personal sector liquid assets*

$$\Delta \ln QLAP = \quad 0.687\,\Delta \ln [100(KNAT + 76.3Q1 + KDEP + 0.57M3S)/CPI$$
$$\qquad\qquad (14.3)$$
$$\qquad\quad -\,0.57QCURC\,]$$

ALS; RHO2 $= 0.550$, SEE $= 0.006$, $CHI_1(8) = 32.5$; 1966(I)–1982(III)
$\qquad\quad$ (5.4) $\qquad\qquad\qquad\qquad\qquad\qquad$ (Nov 1982 data).

(1.3) *Consumption of durable goods*

$$\Delta \ln QDURABLE = -\ 3.624\ -\ 0.515\ \ln(QDURABLE/QRDY)_{-1}$$
$$\qquad\qquad (4.0)\qquad (5.1)$$

$$+\ 0.386 \Delta_4 \ln QRDY\ +\ 0.23 \ln QRDY_{-4}$$
$$\quad (1.4)\qquad\qquad\qquad (3.2)$$

$$-\ 0.039 \Delta_2 \overline{LPER}\ +\ 0.010\ (200 \Delta_2 \ln CPI_{-1} - RLA_{-3})$$
$$\quad (2.8)\qquad\qquad (3.0)$$

$$+\ 1.461 \Delta_2 \ln QLAP_{-1}\ +\ 0.190 D681\ +\ 0.111 D731$$
$$\quad (2.6)\qquad\qquad\qquad (5.5)\qquad\qquad (3.2)$$

$$+\ 0.157 D792$$
$$\quad (4.3)$$

OLS; $R^2 = 0.707$, SEE $= 0.048$, DW $= 1.6$, $CHI_1(8) = 18.3$, LM(4) $= 7.8$; 1965(I)–1981(III) (Nov 1982 data).

(1.4) *Consumers' expenditure*

$$QCE = QCND + QDURABLE$$

II INVESTMENT

In the model total investment (2.8) is divided into nine categories. Of these six are exogenous: local authority dwellings; mainly public industries and services, which includes mining and quarrying,[1] gas, electricity and water, transport and communication and public services; fees; shipping; oil and natural gas; and iron and steel. For the most part these are either in the public sector and hence determined mainly by policy decisions, or subject to discrete changes and large-scale planning. Investment in the remaining three categories (private dwellings, manufacturing and other industries) is determined endogenously.

Private dwellings

Investment in private dwellings is expressed in terms of a demand function for housing (2.1). Here the main determinants are the cost of house purchase, the relative rate of return on investment in housing and the real flow of funds into building societies. The cost of house purchase is expressed in terms of mortgage repayment, incorporating both the relative price of housing and the rate of interest on mortgage advances. Since interest payments on mortgages of up to £25,000 were allowable against income tax, the mortgage interest cost is expressed after tax at

---

[1] Other than oil and natural gas.

the standard rate. Despite high transactions costs owner-occupied housing may be treated by households as an investment as well as a consumption good. This view is represented in the equation by the relative rate of return in the short-run on new housing. The real flow of funds into building societies is the actual net inflow from deposits and shares deflated by the price of new housing (*PNH*) (after incorporating a special low interest government loan which was made to building societies in 1974–5 in an attempt to hold down interest rates).

(2.2) is a simple link between the rate of interest charged to borrowers by building societies and the rate (*RSHR*) which building societies pay to lenders. *RSHR* is explained in the section on the monetary sector of the model (14.16).

The change in shares and deposits (2.3) is explained in terms of the portfolio behaviour of the personal sector. The variables used are the change in the personal sector's financial assets (*DFAPER*) as the increment to the total portfolio, the change in the return available from investment in building society shares and deposits and that available from investment in alternative assets, here represented by local authority temporary debt.

The final equation (2.4) augments the stock of building society shares and deposits (*KDEP*) by the net inflow.

Investment by manufacturing industry

Investment by manufacturing industry (2.5) is defined excluding investment in iron and steel, which is exogenous. The dependent variable includes leasing of capital equipment undertaken by the manufacturing sector. This assumes that *use* of capital goods whether owned or leased is determined by the same set of considerations. These considerations include expected output (modelled by lagged output) and a cash flow term (*CF*), which is defined as real disposable profits (excluding the oil sector).

Other investment

This 'other' category is largely composed of investment by service and distributive trades and is thought to be determined as a lagged function of consumers' expenditure (2.6). There is also an effect from the size of the pre-existing capital stock (2.7).

Investment is allocated between the three sectors (personal, company and public) by use of the weights in 1975 shown in *National Income and Expenditure 1975*, p. 125. Personal sector investment (2.9) includes a share of both stockbuilding and stock appreciation (see sections III and XII) plus most of investment in private dwellings and a third of the residual category of investment after allowing for fees. Investment by the company sector (2.10) also includes an appropriate share of stockbuilding and of stock appreciation, plus the remainder of investment in private dwellings, the whole of investment in manufacturing, iron and steel, petroleum and natural gas and part of the mainly public, shipping and 'other' categories. Investment in plant and machinery (2.13) is a weighted sum of the various sectors' investment. The weights are based on the proportion of investment in plant and machinery in each sector's total investment and are updated from time to time as more recent data become available.

Private dwellings

(2.1)   *Gross investment in private dwellings by the private sector*

$$QDKPD = 95.705 + 0.563\,QDKPD_{-1} - 10.019\left[\frac{PNH}{CPI}RMORT\left(1 - \frac{\overline{SRT}}{100}\right)\right]_{-1}$$
$$\qquad\quad (2.0)\qquad (5.7)\qquad\qquad\qquad (4.7)$$

$$+\,147.680\left[\frac{1 + \Delta_4 PNH/PNH_{-4}}{1 + 0.01RLA}\right] + 5.751\left[\frac{DKDEP + \overline{GLOAN}}{PNH}\right]_{-1}$$
$$\quad (2.3)\qquad\qquad\qquad\qquad\qquad (3.5)$$

OLS; $R^2 = 0.867$, SEE = 32.167, DW = 2.1, CHI$_1$(16) = 19.4, LM(8) = 6.6; 1966(III)–1981(IV) (Nov 1982 data).

(2.2)   *Rate of interest on building society mortgages*

$$RMORT = 1.11\,RSHR\left(1 + \frac{\overline{SRT}}{100}\right)$$

(2.3)   *Change in building society shares and deposits*

$$DKDEP = 48.359 - 0.00224\Delta\left[FAPER\,RLA\left(1 - \frac{\overline{SRT}}{100}\right)\right]$$
$$\qquad\quad (1.5)\qquad (8.4)$$

$$+\,0.00162\,\Delta(FAPER\,RSHR) + 0.066DFAPER + 0.880DKDEP_{-1}$$
$$\quad (2.9)\qquad\qquad\qquad\qquad (2.3)\qquad\qquad (12.9)$$

OLS; $R^2 = 0.950$, SEE = 147.57, DW = 2.4, CHI$_1$(12) = 17.3, LM(6) = 10.4; 1964(I)–1981(II) (Nov 1982 data)

(2.4)   *Building society shares and deposits*

$$KDEP = KDEP_{-1} + DKDEP$$

Manufacturing industry

(2.5)   *Fixed capital formation inclusive of leasing in manufacturing industry (excluding iron and steel)*

$$QDKMF = QDKMFA - \overline{QDKLEASE} + \overline{QDKIS}$$

where

$$QDKMFA = -\ 1.88\ +\ 0.917 QDKMFA_{-1} + 76.097 \overset{4}{\underset{0}{\Sigma}} CF_{-i}$$
$$(0.045)\quad (21.6)\qquad\qquad\qquad (3.1)$$

$$+\ 1.248 \Delta(UTIL\ OMF)_{-2} + 116.9 DG - 128.7 DG_{-1}$$
$$(2.1)\qquad\qquad\qquad (3.7)\qquad\quad (4.0)$$

and $CF = (GTPNO - TXNO - SACO)/(100 PDK)$

DG is a dummy variable which assumes the value of unity in 1968IV and the value of zero in all other periods to take into account the effect of a change in the rate of investment grants.

OLS; $R^2 = 0.905$, SEE $= 31.07$, DW $= 1.8$, CHI$_1$ (16) $= 26.4$, LM(8) $= 10.6$; 1966(III)–1981(IV) (Nov 1982 data)

Other industries
(2.6)   *Investment in other industries*

$$QDKOTH - \overline{QDKLEASE} = 363.26 +\quad 0.011 QKOTH6_{-2}$$
$$(7.6)\quad (15.3)$$

$$+\ 57.903 DH + \Sigma w_i \Delta QCE_{-i}$$
$$(2.3)$$

where DH is a dummy variable which assumes the value of unity between 1969III and 1973I and the value of zero in all other periods to take into account the stimulus given to hotel building in the early 1970s by the Development of Tourism Act (1969).

LAG COEFFICIENTS:	i	w_i t-statistic	i	w_i t-statistic
(Rational lag)	1	0.015 (0.7)	5	0.121 (4.2)
	2	0.038 (1.4)	6	0.148 (5.1)
	3	0.094 (3.2)	7	0.132 (4.8)
	4	0.120 (4.2)	8	0.049 (2.2)
				$\Sigma w_i = 0.717$

ALS; RHO1 $= 0.668$, SEE $= 36.546$, CHI$_1$ (16) $= 21.4$;
$\quad\quad\quad$ (6.3) $\quad\quad\quad\quad\quad\quad\quad\quad$ 1965(IV)–1981(IV) (Nov 1981 data).

(2.7)   *Capital stock in other industries*

$$QKOTH6 = QKOTH6_{-1} + QDKOTH - \overline{QDKLEASE}$$

Total
(2.8)   *Total investment*

$$QDK = QDKPD + \overline{QDKLAD} + QDKMF + QDKOTH + \overline{QDKMP}$$
$$+\ \overline{QDKFEE} + \overline{QDKSH} + \overline{QDKPG} - \overline{QDKIS}$$

Investment by sector
(2.9)   *Investment by the personal sector*

$$GDKPER = 0.1533DS + PDK/100(0.9782QDKPD + 0.342QDKOTH$$
$$- 0.387\overline{QDKFEE}) + 0.1449SA$$

(2.10)   *Investment by the company sector*

$$GDKCO = 0.6199DS + PDK/100[0.0218QDKPD + QDKMF$$
$$- 0.8178\overline{QDKIS} + 0.1734(\overline{QDKMP} + \overline{QDKSH} - \overline{QDKIS})$$
$$+ \overline{QDKPG} + 0.6092QDKOTH] + SACO$$

(2.11)   *Investment by the non-oil company sector*

$$GDKNO = GDKCO - \overline{QDKPG}\,PDK/100$$

(2.12)   *Investment by the public sector*

$$GDKPUB = DK + DS + SA - GDKPER - GDKCO$$

(2.13)   *Investment in plant and machinery*

$$QDKPM = 0.764(QDKMF - \overline{QDKIS}) + 0.366\overline{QDKMP} + 0.405\overline{QDKPG}$$
$$+ 0.021\,\overline{QDKSH} + 0.461QDKOTH$$

III   STOCKS

Stockbuilding (3.4) is divided into three sectors, manufacturing (3.1), distribution (3.2) and a residual (3.3) which is assumed to move in proportion to the first two. Manufacturing stockbuilding is related to manufacturing output with a lag, and also the lagged level of stocks itself. In the long run the equation implies an equilibrium stock—output ratio, but the lags allow this ratio to fall initially following an increase in output. The model for distributors' stocks is similar, except that here the stock—sales ratio depends on a trend, nominal interest rates and inflation. These last two terms can be given an opportunity cost interpretation and introduce an effect of changes in monetary conditions on stockbuilding.

The last three equations, (3.5)–(3.7), simply compute the new stock levels by the addition of stockbuilding to the previous stocks.

(3.1) *Stockbuilding in manufacturing industry*

$$QDSMF = 16.21 + 0.457 QDSMF_{-1} - 0.107 QSMF + 16.684\ OMF$$
$$\quad\ (0.1)\quad (5.7)\qquad\qquad (3.7)\qquad\qquad (2.8)$$

$$+\ 17.812 OMF_{-1} - 15.222 OMF_{-2} + 123.64 SRLD$$
$$\quad (2.1)\qquad\qquad (2.1)\qquad\qquad (2.6)$$

$SRLD$ = Stock relief legislation dummy

OLS; R^2 = 0.768, SEE = 105.71, DW = 2.1, CHI_1 (16) = 13.1, LM(8) = 10.5; 1963(I)–1981(IV) (Nov 1982 data).

(3.2) *Stockbuilding in distributive trades*

$$QDSDT = 265.45 - 0.0678 QSDT_{-1} + 0.0022 (T\ QCE)_{-2}$$
$$\qquad\quad (2.3)\quad (1.6)\qquad\qquad (3.2)$$
$$-\ 0.00176 (T\ QCE)_{-3} +\ 0.00015 (P\ QCE)_{-1}$$
$$\quad (2.5)\qquad\qquad\qquad (1.2)$$

$$-\ 0.00172 (RLA\ QCE)_{-4}$$
$$\quad (5.5)$$

T is a time trend with 1959(I) = 1, $P = 100(PWMF - PWMF_{-4})/PWMF_{-4}$

OLS; R^2 = 0.49, SEE = 83.31, DW = 1.7, CHI_1 (16) = 17.2, LM(8) = 17.9; 1963(I) – 1981(IV) (Nov 1982 data)

(3.3) *Stockbuilding in the rest of industry*

$$QDSRST = \left(\frac{QDSMF + QDSDT}{QSDT + QSMF}\right)(QS - QSDT - QSMF)$$

(3.4) *Total stockbuilding*

$$QDS = QDSMF + QDSDT + QDSRST$$

(3.5) *Stock level in manufacturing*

$$QSMF = QSMF_{-1} + QDSMF_{-1}$$

(3.6) *Stock level in distributive trades*

$$QSDT = QSDT_{-1} + QDSDT_{-1}$$

(3.7) *Total stocks*

$$QS = QS_{-1} + QDS_{-1}$$

IV   EXPORTS

The export sector of the model includes a set of foreign demand functions for UK exports, where the two main determinants of the level of that demand are world trade and the price of UK exports relative to the level of world export prices. Total exports (4.14) are divided initially into goods and services, and there is a further subdivision of goods into six subcategories (4.12), (4.13) and (4.6). This subdivision is partly because exports of oil (*QEXOIL*) are exogenous and partly because manufactured goods (*QEXMF*) are much more elastic with respect to relative price than are food and basic materials.

Exports of oil are forecast exogenously from the forecast for North Sea oil production (imports of oil and gas are forecast as the residual between demand and domestic production which has not been exported). Two further small exogenous items are the residual category of exports not elsewhere specified (*QEXNES*) and the adjustment from the overseas trade accounts to the balance of payments basis for total exports (*QEXADJ*).

Exports of manufactures are estimated (4.1) after excluding items which vary erratically (ships, aircraft, North Sea oil installations and precious stones). For these items (4.5) it is assumed that their ratio to the remainder follows the average of the previous two years. Manufactured exports are determined by the current level of world trade in manufactures and by a long distributed lag on UK export prices relative to world export prices in sterling. Equation (4.2) defines the price ratio, and (4.3) the conversion of world prices into sterling terms.

Exports of food and basic materials (4.7) are determined by total world trade, as these exports are inputs to all categories of final demand in the rest of the world.

(4.1)   *Exports of manufactured goods (excluding erratic items)*

$$\ln QXGMA = \quad 5.359 + \quad 0.625 \ln \overline{WTM} + CSD + \Sigma b_i \ln PRPEX5_{-i}$$
$$\qquad\qquad (108.9) \qquad (55.9)$$

Lag distribution of *PRPEX5*

i	b_i	t-statistic	i	b_i	t-statistic
0	−0.17	1.4	4	−0.067	1.9
1	−0.025	0.5	5	−0.082	2.0
2	−0.0028	0.04	6	−0.070	1.5
3	−0.032	0.6	7	−0.036	0.8

Fifth degree Almon lag, no end point restrictions.

CSD is Composite strike dummy =

−0.07 in 66Q2	−0.02 in 71Q1
0.04 in 66Q3	0.01 in 71Q2
−0.09 in 67Q4	−0.01 in 72Q3
0.05 in 68Q1	0.007 in 72Q4
−0.08 in 70Q3	0 elsewhere
0.05 in 70Q4	

OLS; $R^2 = 0.981$, SEE $= 0.039$, DW $= 1.9$; 1966(I)–1981(IV) (Nov. 1982 data)

(4.2) *Relative price of exports of manufactures*

$PRPEX5 = PXGMA/WPMFC5$

(4.3) *World export price of manufactures in sterling*

$WPMFC5 = WPMF/(0.45\,EXCHRT)$

(4.4) *World export price of manufactures in dollars*

$WPMF = 100 \times 0.45\,\overline{WPMFE}\,EXCHRT/EFFRAT$

(4.5) *Exports of erratic items*

$$QXGER = QXGMA\left[\frac{1}{8}\sum_{i=1}^{8}(QXGER/QXGMA)_{-i}\right]$$

(4.6) *Exports of manufactured goods*

$QEXMF = QXGMA + QXGER$

(4.7) *Exports of food and basics*

$\ln QEXFB = \quad 3.404 + \quad 0.685 \ln\overline{WTTOT} + \quad 1.248\,CSD$
$\qquad\qquad (25.9) \qquad (23.7) \qquad\qquad\qquad (3.0)$

where *CSD* is as in (4.1)
OLS; $R^2 = 0.92$, SEE $= 0.058$, DW $= 1.60$, $CHI_1(12) = 14.29$, LM(6) $= 11.88$; 1967(I)–1980(IV) (Nov. 1982 data).

(4.8) *Relative price of exports of food and basics*

$PRPEXFB4 = PEXFB/WPFBC4$

(4.9) *World export price of primary products in sterling*

$$WPFBC4 = \left(\frac{WPFB}{0.45\,EXCHRT} - 0.1\,PEXFB\right)\bigg/\ 0.9$$

(4.10)   *World export price of primary products in dollars*

$WPFB = 100 \times 0.45 \overline{WPFBE} \; EXCHRT/EFFRAT$

(4.11)   *Exports of services*

$\ln QEXSER = \quad 9.285 + 0.316 \ln \overline{WTTOT} + 0.338 + \ln \overline{WTTOT}_{-1}$
$\qquad\qquad\quad (21.4) \quad\;\; (9.0) \qquad\qquad\qquad (3.3)$

$\qquad\qquad\quad + \Sigma a_i \ln (EFFRAT \; PEXSER/\overline{PMSER})_{-i}$

i	a_i	t-statistic	i	a_i	t-statistic
1	−0.361	4.4	4	−0.128	2.6
2	−0.278	12.5	5	−0.061	1.6
3	−0.200	5.5	Σ	−1.028	12.4

OLS; $R^2 = 0.99$, SEE $= 0.0233$, DW $= 1.34$, $CHI_1(12) = 20.54$, LM(6) $=$ 5.01; 1969(I)−1980(IV) (Nov. 1982 data).

(4.12)   *Exports of goods*

$QEXG = QEXMF + QEXFB + QEXOTH + \overline{QEXOIL}$

(4.13)   *Other exports*

$QEXOTH = \overline{QEXADJ} + \overline{QEXNES}$

(4.14)   *Total exports*

$QEX = QEXG + QEXSER$

V   IMPORTS

Total imports are disaggregated into imports of manufactures, other goods excluding crude oil and gas, and services. Oil imports are exogenous to the model, see (5.4).

Imports of manufactures are given by a demand function (5.1) and depend on expenditures and import prices of manufactures relative to domestic prices of manufactured goods. The specification of the equation is such as to make the marginal propensity to import out of Total Final Expenditure (*QTFE*) depend upon relative prices. Additionally, since the components of expenditure enter the equation, the marginal propensity to import depends on the composition of total expenditures. An allowance for an effect from the domestic supply of manufactures is made by including *OMF* in the equation.

The specification for imports of other goods (5.2) is similar to that for manufactures, but here the output of manufactures enters with a positive sign as the demand for industrial inputs varies directly with output.

Finally, imports of services (5.5) are determined by total final expenditure and their own lagged value.

(5.1)   *Imports of manufactures*

$$QMMF = -3489.56 + aQTFE - 0.356(QDK - QDKPM + \overline{QPAC})$$
$$(4.6)(4.5)$$

$$+ 0.122QEX + 0.424QDKPM - 25.64OMF$$
$$(1.2)(1.2)(2.5)$$

where $a_i = 0.356 + \Sigma c_i \left(\dfrac{\overline{TMMF}\ \overline{UVIMMF}\ 100}{PWMF\ EFFRAT \times 1.035} \right)_{-i}$
$$(4.5)$$

and $QTFE = QCE + QDK + QEX + QDS + \overline{QPAC}$

Lag distribution on relative price term

i	c_i	t-statistic	i	c_i	t-statistic
6	−0.00236	0.5	10	−0.00628	1.6
7	−0.00447	0.7	11	−0.00547	1.1
8	−0.00581	0.8	12	−0.00399	0.6
9	−0.00641	1.1	13	−0.00188	0.3

3rd degree Almon lag, no end point restrictions.

OLS; SEE = 0.00439, DW = 1.4, $CHI_1 (8) = 9.7$; 1968(III)–1980(IV) (Nov. 1982 data)

Both the above equation and the next were estimated after division by *QTFE,* and error statistics refer to the estimation equation.

(5.2)   *Imports of other goods*

$$QMOTH = -211.8 + bQTFE + 0.0647(\overline{QPAC} + QEX + 2QDK)$$
$$(0.4)(3.9)$$

$$+ 15.765OMF$$
$$(3.6)$$

$$b = \Sigma c_i \left(\dfrac{\overline{PMOTH}\ QGDPMP}{GDPMP\ EFFRAT} \right)_{-i}$$

Lag distribution on relative price term

i	c_i	t-statistic	i	c_i	t-statistic
0	−0.01672	1.7	3	−0.00495	0.4
1	0.00680	0.6	4	−0.01446	1.5
2	0.00565	0.5	Σ	−0.02368	

OLS; SEE = 0.00279, DW = 1.4, $CHI_1(8) = 8.30$, 1971(III)–1981(IV) (Nov. 1982 data).

(5.3)   *Imports of goods excluding oil and gas*

$QMGEO = QMMF + QMOTH + \overline{QMADJ}$

(5.4)   *Imports of goods*

$QMG = QMGEO + \overline{QMOILG}$

(5.5)   *Imports of services*

$\ln QMSER = -1.21 + 0.637 \ln QMSER_{-1} + 0.372 \ln QTFE$
$\quad\quad\quad\quad (1.7)\quad\quad (6.3)\quad\quad\quad\quad\quad\quad\quad (2.9)$

OLS; $R^2 = 0.91$, SEE $= 0.367$, DW $= 2.1$, CHI$_1(12) = 21.3$, LM(6) $=$ 8.8; 1967(I)–1980(II) (Nov. 1982 data) .

(5.6)   *Total imports*

$QM = QMG + QMSER$

VI   OUTPUT

Gross Domestic Product as measured by output (6.6) is assumed to move in direct proportion to GDP as measured by expenditure, so the residual error in the accounts is assumed to be a constant proportion. The disaggregated sectors of output are determined either exogenously, as in the case of agriculture (OAG) and dwellings ($ODWL$), or through a stylised input—output matrix, based on the coefficients published in *Economic Trends,* table 113, June 1978, as in the case of manufacturing (with an adjustment lag) (6.1), mainly public industries excluding oil (6.2) and public administration and defence (6.3). Output of other industries is then treated as a residual (6.4). All these output categories are expressed as index numbers. One further subdivision is used in other parts of the model, output of other industries including agriculture (6.5).

   UTIL (6.7) is a broadly based measure of capacity utilisation used in the equation for manufacturing investment (2.5).

   This section is concluded by five equations defining productivity as output divided by employment, the categories being the same as those used in the determination of employment in the next section.

(6.1)   *Output of manufacturing industry*

$\Delta \ln OMF = 0.323 \Delta \ln QD - 0.229 \ln OMF_{-1} + 0.119 \ln QD_{-1}$
$\quad\quad\quad\quad\quad (6.8)\quad\quad\quad\quad\quad (3.6)\quad\quad\quad\quad\quad\quad (3.6)$

where $QD = 0.15QCE + 0.13\overline{QPAC} + 0.3QDK + 0.4QEX + 0.5QDS$

OLS; $\bar{R}^2 = 0.56$, DW = 2.14, h = -0.56; 1963(I)–1977(III) (Nov. 1978 data)

(6.2)   *Output of mainly public industries excluding oil*

$$OMP = \frac{100}{3057}(0.091QCE + 0.046\overline{QPAC} + 0.074QDK + 0.142QEX)$$

(6.3)   *Output of public administration and defence*

$$OPAD = \frac{400}{22950}\overline{QPAC}$$

(6.4)   *Output of other industries*

$$OOTH6 = \frac{1}{438}\left(1000OGDP - 283OMF - 80OPAD - 61\overline{ODWL}\right.$$
$$\left. - 136.9OMP - 1.1 \times 100\frac{\overline{QOIL}}{56.1}\right)$$

(6.5)   *Output of other industries including agriculture*

$$OOTH = (336OOTH6 + 28\overline{OAG})/364$$

(6.6)   *Output GDP*

$$\frac{OGDP - OGDP_{-1}}{OGDP_{-1}} = \frac{QGDP - QGDP_{-1}}{QGDP_{-1}}$$

(6.7)   *Capacity utilisation in the whole economy*

$$\ln UTIL = -0.126 + 0.875 \ln UTIL_{-1} + 5.967 \Delta\ln EMP + 3.774 \Delta\ln OMF$$
$$\qquad\quad (3.1) \qquad (20.7) \qquad\qquad (2.2) \qquad\qquad\quad (6.3)$$

OLS; $R^2 = 0.902$, SEE = 0.101, DW = 2.5; 1963(II)–1982(II) (Nov. 1982 data)

Productivity
$PRODMF\ \ \ = 100(OMF/EMPMF)$
$PRODOTH = 100(OOTH6/EMPOTH)$
$PRODMP\ \ \ = 100(OMP/EMPMP)$
$PRODPAD = 100(OPAD/EMPAD)$
$PRODGDP = 100(OGDP/EMP)$

VII   EMPLOYMENT

Total employment (7.5) is divided into four categories: manufacturing (7.1), mainly public industries (7.3), other industries (7.2) and public administration and defence (7.4). In the last case, since output is in fact measured largely by employment, employment is calculated directly as as fixed proportion of output. In the other three cases employment is related to output with a lag (and with a time trend in the case of manufacturing and mainly public industries). For manufacturing and other industries each equation imposes constant returns to labour in the steady state.

Unemployment is determined as the residual between the exogenous labour force projection and employment (7.6) allowing for a proportion of non-registration of those becoming unemployed.

Finally, this section also includes (7.7) the explanation of average hours in manufacturing industry. This equation implies that hours are positively related to manufacturing output in the short run but not in the long run.

(7.1)   *Employment in manufacturing*

$$\Delta \ln EMPMF = \quad 0.088 + \quad 0.685 \; \Delta \ln EMPMF_{-1} + \quad 0.114 \ln(OMF/EMPMF_{-1})$$
$$\qquad\qquad\qquad (1.8) \qquad (11.6) \qquad\qquad\qquad (8.0)$$

$$\quad - \; 0.036 \ln(OMF/EMPMF)_{-1} - \; 0.0575 \ln(OMF_{-2}/EMPMF_{-1})$$
$$\quad (1.7) \qquad\qquad\qquad\qquad\qquad (3.6)$$

$$\quad - \; 0.00015 TIM$$
$$\quad (1.8)$$

OLS; $R^2 = 0.92$, SEE $= 0.0025$, DW $= 2.02$, $CHI_1(16) = 12.96$, LM(8) $=$ 2.16; 1965(I)–1982(II) (Nov. 1982 data)

(7.2)   *Employment in other industries*

$$\Delta \ln EMPOTH = \quad 0.345 + \quad 0.227 \ln(OOTH6/EMPOTH_{-1})$$
$$\qquad\qquad\qquad (3.0) \qquad (3.0)$$

$$\quad - \; 0.153 \ln(OOTH6_{-1}/EMPOTH_{-2}) + \quad 0.356 \; \Delta \ln EMPOTH_{-1}$$
$$\quad (1.9) \qquad\qquad\qquad\qquad\qquad (2.6)$$

$$\quad - \; 0.00009 TIM$$
$$\quad (1.5)$$

OLS; $R^2 = 0.29$, SEE $= 0.0069$, DW $= 2.18$, $CHI_1(16) = 19.74$; 1966(I)–1982(II) (Nov. 1982 data)

(7.3)   *Employment in mainly public industries*

$$\ln EMPMP = \quad 0.461 + \quad 0.745 \ln EMPMP_{-1} + 0.157 \ln EMPMP_{-2}$$
$$\qquad\qquad (1.6) \qquad (6.1) \qquad\qquad\qquad (1.3)$$

$$\qquad + \; 0.0623 \ln OMP - \; 0.00074 TIM$$
$$\qquad (2.0) \qquad\qquad\qquad (2.1)$$

OLS; $R^2 = 0.99$, SEE $= 0.008$, DW $= 2.0$, $CHI_1(16) = 7.2$, LM(8) $= 4.6$; 1965(I)–1981(IV) (Nov. 1982 data)

(7.4)   *Employment in public administration and defence*

$EMPAD = 16.086\,OPAD$

(7.5)   *Total employment*

$EMP = EMPMF + EMPOTH + EMPMP + EMPAD$

(7.6)   *Unemployment*

$\Delta UNEMP = 0.95\,\Delta\overline{LAB} - 0.95\,\Delta EMP$

(7.7)   *Average hours worked in manufacturing industry*

$$\ln AVHMF = \underset{(3.6)}{0.965} + \underset{(12.3)}{0.782}\ln AVHMF_{-1} + \underset{(8.4)}{0.248}\ln OMF - \underset{(4.2)}{0.180}\ln OMF_{-1}$$

$$- \underset{(2.7)}{0.059}\ln OMF_{-3} - \underset{(10.7)}{0.051}TDW + \underset{(6.2)}{0.036}TDW_{-1} - \underset{(1.9)}{0.00017}TIM$$

TDW is three day week dummy $= 1$ in 1974(II) and 0 elsewhere.
OLS; $R^2 = 0.98$, SEE $= 0.0044$, DW $= 2.03$, $CHI_1(16) = 15.34$, LM(8) $= 12.20$; 1966(I)–1982(II) (Nov. 1982 data).

VIII   INCOMES

This section refers largely to incomes of the private sector, taxation is dealt with separately in the next section, IX. Equations (8.1)–(8.5) determine income from employment, including forces' pay which is estimated exogenously, the national insurance contribution paid by employers (8.4), which is a function of the wages and salaries bill and wages and salaries themselves. Wages and salaries are the product of the wage rate, the average hours worked and the number of employees (8.2) and (8.3).

The first behavioural equation is that for the wage rate (8.1). The equation allows for a number of important influences which have been identified in research on wage inflation. These are real earnings targets, represented in this equation by the variable *RTT*, aggregate demand effects proxied by unemployment, and the effect on nominal wage inflation of movements in expected price inflation (percentage changes in P^e). The effect of purely cyclical influences on wages is also proxied by the level and rate of change of average hours worked.

Rent is derived for company, personal and public sectors as a function of GDP (at market prices) (8.6)–(8.8). Income from self-employment (8.9) on a *per capita* basis is a function of both average earnings and disposable profits. To obtain the total of 'other' personal incomes, (8.10) and (8.11) personal sector net property incomes are added, as are transfers by companies to charities and net transfers from abroad.

After calculating employees' national insurance contributions (8.12) real personal disposable incomes are calculated (8.13) by the addition of transfer payments, principally current grants which are exogenously derived, less taxes and transfers out of the country.

Equations (8.14), (8.15) and (8.16) define the incomes of the company and public sectors and (8.18) and (8.20) define net property income by sector as a function of the average rate of interest on the weighted financial assets of the sectors over the previous year. Net property income of the overseas sector is exogenously derived and net property income of the company sector is defined as the residual (8.19). Debt interest payable by the public sector is related to interest rates and the debt on which they are charged (8.21).

The income measure of GDP is assumed to move in line with the expenditure measure (8.17).

(8.1)   *Wage rates*

$$\Delta \ln WAGERATE = \ 0.446 - \ 0.205 RTT_{-3} + \ 0.759 \Delta \ln P^e$$
$$\qquad\qquad (3.0) \qquad (2.8) \qquad\qquad (3.6)$$

$$- \ 5.172 \Delta^2 UPC_{-1} - \ 3.160 \Delta UPC_{-3}$$
$$\quad (3.3) \qquad\qquad\qquad (3.5)$$

$$- \ 0.372 UPC_{-4} - \ 0.004 AVHMF - \ 0.004 \Delta AVHMF$$
$$\quad (2.2) \qquad\qquad (2.9) \qquad\qquad (2.6)$$

where real earnings growth $RTT = \ln[(AVEARN/CPI)/(0.462 (1 + 0.00610)^{TIM}]$ $UPC = UNEMP/(UNEMP + EMP)$
I.V. Instruments for P are lagged prices $(t-1, \ldots, t-4)$, and for H are $AVHMF_{-1}$, UPC_{-1}, ΔUPC_{-1} and time.
$R^2 = 0.55$, DW = 1.83, $CHI_1(16) = 17.8$, LM(8) = 10.7;
1963(IV)–1982(II) (Nov. 1982 data).

(8.2)   *Wages and salaries*

$$WS = \frac{AVEARN\ EMP}{76.92}$$

(8.3) *Average earnings*

$AVEARN = WAGERATE \, AVHMF$

(8.4) *Employers' contributions*

$EC = \overline{RATEC} \, WS$

(8.5) *Income from employment*

$IE = WS + \overline{FP} + EC$

(8.6) *Company sector rent*

$RCO = -9.64 + 0.00735 \, GDPMP_{-1}$

(8.7) *Personal sector rent*

$RPER = -141.66 + 0.0475 \, GDPMP_{-1}$

(8.8) *Public sector rent*

$RPUB = 23.63 + 0.0214 \, GDPMP_{-1} + 1.657 \, TIM$

(8.9) *Income from self-employment*

$$\ln[1000(ISE - SAPER)/\overline{LABSE}] = \underset{(1.0)}{0.222} + \underset{(2.0)}{0.127 \ln AVEARN}$$

$$+ \underset{(1.8)}{0.0223 \ln(GTPCO - TXCO - SACO)}$$

$$+ \underset{(13.6)}{0.880 \ln[1000(ISE - SAPER)/\overline{LABSE}]_{-1}}$$

$\text{OLS}; R^2 = 1.00, \text{SEE} = 0.024, \text{DW} = 1.70, \text{h} = -1.32$

(8.10) *Income from rent and self-employment*

$IRSE = RPER + RCO + RPUB + ISE$

(8.11) *Other personal income*

$OPI = IRSE + \overline{TC} + NPIPER - RCO - RPUB + \overline{TTAPER} - \overline{NTAPER}$

(8.12) *National insurance contributions*

$NIC = \overline{RATNIC} \, WS$

(8.13)   *Real personal disposable income*

$$QRDY = \frac{100}{CPI}(IE + \overline{CG} + OPI - \overline{TTAPER} - NIC - TXPER)$$

(8.14)   *Gross trading profits of the non-oil company sector*

$$GTPNO = 0.674(PGDP\ QYGDP/100 - IE - IRSE + SA - GTPOIL)$$

(8.15)   *Gross trading profits of the company sector*

$$GTPCO = GTPNO + GTPOIL - \overline{GTOILPUB}$$

(8.16)   *Gross trading surplus of the public sector*

$$GTSPUB = PGDP\ QYGDP/100 - IE - IRSE + SA - GTPCO$$

(8.17)   *Income GDP*

$$\frac{QYGDP - QYGDP_{-1}}{QYGDP_{-1}} = \frac{QGDP - QGDP_{-1}}{QGDP_{-1}}$$

(8.18)   *Net property income of the personal sector*

$$NPIPER = 345 + 0.332NPIPER_{-4}$$
$$+ \Sigma w_i[(FAPER_{-i} - 39710)(0.5RCNSL_{-i} + 0.25RMORT_{-i} + 0.25\overline{RTB}_{-i})]$$

i	w_i	i	w_i
0	0.000476	2	0.000238
1	0.000357	3	0.000119

(8.19)   *Net property income of the company sector*

$$NPICO = -(\overline{NPIOS} + NPIPUB + NPIPER)$$

(8.20)   *Net property income of the public sector*

$$NPIPUB = -676 + 0.332NPIPUB_{-4} + ROYS$$
$$+ \Sigma w_i[(FAPUB_{-i} + 52275)(0.5RCNSL_{-i} + 0.25RMORT_{-i} + 0.25\overline{RTB}_{-i})]$$

i	w_i	i	w_i
0	0.00048	2	0.00024
1	0.00036	3	0.00012

(8.21)   *Debt interest for the public sector*

$$DETINT = 94.24 - 0.00199DFAPUB(RCNSL + \overline{RTB}) + 0.883DETINT_{-1}$$

IX TAXES

Taxes on Income

The tax model is set up to provide a simple series of rules from which tax yields can be calculated given the size of the relevant tax bases and average tax rates. The income tax model permits computation of the effects of changes in the allowances against tax (married person's (9.1), single person's (9.2), child (9.3), age (9.4)) as well as changes in tax rates. In this latter case specific treatment is given for the special reduced rate of tax which was introduced for a period in the mid-1970s (*RRT*) and for the differential between higher rates and the standard rate (*URT*). The average and marginal tax rates (9.11) and (9.12) are then computed from a polynomial approximation which allows for the fact that as average incomes and hence the tax base rise the average tax rate rises for a given level of tax allowances. The tax coefficients used in this calculation are derived in equations (9.5) to (9.9). The level of personal income tax can then be computed by multiplication of the average tax rate by the tax base (9.13) allowing for the fact that income from rent and self-employment is taxed approximately five quarters in arrears. In both (9.13) and (9.10), income is computed as the sum of wages and salaries and forces' pay less national insurance contributions (in so far as they are not taxable), retirement pensions, property income and the taxable portion of income from rent and self-employment.

Company income taxes comprise taxes levied on North Sea operations (for which see section XV) and other company income taxes. These non-oil taxes (9.14) are levied on taxable profits allowing for the 1½–2½ year lag between accrual and payment.

Net taxes on expenditure

Expenditure taxes less subsidies equal the adjustment to factor cost — the difference between GDP at market prices and GDP at factor cost. At constant prices the adjustment to factor cost (12.4) is a weighted sum of the components of final demand with the weights reflecting the average incidence of taxation and subsidy in the base year, 1975. This method differs from the CSO's method of calculation only in degree of aggregation.

A similar framework for calculating the current price adjustment to factor cost based on the components of demand at current prices and current average tax rates was formerly used to calculate tax yields at current prices and this has been retained as an option in the new model. The new indirect tax model is based on the composition of the adjustment to factor cost by type of tax (9.17). Many of the individual categories are exogenous or based on a rule of thumb but the yields of VAT (9.24) and other customs and excise duties (OCE) (9.25), which together account for most of the revenue from expenditure taxes, are calculated using a framework which allows for substitution effects in consumer demand using Treasury estimates of the various price and income elasticities and other parameters. (See 'The change in revenue from an indirect tax change', *Economic Trends*, March 1980.)

(9.1)   *Aggregate married person's income tax allowance*

$$MP = MP_{-1}\ \overline{MPA}/\overline{MPA}_{-1}$$

(9.2)   *Aggregate single person's income tax allowance*

$$SP = SP_{-1}\ \overline{SPA}/\overline{SPA}_{-1}$$

(9.3)   *Aggregate income tax child allowance*

$$CH = CH_{-1}\ \overline{CHA}/\overline{CHA}_{-1}$$

(9.4)   *Aggregate income tax age allowance*

$$AGE = AGE_{-1}\ \overline{AGEA}/\overline{AGEA}_{-1}$$

Tax coefficients

(9.5) $TXCOEFF0 = TXCOEFF0_{-1}\,DR$

(9.6) $TXCOEFF1 = TXCOEFF1_{-1}(1 - DA)DR$

(9.7) $TXCOEFF2 = TXCOEFF2_{-1}(1 - DA)^2 DR$

(9.8) $TXCOEFF3 = TXCOEFF3_{-1}(1 - DA)^3 DR$

(9.9) $TXCOEFF4 = TXCOEFF4_{-1}(1 - DA)^4 DR$

where $DA = (\Delta MP + \Delta SP + \Delta CH + \Delta AGE)/\sum\limits_{i=1}^{4} YG_{-i}$

$$DR = 0.93\,X/X_{-1} + 0.07\,\overline{URT}/\overline{URT}_{-1}$$

$$\leqslant\ = SRTA - 0.312(SRTA - \overline{RRT})$$

($SRTA$ is $7/9\ \overline{SRT}$ before 1973(II) and $\overline{SRT}$ thereafter).

(9.10)   *Income definition for tax allowances*

$$YG = 0.97(WS + \overline{FP}) + EC - NIC\,\overline{NICSR} + 0.42\overline{PR}\ \overline{CG} + NPIPER$$
$$+ (IRSE - RPUB - RCO)(1 - \overline{IRR})$$

(9.11)   *Average tax rate*

$$ATXR = TXCOEFF0/G + TXCOEFF1 + TXCOEFF2G + TXCOEFF3\,G^2$$
$$+ TXCOEFF4G^3/100$$

where $G = YG/(35124/4)$

(9.12)   *Marginal tax rate*

$$MTXR = TXCOEFF1 + 2\,TXCOEFF2\,G + 3\,TXCOEFF3\,G^2$$
$$+ 4\,TXCOEFF4\,G^3/100$$

(9.13)   *Personal income tax revenue*

$$TXPER = ATXR\,[0.97\,(WS + \overline{FP}) + EC - NIC\,\overline{NICSR} + 0.42\,\overline{PR}\,\overline{CG}$$
$$+ NPIPER] + ATXR_{-5}(IRSE_{-5} - RCO_{-5} - RPUB_{-5})(1 - \overline{IRR}_{-5})$$

(9.14)   *Companies' income taxes, excluding taxes on North Sea operations*

$$TXNO = 52 + 0.00148 \sum_{i=6}^{10} \overline{TRCORP}_{-i}[GTPNO_{-i} + RCO_{-i}$$

$$- 0.8(GDKNO_{-i} - SACO_{-i} - 0.777DS_{-i})]$$

(9.15)   *Corporate income tax*

$$TXCO = TXNO + TXOIL$$

(9.16)   *Taxes on imports*

$$TXM = \overline{RM}\,QMG\,PMG/EFFRAT$$

(9.17)   *Adjustment to factor cost*

$$AFC = RATES - SUBS + INDTX + \overline{NIS} + AFCOTH$$

(9.18)   *Indirect taxes*

$$INDTX = RVAT + ROCE + RMPS + ROTH$$

Rules of thumb

(9.19)   *Local Authority rates*

$$RATES = UPRF\,RATES_{-1}$$

where $UPRF = \Delta_4 CPI_{-2}$ in Q2 and 1 elsewhere.

(9.20)   *Central government and local authority subsidies*

$SUBS = UPRF\ SUBS_{-1}$

(9.21)   *Residual items in AFC*

$AFCOTH = UPRF\ AFCOTH_{-1}$

(9.22)   *Yield of other customs and excise taxes*

$ROTH = ROTH_{-1}\ CE/CE_{-1}$

(9.23)   *Yields of customs/protective duties*

$RMPS = RMPS_{-1}\ MG/MG_{-1}$

where $MG = M - 100\ QMSER\ PMSER/EFFRAT$

It is anticipated that these rules of thumb will be replaced by exogenous projections when the model is being used for forecasting.

Consumer Taxes
General model

$$
R = R_{-4}\Bigg\{1 + \frac{1}{P}\Bigg[\left(\frac{TRN(1 + TR)}{(1 + TRN)TR} - 1\right) + \left(\frac{T}{T_{-4}} - \frac{TRN(1 + TR\ T/T_{-4})}{(1 + TRN)TR}\right)
$$
$$
\left(\frac{1 + TR\ T/T_{-4}}{1 + TR}\right)^{EP}\left(\frac{1 + TR\left\{1 + (T/T_{-4} - 1)S\right\}}{1 + TR}\right)^{-EY}\Bigg]
$$
$$
+ \left[\left(\frac{CPI}{CPI_{-4}}\right)^{\delta - EY} - 1\right] + \left[\left(\frac{QCE}{QCE_{-4}}\right)^{EY} - 1\right]\Bigg\}
$$

(9.24)   *Yield of VAT*

Variables:	$R = RVAT$	
	$T = \overline{TVAT}$	
	$S = \overline{SVAT}$	
Parameters:	$P =$	Proportion of *VAT* yield derived from consumers' expenditure
	$TR =$	Proportion of tax in the price of goods subject to *VAT*
	$TRN =$	Proportion of tax in the price of other goods
	$EP =$	Price elasticity of demand for goods subject to *VAT*
	$EY =$	Income elasticity of demand for goods subject to *VAT*
	$\delta = 1$	

(9.25)   *Yield of other Customs and Excise taxes*

Variables: $R = \overline{ROCE}$
                   $T = \overline{TOCE}$
                   $S = \overline{SOCE}$

Parameters: P = Proportion of other customs and excise taxes (OCE) yield derived from consumers' expenditure

                  TR = Proportion of tax in the price of goods subject to OCE

                  TRN = Proportion of tax in the price of other goods

                  EP = Price elasticity of demand for goods subject to OCE

                  EY = Income elasticity of demand for goods subject to OCE

                  $\delta = 0$

X   PRICES

The rate of inflation in consumer prices (10.1) is specified as a function of unit import prices (MC) and unit labour costs (LAC). The change in output of manufacturing is included as an indicator of demand pressure, and allowance is also made for the effect on prices of a change in the rate of net taxation on consumer expenditure.

Wholesale prices of manufactures (10.3) are determined in a broadly similar way. The specification used for investment goods (10.4) depends upon cost indices, not unit values. The price of new houses (10.5) is determined by building costs and the deviation of investment in private dwellings from its trend over time.

Prices of expenditure by public authorities (10.6) are dominated by wage costs with a small allowance for import prices and net indirect tax changes and with adjustment for changes in productivity.

Export prices (10.7)–(10.15) are divided into seven categories reflecting the disaggregation of exports themselves in section IV. Export prices of manufactured goods excluding erratic items are determined almost equally by domestic wholesale prices of manufactures and by world prices in sterling. The prices of erratic items are assumed to maintain their average relation to non-erratic items over the previous two years (10.8) and this makes possible the use of a simple weighted average (10.9) to obtain the price of exports of manufactures as a whole.

Export prices of food and basic materials (10.10) are determined by lagged adjustment to domestic wholesale prices and to competitors' prices.

Changes in prices of exports of services (10.11) are affected by the changes in the general level of domestic prices as reflected by consumer prices and in the prices of directly competing imports of services in sterling terms. In the equation for total export prices (10.12), the export price deflator is calculated as the weighted sum of its components, which, in addition to the items already identified in equations (10.7)–(10.11), include the exogenously determined prices of other exports and exports of oil. Other exports' prices (10.15) are further sub-divided into exports not elsewhere specified (10.13) and the *OTS* to *BOP* adjustment (10.14), both of which move in proportion to the price of exports of goods (*PEXGE*).

The import price deflator for goods (10.16) is similarly obtained from its components, but the remaining deflators, total imports (10.18) and stocks (10.19) are defined directly by dividing current price values by 1975 price values.

(10.1)　*Consumer price index*

$$\Delta \ln CPI = \; 0.0394 + \; 0.0468 \; \Delta \ln MC + 0.2008 \Delta_2 \Delta \ln CPI_{-1}$$
$$\quad\quad (3.0) \quad\quad (1.3)$$

$$+ \, 0.0898 \Delta \ln LAC_{-3} + \; 0.085 \Delta \ln OMF_{-4}$$
$$\quad (1.7) \quad\quad\quad\quad\quad (2.0)$$

$$+ \, 0.0398 \Delta \ln \overline{TRCE} - \; 0.156 \ln(CPI/LAC)_{-1}$$
$$\quad (2.1) \quad\quad\quad\quad\quad (3.7)$$

$$- \; 0.0815 \ln(CPI/MC)_{-1} - \; 0.0274 \ln(CPI/\overline{TRCE})_{-1}$$
$$\quad (8.2) \quad\quad\quad\quad\quad\quad (4.8)$$

where $LAC = (WS + EC + \overline{NIS})/OGDP$

and $MC = M/OGDP$

IV; SEE $= 0.0068$, DW $= 2.01$, CHI$_1$(16) $= 14.8$; 1965(III)–1981(IV) (May 1982 data)

(10.2)　*Retail price index*

$$\Delta \ln RPI = - \; 0.103 + \; 1.016 \, \Delta \ln CPI - 0.468 \, \ln(RPI/CPI)_{-1}$$
$$\quad\quad (4.0) \quad\quad (12.6) \quad\quad\quad\quad (2.7)$$

$$+ \, 0.0157 \ln \left(\sum_{i=1}^{16} \frac{PNH_{-i}}{16} (1 - \overline{SRT}_{-1}/100) RMORT_{-1} \right) + \; 0.0042 Q1 + \; 0.0125$$
$$\quad (3.7) \quad\quad\quad\quad\quad\quad\quad\quad\quad\quad\quad\quad\quad\quad\quad\quad\quad (1.7) \quad\quad (5.3)$$

OLS; $R^2 = 0.949$, SEE $= 0.0045$, $CHI_1(8) = 6.1$, $LM(4) = 2.2$; 1973(I)–1980(IV) (Nov. 1982 data).

(10.3)   *Wholesale price of manufactured goods*

$$\Delta\ln PWMF = \underset{(0.6)}{0.010} + \underset{(4.3)}{0.305}\,\Delta_2\Delta\ln PWMF_{-1} + \underset{(2.3)}{0.129}\,\Delta\ln LAC_{-2}$$

$$+ \underset{(2.5)}{0.0627}\,\Delta\ln MC_{-3} + \underset{(1.9)}{0.0486}\,\Delta\ln MC_{-4}$$

$$- \underset{(2.5)}{0.0849}\,\ln(PWMF/LAC)_{-1} - \underset{(7.0)}{0.0620}\,\ln(PWMF/MC)_{-1}$$

OLS; $R^2 = 0.82$, SEE $= 0.0082$, DW $= 1.92$, $CHI_1(16) = 15.0$, $LM(8) = 13.3$; 1965(II)–1981(IV) (May 1982 data).

(10.4)   *Price of investment goods*

$$DR1(PDK) = - \underset{(0.1)}{0.0005} + \underset{(2.6)}{0.157}DR1(PM_{-1}) + \underset{(2.2)}{0.138}DR1(PM_{-2})$$

$$+ \underset{(1.1)}{0.117}DR1(W) + \underset{(2.5)}{0.231}DR1(W_{-1}) + \underset{(3.2)}{0.302}DR1(W_{-2})$$

$$- \underset{(0.6)}{0.0501}DR1\left(\frac{PRODMF}{100}\right)_{-1} - \underset{(1.4)}{0.108}DR1\left(\frac{PRODMF}{100}\right)_{-3}$$

where $DR1(x) = (x - x_{-1})/x_{-1}$

$$W = \frac{1000}{13}(WS + EC)/EMP$$

OLS; $\bar{R}^2 = 0.67$, SEE $= 0.0112$, DW $= 1.89$; 1964(I)–1978(IV) (May 1979 data).

(10.5)   *Price of new houses*

$$\Delta PNH = - \underset{(3.9)}{6.738} + \underset{(2.9)}{0.270}\Delta\overline{PBC} + \underset{(4.6)}{7.851}\,\frac{QDKPD}{(558.39 + 2.362TIM)}$$

OLS; $\bar{R}^2 = 0.32$, DW $= 1.2$; 1963(I)–1977(III) (Nov. 1978 data).

(10.6)   *Price of public authorities' current expenditure*

$$\ln PPAC = \underset{(3.3)}{0.817} + \underset{(4.5)}{0.346} \ln \left[0.856 \frac{(129.2IE)}{EMP} + \underset{(3.3)}{0.093} PM + 0.05 \frac{(100AFC)}{QAFC} \right]$$

$$- \underset{(3.3)}{0.203} \ln \left[22183 \frac{OGDP}{EMP} \right] + \underset{(8.8)}{0.686} \ln PPAC_{-1}$$

OLS; $\bar{R}^2 = 0.998$, SEE $= 0.017$, DW $= 1.72$, h $= 1.47$;
1960(II)–1976(III).

(10.7)   *Export price of manufactures excluding erratic items*

$$\ln PXGMA = \underset{(6.2)}{0.0721} + \underset{(2.6)}{0.199} \ln PWMF + \underset{(5.4)}{0.211} \ln WPMFC5 + \underset{(8.5)}{0.579} \ln PXGMA$$

GIVE; $R^2 = 0.999$, SEE $= 0.014$, DW $= 2.05$, CHI$_1$(12) $= 9.37$, LM(6) $=$
5.36; 1964(II)–1978(I) (Feb. 1981 data).

(10.8)   *Price of erratic exports of goods*

$$PXGER = PXGMA \left[\frac{1}{8} \sum_{i=1}^{8} (PXGER/PXGMA)_{-i} \right]$$

(10.9)   *Price of exports of manufactures*

$$PEXMF = \frac{PXGMA \; QXGMA + PXGER \; QXGER}{QEXMF}$$

(10.10)   *Price of exports of food and basic materials*

$$\ln PEXFB = - \underset{(3.3)}{0.343} + \underset{(6.1)}{0.622} \ln PEXFB_{-1} + \underset{(6.3)}{0.229} \ln WPFBC4_{-1}$$

$$+ \underset{(2.2)}{0.227} \ln PWMF$$

OLS; $R^2 = 0.997$, SEE $= 0.0332$, DW $= 1.65$, CHI$_1$(12) $= 14.11$, LM(6) $=$
10.66; 1967(I)–1980(IV) (Nov. 1982 data).

(10.11)   *Price of exports of services*

$$\Delta\ln PEXSER = \underset{(2.7)}{0.0164} + \underset{(2.6)}{0.413}\,\Delta\ln CPI + \underset{(5.6)}{0.360}\,\Delta\ln PMSERS$$
$$+ \underset{(5.6)}{0.236}\,\ln(CPI/PEXSER)_{-1} + \underset{(1.1)}{0.0475}\,\ln\left(\frac{PMSERS}{PEXSER}\right)_{-1}$$

where $PMSERS = 100\overline{PMSER}/EFFRAT$

OLS; $R^2 = 0.56$, SEE $= 0.0146$, DW $= 1.73$, $CHI_1(12) = 14.05$, LM(6) $=$ 11.42; 1966(I)–1980(IV) (Nov. 1982 data).

(10.12)   *Exports deflator*

$$PEX = \frac{1}{QEX}(PEXMF\ QEXMF + PEXFB\ QEXFB + PEXOTH\ QEXOTH$$
$$+ 100PFEXOIL\left(\frac{\overline{QEXOIL}}{EFFRAT}\right) + PEXSER\ QEXSER)$$

(10.13)   *Price of exports not elsewhere specified*

$$PEXNES = PEXNES_{-1}PEXGE/PEXGE_{-1}$$

where $PEXGE = [100PFEXOIL\ \overline{QEXOIL}/EFFRAT + PEXMF\ QEXMF$
$$+ PEXFB\ QEXFB]/(QEXFB + QEXMF + \overline{QEXOIL})$$

(10.14)   *Price of exports adjusted from OTS to BOP basis*

$$PEXADJ = PEXADJ_{-1}PEXGE/PEXGE_{-1}$$

(10.15)   *Price of other exports*

$$PEXOTH = [PEXNES\ \overline{QEXNES} + PEXADJ\ \overline{QEXADJ}]/QEXOTH$$

(10.16)   *Imports of goods deflator*

$$PMG = [PMGEO\ QMGEO + PMOILG\ \overline{QMOILG}]/(QMGEO + \overline{QMOILG})$$

(10.17)   *Imports of goods excluding oil deflator*

$$PMGEO = (PMMF\ QMMF + \overline{PMOTH}\ QMOTH + \overline{PMADJ}\ \overline{QMADJ})/QMGEO$$

(10.18)   *Imports deflator*

$$PM = 100M/QM$$

(10.19)   *Stocks deflator*

$PS = 100S/QS$

(10.20)   *Total final expenditure deflator*

$$PTFE = 100 \, \frac{(CE + PAC + DK + DS + EX)}{(QCE + \overline{QPAC} + QDT + QDS + QEX)}$$

(10.21)   *Linking equation for the deflator for imports of manufactured goods, in foreign currency*

$$\Delta \ln PMMF = - \underset{(1.1)}{0.00279} + \underset{(14.3)}{0.944} \Delta \ln \overline{UVIMMF}$$

$$- \underset{(1.0)}{0.0567} \ln(PMMF_{-1}/\overline{UVIMMF}_{-1})$$

OLS; $R^2 = 0.83$, SEE $= 0.0128$, DW $= 2.74$, $CHI_1(8) = 12.78$;
1970(III)–1980(IV) (Nov. 1982 data).

XI   EXCHANGE RATES

The equation for the effective rate (11.1) is an estimated equation based on a model determining the *real* effective rate. It is based on two considerations. The first is that the real exchange rate is determined by real factors. Among these factors are real interest rate differentials (measured by the differential between the 3 month Treasury Bill rate and the Eurodollar rate), the real value of the current balance, and 'special' factors, such as the real value of North Sea oil reserves evaluated at the dollar export price. All variables are deflated by the wholesale price index. However, since changes in the price level produce transitory effects on the real exchange rate, this was allowed for by introducing lagged values of changes in relative prices in the equation. The second consideration concerned the behaviour of the authorities who seek by manipulating interest rates to moderate nominal exchange rate movements. To incorporate such behaviour, a reaction function for the domestic interest rate (given expected prices) was substituted into the real exchange equation, and the resulting equation estimated by an iterative instrumental variable (IV) method.

(11.1)   *Effective exchange rate (EFFRAT)*

$$\Delta RRI = \underset{(12.6)}{0.348} G + \underset{(3.2)}{0.506} \Delta_2 QCURB - \underset{(0.8)}{50.8} \Delta^2 RP$$

$$- \underset{(2.0)}{116.0} \Delta^2 RP_{-2} + \underset{(2.2)}{0.00162} \Delta OR$$

where RRI = real exchange rate

$$= EFFRAT\ PWMF/PF6$$

$$G = RTB - \left(\frac{PWMF}{PWMF_{-1}} - 1\right) 100 - \left(RTB\left(\frac{PWMF}{PWMF_{-1}} - 1\right)\right)$$

$$-REU + \left(\frac{USIP}{USIP_{-1}} - 1\right) 100 + \left(REU\left(\frac{USIP}{USIP_{-1}} - 1\right)\right)$$

$QCURB$ = real value of the current balance
$\qquad = CURB/PWMF$
RP = relative prices
$\qquad = PF6/PWMF$
OR = real value of oil reserves
$\qquad = \overline{ORES}\ POIL/PWMF$

Iterative estimation technique; $R^2 = 0.66$, SEE $= 3.57$, DW $= 1.9$, $CHI_1(16) = 16.2$, LM(8) $= 5.2$; 1972(I)–1982(II) (Nov. 1982 data).

(11.2) *Dollar exchange rate*

$$\frac{EXCHRT}{EXCHRT_{-1}} = \frac{EFFRAT}{EFFRAT_{-1}}$$

(11.3) *Current balance*

$$CURB = EX - M - \overline{NTAPER} - NTAPUB - \overline{NPIOS}$$

(11.4) *Balance of visible trade*

$$VISBAL = (QEXMF\ PEXMF + QEXOTH\ PEXOTH + QEXFB\ PEXFB$$
$$+ \overline{QEXOIL}\ PFEXOIL/(EFFRAT/100)$$
$$- QMG\ PMG/(EFFRAT/100))/100$$

XII GDP IDENTITIES AND CURRENT PRICE VARIABLES

This section of the model is simply a set of definitions. GDP at factor cost (12.1) is composed of total final sales, stockbuilding less imports and the adjustment to factor cost. The total of final sales is consumers' expenditure plus investment, exports and public authorities current expenditure. This becomes total final expenditure if stockbuilding is also included. GDP at market prices is related to GDP at factor cost (12.2) by adding back the adjustment to factor cost. (12.3) defines the average estimate of GDP.

Equations (12.7) to (12.15) define the current price components of GDP (12.13). The first five of these, consumers' expenditure (12.7), public authorities current expenditure (12.12), gross fixed investment (12.8), stockbuilding (12.9) and exports (12.10) are simply expenditure at 1975 prices multiplied by the appropriate price deflator. Imports (12.11) are totalled and require division by the effective exchange rate to express the prices in sterling terms. The remaining item, the adjustment to factor cost, was defined in equation (9.17). (12.14) defines GDP at market prices using a current price equivalent of (12.2). (12.15) completes the national accounts by the definition of the residual error as the discrepancy between the expenditure and income estimates of GDP.

The final four equations define the level of stocks in current prices (12.16) as the previous level plus stockbuilding and stock appreciation where stock appreciation is defined in (12.17). In turn stock appreciation is allocated to the company and personal sectors in (12.18) and (12.19). (The residual is stock appreciation in the public sector.)

Real GDP identities
(12.1)   *Real GDP at factor cost (expenditure estimate)*

$$QGDP = QCE + QDK + QEX + \overline{QPAC} + QDS - QM - QAFC$$

(12.2)   *Real GDP at market prices*

$$QGDPMP = QGDP + QAFC$$

(12.3)   *Real GDP at factor cost (average estimate)*

$$QGDPC4 = (QGDP + QYGDP + 235.8\,OGDP)/3$$

(12.4)   *Adjustment to factor cost*

$$QAFC = 0.1245\,QCE + 0.0403\,\overline{QPAC} + 0.0466(QDK + QDS) + 0.0278\,QEX$$

(12.5)   *Deflator for GDP at factor cost*

$$PGDP = 100\,GDP/QGDP$$

(12.6)   *Deflator for GDP at market prices*

$$PMP = 100\,GDPMP/QGDPMP$$

Current price variables
(12.7)   *Consumers' expenditure*

$$CE = QCE\,CPI/100$$

(12.8)   *Gross fixed investment*

$DK = QDK\,PDK/100$

(12.9)   *Stockbuilding*

$DS = QDS\,PDK/100$

(12.10)   *Exports*

$EX = QEX\,PEX/100$

(12.11)   *Imports*

$M = (QMG\,PMG + QMSER\,\overline{PMSER})/EFFRAT$

(12.12)   *Public authorities' current consumption*

$PAC = \overline{QPAC}\,PPAC/100$

(12.13)   *GDP at factor cost*

$GDP = CE + PAC + DK + DS + EX - M - AFC$

(12.14)   *GDP at market prices*

$GDPMP = GDP + AFC$

(12.15)   *Residual error*

$ERR = GDP - QYGDP\,PGDP/100$

Stock appreciation
(12.16)   *Value of stocks*

$S = S_{-1} + DS_{-1} + SA_{-1}$

(12.17)   *Stock appreciation, total*

$$SA = 0.5\left[S\left(\frac{PS}{PS_{-1}} - 1 \right) + S_{-1}\left(1 - \frac{PS_{-1}}{PS} \right) \right]$$

(12.18)   *Stock appreciation, company sector*

$SACO = 0.83SA$

(12.19)   *Stock appreciation, personal sector*

$SAPER = 0.14SA$

XIII   FINANCIAL ASSETS

This section of the model is composed entirely of definitions. Equations (13.1)–(13.4) define the net acquisition of financial assets, *NAFA*, by the four sectors of the economy, personal (13.1), company (13.2), public (13.3) and overseas (13.4) which sum to the residual error in the national accounts. The remaining three equations (13.5)–(13.7) augment the stock of financial assets by the *NAFA*s and a share of the residual error. The *NAFA*s are the residuals from the sum of each sector's incomes less its expenditures. Thus in the case of the personal sector (13.1) the *NAFA* is equal to income from employment, other personal income, current grants, and net current and capital transfers from abroad less consumers' expenditure, personal sector investment (2.9), income taxation and national insurance contributions. Similarly, the *NAFA* of the company sector (13.2) is equal to income from trading profits, and other sources, less expenditures on investment and taxation. The public sector sources of income are, in the order in (13.3), national insurance contributions, rent, income tax, company tax, trading surpluses, net property income, net capital transfers to the other sectors, and the adjustment to factor cost (net indirect taxes). Its expenditures are on current goods and services, current grants, current transfers abroad and investment. Finally the overseas sector (13.4) has net income from net current and capital transfers from the other sectors, and imports less exports.

(13.1)   *Net acquisition of financial assets by the personal sector*

$$DFAPER = IE + OPI + \overline{CG} - \overline{TTAPER} + \overline{KTPER} - CE - NIC$$
$$- TXPER - GDKPER$$

(13.2)   *NAFA by the company sector*

$$DFACO = GTPCO + RCO + NPICO + \overline{KTCO} - \overline{TC} - TXCO - GDKCO$$

(13.3)   *NAFA by the public sector*

$$DFAPUB = NIC + RPUB + TXPER + TXCO + GTSPUB + NPIPUB$$
$$- \overline{KTPER} - \overline{KTCO} - \overline{KTOS} + AFC - PAC - \overline{CG}$$
$$- \overline{NTAPUB} - GDKPUB$$

(13.4)   *NAFA by the overseas sector*

$$DFAOS = \overline{NTAPER} + \overline{NTAPUB} + \overline{NPIOS} + \overline{KTOS} - EX + M$$

(13.5) *Stock of financial assets of the personal sector*

$$FAPER = FAPER_{-1} + DFAPER_{-1} + 0.5\,ERR_{-1}$$

(13.6) *Stock of financial assets of the company sector*

$$FACO = FACO_{-1} + DFACO_{-1} + 0.25\,ERR_{-1}$$

(13.7) *Stock of financial assets of the public sector*

$$FAPUB = FAPUB_{-1} + DFAPUB_{-1} + 0.25\,ERR_{-1}$$

XIV MONETARY SECTOR

The monetary sector of the model seeks to explain some of the main financial transactions between the sectors of the economy. Starting with the public sector (14.1) the public sector's borrowing requirement is by definition financed by bank lending to the public sector, debt sales to the private sector, by issuing currency and by borrowing from the overseas sector, the latter being treated as exogenous. The PSBR is determined by the income and expenditure sectors of the model. Behavioural equations for the banking sector are designed to leave bank lending to the public sector as a residual item. Debt sales are divided into two components, total debt sales to the non-bank private sector (14.9) and national savings which is treated exogenously. The change in currency is explained in real terms (14.7). These categories are treated as demand determined. In the case of currency, demand depends on transactions which relate to consumers' expenditure. Sales of long- and short-term debt (including National Savings) are determined by portfolio demand (14.9), with the difference between the CD rate and the yield on consols as the representative relative interest rate. The cumulative sum of the net acquisition of financial assets of the non-bank private sector is entered as a proxy for wealth in this equation.

The identity for the change in the broad money supply (*M3S* defined in (14.2)) introduces only one further element to be explained, bank lending to the private sector, as the remaining small elements in the identity are exogenous.

Bank lending to the private sector (14.3) is divided into six components, the first of which, bank lending to the other financial institutions, is exogenous. The remaining five are lending to the personal sector, lending to industrial and commercial companies, loans for house purchase, the Issue Department's transactions in commercial bills and a residual.

The behavioural equation for bank lending to the personal sector (10.4) is a demand equation, dependent on interest rates, real disposable income, and the change in the net acquisition of financial assets by the personal sector, used here to proxy changes in personal wealth. Bank lending to industrial and commercial companies (14.5) is a transactions demand equation. It depends on real output and there is a significant effect from the real borrowing requirement of this sector, which, in turn, is given by the linking equation (14.6). There is also an effect from relative interest rates, including foreign rates, which are included to capture switching between domestic and foreign sources of borrowing.

The demand for currency (14.7) is given by a simple distributed lag on total consumers' expenditure. Equation (14.8) is the demand equation for narrow money (*M*1).

The model is completed by the explanation of the interest rates used. The equation for the interest rate on bank lending (14.12) links it to the lagged certificate of deposit rate. In turn the CD rate is linked to the Treasury bill rate via the identity in (14.13). The same procedure is followed for the interest rate on local authority debt (14.14) and building society rates are assumed to move with local authority rates. The Treasury bill rate is forecast exogenously. The remaining interest rate used in the model is the long rate — represented by the yield on 2½% consols — which is determined by an equation using the lagged Treasury bill rate and consumer prices.

(14.1)   *Financing the PSBR*

$$DBLPUB = FINT - DFAPUB - \Delta SGDETPRI - DCUR - \overline{PDOAS} - \overline{IDCB}$$

where $DCUR = \Delta(QCURC\, CPI/100)$

(14.2)   *Broad money supply*

$$\Delta M3S = DBLPUB + DBLPRIVS - \overline{NNDL} + \overline{EFC} + DCUR + \overline{PDOAS} + \overline{IDCB}$$

(14.3)   *Bank lending to the private sector*

$$DBLPRIVS = \overline{DBLOFIS} + \overline{DBLHS} + \Delta BLOPERS + \Delta BLICS - \overline{IDCB} + \overline{DBLRESS}$$

(14.4)   *Change in (£) bank lending to the personal sector (other than for house purchase)*

$$\Delta \ln BLOPERS = -\ 0.155 + 0.516 \Delta \ln(QRDY\, CPI/100)$$
$$(2.7) \qquad (1.9)$$

$$-\ 0.123\ \ln[BLOPERS/(QRDY\, CPI/100)]_{-1} - 0.0052 \Delta RBL_{-}$$
$$(3.8) \qquad\qquad\qquad\qquad\qquad\qquad (1.0)$$

$$-\ 0.0006 RBL_{-3} + 0.143 SCC + 0.019 DFAPER/1000$$
$$(0.2) \qquad\qquad (7.5) \qquad\quad (2.7)$$

SCC = 'Short' competition and credit control dummy, taking the value of unity. 1971(IV)–1973(IV); zero elsewhere.
OLS; R^2 = 0.575, SEE = 0.043, DW = 2.0, $CHI_1(16)$ = 14.2, LM(8) = 8.9; 1965(I)–1981(II) (Nov. 1982 data).

(14.5) *Bank lending to industrial and commercial companies*

$$\Delta_4 \ln QBL = -\ 0.126 + \underset{(7.4)}{0.575}\ \Delta_2 \ln QBL_{-1} + \underset{(9.3)}{0.878}\ \Delta \ln QBL_{-3}$$
$$\underset{(4.2)}{}$$

$$+\ \underset{(2.4)}{0.322}\ \Delta_4 \ln QGDP - \underset{(6.9)}{0.273}\ \ln(QBL/QGDP)_{-4}$$

$$-\ \underset{(1.4)}{0.00348}\ \Delta RBL_{-2} - \underset{(3.4)}{0.00350}(RBL_{-5} + RBL_{-6})$$

$$+\ \underset{(5.9)}{0.003}ICCBR/PTFE + \underset{(0.7)}{0.00286}(RLA - RBL)$$

$$+\ \underset{(0.7)}{0.00277}(RLA - RBL)_{-2} + \underset{(2.4)}{0.00174}(\overline{REU}_{-2} + \overline{REU}_{-3})$$

$$+\ \underset{(6.8)}{0.0820}CCC + \underset{(2.8)}{0.018}Q2 + \underset{(3.2)}{0.020}\ Q3$$

where: $\quad QBL = 100 \left(\dfrac{BLICS + \overline{BILK}}{PTFE} \right), \quad CCC = 1$ from 1971(IV) inclusive
$$= 0 \text{ elsewhere}$$

OLS; R^2 = 0.96, SEE = 0.0189, DW = 2.0, $CHI_1(16)$ = 12.6, LM(8) = 10.8; 1965(I)–1980(III) (Nov. 1982 data).

(14.6) *Net borrowing requirement of industrial and commercial companies*

$$\frac{ICCBR}{PTFE} = -\ \underset{(4.4)}{1.053}\ \frac{DFACO}{PTFE} + \underset{(4.6)}{5.638}$$

OLS; R^2 = 0.4, SEE = 611.0, DW = 1.7, $CHI_1(8)$ = 7.0, LM(4) = 1.3; 1973(I)–1980(III) (June 1982 data).

(14.7) *Demand for currency*

$$\Delta \ln QCURC = -\ 0.172 - \underset{(2.3)}{0.00117}TIM + \underset{(3.5)}{0.606}\Delta \ln QCE + \underset{(1.4)}{0.231}\ \Delta \ln QCE_{-1}$$
$$\underset{(2.1)}{}$$

$$-\ \underset{(2.0)}{0.161}\ \ln(QCURC/QCE)_{-1}$$

OLS; R^2 = 0.2, SEE = 0.019, DW = 2.0, $CHI_1(12)$ = 5.9, LM(6) = 1.8; 1964(I)–1982(II) (Nov. 1982 data).

(14.8)   *Demand for narrow money*

$$\Delta \ln QM1 = \;\; 0.025 \; - \;\; 0.069 \ln(M1/GDPMP)_{-1} \; + \;\; 0.316 \, \Delta \ln QGDMP_{-1}$$
$$\qquad\quad (3.2) \qquad (3.6) \qquad\qquad\qquad\qquad (2.1)$$

$$- \;\; 0.0076 \, \Delta RLA \; - \;\; 0.0025 \, \Delta RLA_{-2} \; - \;\; 0.0055 \, RLA_{-2}$$
$$(4.6) \qquad\qquad (1.5) \qquad\qquad (4.6)$$

where $QM1 = \dfrac{M1}{PMP}$

OLS; $R^2 = 0.46$, SEE $= 0.018$, DW $= 2.1$, $CHI_1(12) = 11.9$, LM(6) $=$
5.0; 1964(I)–1982(II) (Nov. 1982 data).

(14.9)   *Sales of long- and short-term public debt*

$$\Delta \ln SGDETPRI = - \;\; 0.81 \; + \;\; 0.0027 RCNSL \; + \;\; 0.0016(RCNSL - CDR)_{-1}$$
$$(1.6) \qquad (1.8) \qquad\qquad (1.4)$$

$$+ \;\; 0.278 LF \; - \;\; 0.392 LF_{-1} \; + \;\; 0.185 LF_{-2} \; - \;\; 0.113 LGF_{-1}$$
$$(1.0) \qquad\;\; (0.9) \qquad\quad (0.6) \qquad\qquad (1.2)$$

where $LF_{-1} = \ln(FACO + FAPER)$
$\qquad\;\; LGF = \ln[SGDETPRI/(FACO + FAPER)]$

NB: *SGDETPRI* is the stock of debt at the end of quarter, whereas
FACO and *FAPER* are beginning of period stocks.
OLS; $R^2 = 0.321$, SEE $= 0.0142$, DW $= 1.9$, $CHI_1(16) = 12.55$, LM(8) $=$
7.838; 1972(II)–1981(II) (Nov. 1982 data).

(14.10)   *Sales of government long- and short-term debt*

$$GDETLS = \Delta SGDETPRI - \overline{NATSAV}$$

(14.11)   *National savings*

$$KNAT = \overline{NATSAV} + KNAT_{-1}$$

(14.12)   *Bank lending rate*

$$\Delta RBL = \;\; 0.672 \, \Delta CDR \; + \;\; 0.155 \, CDR_{-1} \; - \;\; 0.34(RBL - CDR)_{-1} \; + \;\; 1.62$$
$$(10.0) \qquad\qquad (2.1) \qquad\qquad (3.1) \qquad\qquad\qquad\quad (3.1)$$
OLS; $R^2 = 0.82$, SEE $= 0.66$, DW $= 1.85$, $CHI_1(8) = 5.0$, LM(4) $= 2.8$;
1973(I)–1981(III) (Nov. 1982 data).

(14.13) *Certificate of deposit rate*

$$CDR = \overline{RTB}$$

(14.14) *Rate of interest on local authority temporary debt*

$$RLA = \overline{RTB}$$

(14.15) *Yield on 2½% consols*

$$\Delta RCNSL = \underset{(0.6)}{0.0333} + \underset{(4.8)}{\Sigma a_i\, \Delta \overline{RTB}_{-i}} + \underset{(1.3)}{\Sigma b_i\, (\%CPI - \%CPI_{-1})_{-i}}$$

where $\%CPI$ is the percentage rate of change of the CPI over the previous quarter.

Almon lags	i	a_i	b_i
Lag coefficients	0	0.2614	0.1103
	1	0.0748	0.0698
	2	0.0439	0.0507
	3	0.0949	0.0451
	4	0.1538	0.0450
	5	0.1468	0.0428
	6		0.0304
		0.7757	0.3941

OLS; $\overline{R}^2 = 0.46$, DW = 2.1; 1963(I)–1977(III) (Nov. 1978 data).

(14.16) *Building society share and deposit rate*

$$\Delta RSHR = \Delta RLA$$

XV NORTH SEA OIL

The three equations which comprise the oil sector are for gross trading profits ($GTPOIL$) from the North Sea oil sector, government tax royalties ($ROYS$) from the North Sea and 'direct taxes' from the North Sea. Direct tax ($TXOIL$) is the sum of Corporation Tax, Petroleum Revenue Tax and Advanced Petroleum Revenue Tax. These three equations are not estimated directly; they are derived as a Taylor series approximation to a larger computer model of the North Sea sector developed at the National Institute. Variables with the suffix BR are the base point around which the Taylor expression has been calculated, and the others are the current model values.

(15.1)　*Taxes on income*

$$TXOIL = \overline{TXOILBR}\left[1 + \sum_i a_i\left(\frac{POIL - \overline{POILBR}}{\overline{POILBR}}\right)_{-i} + \sum_i b_i\left(\frac{QOIL - \overline{QOILBR}}{\overline{QOILBR}}\right)_{-i}\right.$$

$$+ \sum_i c_i\left(\frac{EXCHRT - \overline{EXCHRTBR}}{\overline{EXCHRTBR}}\right)_{-i} + \sum_i d_i\left(\frac{PRTR - \overline{PRTRBR}}{\overline{PRTRBR}}\right)_{-i}$$

$$\left. + \sum_i e_i\left(\frac{TRCORP - \overline{TRCORPBR}}{\overline{TRCORPBR}}\right)_{-i}\right]$$

Lag weights

i	a	b	c	d	e
1	0.405	0.430	−0.362	0.05	
2	0.405	0.430	−0.362	0.05	
3	0.405	0.430	−0.362	0.05	
4	0.405	0.430	−0.362	0.05	
5	−0.068	−0.082	0.057		0.055
6	−0.068	−0.082	0.057		0.055
7	−0.068	−0.082	0.057		0.055
8	−0.068	−0.082	0.057		0.055
9	0.013	0.0013	−0.012		
10	0.013	0.0013	−0.012		
11	0.013	0.0013	−0.012		
12	0.013	0.0013	−0.012		

(15.2)　*Royalties (taxes on expenditure)*

$$ROYS = \overline{ROYSBR}\left[1 + \sum_i a_i\left(\frac{POIL - \overline{POILBR}}{\overline{POILBR}}\right)_{-i} + \sum_i b_i\left(\frac{QOIL - \overline{QOILBR}}{\overline{QOILBR}}\right)_{-i}\right.$$

$$\left. + \sum_i c_i\left(\frac{EXCHRT - \overline{EXCHRTBR}}{\overline{EXCHRTBR}}\right)_{-i}\right]$$

i	a_i	b_i	c_i
1	0.262	0.254	−0.238
2	0.262	0.254	−0.238
3	0.262	0.254	−0.238
4	0.262	0.254	−0.238

(15.3) *Profits*

$$GTPOIL = \overline{GTPOILBR}\left[1 + \sum_i a_i\left(\frac{POIL - \overline{POILBR}}{\overline{POILBR}}\right)_{-i}\right.$$

$$\left. + \sum_i b_i\left(\frac{\overline{QOIL}\ \overline{QOILBR}}{\overline{QOILBR}}\right)_{-i} + \sum_i c_i\left(\frac{EXCHRT - \overline{EXCHRTBR}}{\overline{EXCHRTBR}}\right)_{-i}\right]$$

i	a_i	b_i	c_i
1	0.257	0.249	−0.235
2	0.257	0.249	−0.235
3	0.257	0.249	−0.235
4	0.257	0.249	−0.235

(15.4) *Exports of oil deflator*

$$PFEXOIL = \overline{PFEXOILD}\ EFFRAT/[100(0.45 EXCHRT)]$$

(15.5) *Imports of oil and natural gas deflator*

$$PMOILG = \overline{PMOILGD}\ EFFRAT/[100(0.45 EXCHRT)]$$

(15.6) *Price of oil in dollars*

$$POIL = 100\ PFEXOIL\ EXCHRT/EFFRAT$$

DEFINITIONS AND SOURCES OF VARIABLES

This listing shows the variable model name followed by its number, the definition of the variable and its source.

The following conventions are used with respect to notation:

Q	as	prefix is 1975 prices
P	as	prefix is price (except PAC)
PER	as	suffix is personal sector
CO	as	suffix is company sector
OS	as	suffix is overseas sector
PUB	as	suffix is public sector
O	as	prefix is output
EMP	as	prefix is employment
M	as	prefix is imports
EX	as	prefix is exports
NPI	as	prefix is net property income (dividend and interest)
FA	as	prefix is financial assets

Data sources are:

BB	National Income and Expenditure Blue Book
BOE	Bank of England Quarterly Bulletin
CS	UK Chamber of Shipping
DED	Department of Economic Development (Northern Ireland)
DEG	Department of Employment Gazette
DOI	Department of Industry 'British Business'
ET	Economic Trends
FS	Financial Statistics
HMT	Treasury
MDS	Monthly Digest of Statistics
MRETS	Monthly Review of External Trade Statistics
OECD(MEI)	Main Economic Indicators
RICS	Royal Institute of Chartered Surveyors
UNMBS	United Nations Monthly Bulletin of Statistics

VARIABLE	NO.	EQUATION	DEFINITION	UNITS AND SOURCE
AFC	99	9.17	Adjustment to factor cost	£m/ET
AFCOTH	155	9.21	Residual item in AFC identity	£m/Transformed
AGE	173	9.4	Aggregate income tax age allowance	£m/Inland Revenue
AGEA	216	EXOG	Individual income tax age allowance	£/Inland Revenue
ATXR	174	9.11	Average rate of income tax	Internal definition
AVEARN	59	8.3	Average earnings	£ per week/Transformed
AVHMF	54	7.7	Average hours worked per operative (GB) index	1975 = 100/ET
BILK	122	EXOG	Bill leak	£m/HMT
BLICS	142	14.5	Outstanding sterling bank lending to ICC	£m/BOE
BLOPERS	140	14.4	Outstanding sterling bank lending to persons excluding for house purchase	£m/BOE
CDR	212	14.13	Interest rate on sterling certificates of deposit	Per cent/FS
CE	100	12.7	Consumers' expenditure	£m/ET
CG	68	EXOG	Current grants	£m/ET
CH	172	9.3	Aggregate income tax child allowance	£m/Inland Revenue
CHA	215	EXOG	Individual income tax child allowance	£/Inland Revenue
CPI	73	10.1	Consumer price index	1975 = 100/Transformed
CURB	268	11.3	Current balance	£m/ET
DBLHS	141	EXOG	Flow of sterling bank lending to persons for house purchase	£m/BOE
DBLOFIS	218	EXOG	Flow of sterling bank lending to OFI's	£m/BOE
DBLPRIVS	139	14.3	Flow of sterling bank lending to private sector	£m/BOE
DBLPUB	247	14.1	Flow of sterling bank lending to public sector	£m/BOE
DBLRESS	194	EXOG	Residual category of sterling bank lending flows	£m/Transformed
DETINT	189	8.21	Debt interest payments by public sector	£m/FS
DFACO	144	13.2	Net acquisition of financial assets, company sector	£m/FS
DFAOS	146	13.4	Net acquisition of financial assets, overseas sector	£m/FS
DFAPER	143	13.1	Net acquisition of financial assets, persons	£m/FS
DFAPUB	145	13.3	Net acquisition of financial assets, public sector	£m/FS

VARIABLE	NO.	EQUATION	DEFINITION	UNITS AND SOURCE
DHP	243	EXOG	Change in hire purchase debt outstanding	£m/ET
DK	102	12.8	Gross investment, total	£m/ET
DKDEP	110	2.3	Net increase in building society shares and deposits	£m/FS
DS	106	12.9	Stock changes, total	£m/Transformed
EC	56	8.4	Employers contributions	£m/ET
EFC	246	EXOG	External and foreign currency counterparts	£m/BOE
EFFRAT	199	11.1	Sterling effective exchange rate	1975 = 100/FS
EMP	48	7.5	Employment, UK total	Thous/DEG
EMPAD	52	7.4	Employment, public administration and defence, UK	Thous/DEG and DED
EMPMF	49	7.1	Employment, manufacturing, UK	Thous/Transformed from ET
EMPMP	51	7.3	Employment, mainly public, UK	Thous/DEG and DED
EMPOTH	50	7.2	Employment, other, UK	Thous/Transformed
ERR	196	12.15	Residual error in national accounts	£m/ET
EX	104	12.10	Exports, total	£m/ET
EXCHRT	206	11.2	Sterling/dollar exchange rate	$per £/FS
EXCHRTBR	262	EXOG	Baseline value for EXCHRT in oil sector	$per £/FS
FACO	148	13.6	Stock of financial assets, company sector	£m/Transformed
FAPER	147	13.5	Stock of financial assets, persons	£m/Transformed
FAPUB	149	13.7	Stock of financial assets, public sector	£m/Transformed
FINT	190	EXOG	Financial transactions, public sector	£m/Transformed
FP	62	EXOG	Forces' pay	£m/ET
GDETLS	192	14.10	Sales of government long- and short-term debt	£m/Transformed
GDKCO	167	2.10	Gross capital formation, company sector	£m/ET
GDKNO	85	2.11	Gross capital formation, non-oil company sector	£m/Transformed
GDKPER	166	2.9	Gross capital formation, persons	£m/ET
GDKPUB	168	2.12	Gross capital formation, public sector	£m/ET
GDP	101	12.13	Gross domestic product	£m/ET
GDPMP	185	12.14	Gross domestic product at market prices	£m/Transformed

VARIABLE	NO.	EQUATION	DEFINITION	UNITS AND SOURCE
GLOAN	113	EXOG	Government loan to building societies	£m/FS
GTOILPUB	229	EXOG	Gross trading profits, BNOC	£m/Transformed
GTPCO	127	8.15	Gross trading profits, company sector	£m/ET
GTPNO	83	8.14	Gross trading profits, non-oil company sector	£m/Transformed
GTPOIL	82	15.3	Gross trading profits, oil sector	£m/ET
GTPOILBR	264	EXOG	Baseline value for GTPOIL in oil sector	£m/ET
GTSPUB	165	8.16	Gross trading surplus, public sector	£m/ET
ICCBR	121	14.6	Net borrowing requirement of ICC	£m/ET
IDCB	224	EXOG	Transactions in Issue Department commercial bills	£m/FS
IE	63	8.5	Income from employment	£m/ET
INDTX	274	9.18	Income from indirect taxes	£m/FS
IRR	164	EXOG	Proportion of 'other' income exempt from tax	Internal definition
IRSE	61	8.10	Income from rent and self-employment	£m/ET
ISE	251	8.9	Income from self employment	£m/Transformed
KDEP	111	2.4	Level of building society deposits	£m/Transformed
KNAT	163	14.11	Stock of national savings outstanding	£m/Transformed
KTCO	137	EXOG	Capital transfers, company sector	£m/ET
KTOS	138	EXOG	Capital transfers, overseas sector	£m/ET
KTPER	136	EXOG	Capital transfers, persons	£m/ET
LAB	237	EXOG	Labour supply, UK	Thous/Transformed
LABSE	236	EXOG	Self-employment, UK	Thous/DEG
LCO	38	EXOG	Bank lending requests dummy, company sector	Internal definition
LPER	14	EXOG	Bank lending requests dummy, persons	Internal definition
M	105	12.11	Imports, total	£m/ET
MP	170	9.1	Aggregate married person's income tax allowance	£m/Inland Revenue
MPA	213	EXOG	Individual married person's income tax allowance	£/Inland Revenue
MTXR	175	9.12	Marginal income tax rate	Transformed
M1	242	14.8	Money supply, M1 definition	£m/Transformed

VARIABLE	NO.	EQUATION	DEFINITION	UNITS AND SOURCE
M3S	245	14.2	Money supply, £M3 definition	£m/Transformed
NATSAV	191	EXOG	Sales of national savings	£m/FS
NIC	58	8.12	National insurance contributions	£m/ET
NICSR	158	EXOG	Proportion of NIC exempt from tax	BB
NIS	150	EXOG	National Insurance employers' surcharge	£m/FS
NNDL	220	EXOG	Net non-deposit liabilities of public sector	£m/BOE
NPICO	128	8.19	Dividends and interest income, company sector	£m/Transformed
NPIOS	130	EXOG	Dividends and interest income, overseas sector	£m/ET
NPIPER	66	8.18	Dividends and interest income, persons	£m/Transformed
NPIPUB	129	8.20	Dividends and interest income, public sector	£m/Transformed
NTAPER	70	EXOG	Net transfers abroad, persons	£m/ET
NTAPUB	133	EXOG	Net transfers abroad, public sector	£m/Transformed
OAG	40	EXOG	Output index, agriculture	1975 = 100/ET
ODWL	44	EXOG	Output index, dwellings	1975 = 100/ET
OFB	208	EXOG	Output index, food and basics	1975 = 100/MDS
OGDP	188	6.6	Output index, GDP	1975 = 100/ET
OMF	41	6.1	Output index, manufacturing	1975 = 100/ET
OMP	42	6.2	Output index, mainly public	1975 = 100/Transformed
OOTH6	43	6.4	Output index, other	1975 = 100/Transformed
OPAD	45	6.3	Output index, public administration and defence	1975 = 100/ET
OPI	67	8.11	Other personal income	£m/Transformed
ORES	269	EXOG	Oil reserves	£m/Brown Book
PAC	103	12.12	Public authorities' consumption	£m/ET
PBC	98	EXOG	Building costs	1975 = 100/RICS
PDK	75	10.4	Deflator, fixed investment	1975 = 100/Transformed
PDOAS	219	EXOG	Financing of the PSBR, external transactions	£m/BOE
PEX	80	10.12	Deflator, total exports	1975 = 100/Transformed
PEXADJ	95	10.14	Deflator, exports OTS to BOP adjustment	1975 = 100/Transformed

VARIABLE	NO.	EQUATION	DEFINITION	UNITS AND SOURCE
PEXFB	81	10.10	Deflator, exports of food and basics	1975 = 100/Transformed
PEXMF	77	10.9	Deflator, exports of manufactures	1975 = 100/Transformed
PEXNES	46	10.13	Deflator, exports rest (OTS)	1975 = 100/Transformed
PEXOTH	78	10.15	Deflator, exports, other (BOP)	1975 = 100/Transformed
PEXSER	79	10.11	Deflator, exports of services	1975 = 100/Transformed
PFB	209	EXOG	Price of food and basics	1975 = 100/MDS
PFEXOIL	227	15.4	Deflator, exports of oil (in foreign currency)	1975 = 100/Transformed
PFEXOILD	249	EXOG	Deflator, exports of oil (in US $)	1975 = 100/Transformed
PF6	197	EXOG	World wholesale prices	1975 = 100/internal definition
PGDP	74	12.5	Deflator, GDP	1975 = 100/Transformed
PM	89	10.18	Deflator, total imports	1975 = 100/Transformed
PMADJ	87	EXOG	Deflator, imports OTS to BOP adjustment	1975 = 100/Transformed
PMFL	84	EXOG	Deflator, imports of fuel (in foreign currency)	1975 = 100/Transformed
PMG	94	10.16	Deflator, imports of goods excl. oil (in foreign currency)	1975 = 100/Transformed
PMGEO	226	10.17	Deflator, imports of goods excl. oil (in foreign currency)	1975 = 100/Transformed
PMMF	90	10.21	Deflator, imports of manufactures (in foreign currency)	1975 = 100/Transformed
PMOILG	225	15.5	Deflator, imports of oil and natural gas (in foreign currency)	1975 = 100/Transformed
PMOILGD	248	EXOG	Deflator, imports of oil and natural gas (in US $)	1975 = 100/Transformed
PMOTH	91	EXOG	Deflator, imports, other	1975 = 100/Transformed
PMP	161	12.6	Deflator, GDP at market prices	1975 = 100/Transformed
PMSER	88	EXOG	Deflator, imports of services	1975 = 100/Transformed
PNH	97	10.5	Price of new houses	1975 = 100/ET
POIL	92	15.6	Price of oil (in US $)	Transformed
POILBR	260	EXOG	Baseline for POIL in oil model	Transformed
PPAC	76	10.6	Deflator, public authority consumption	1975 = 100/Transformed
PR	157	EXOG	Proportion of retirement pensions in CG	BB
PRPEXFB4	205	4.8	Relative price of exports of food and basics	Ratio/Transformed

VARIABLE	NO.	EQUATION	DEFINITION	UNITS AND SOURCE
PRPEX5	162	4.2	Relative price of exports of manufactures	Ratio/Transformed
PRTR	258	EXOG	Rate of petroleum revenue tax	Brown Book
PRTRBR	259	EXOG	Base line for PRTR in oil model	Brown Book
PS	96	10.19	Deflator, stocks	1975 = 100/Transformed
PSHIP	210	EXOG	Time charter index for dry cargo	1975 = 100/CS
PTFE	120	10.20	Deflator, total final expenditure	1975 = 100/Transformed
PWMF	71	10.3	Wholesale price of manufactures	1975 = 100/MDS
PXGER	255	10.8	Price of exports of erratic goods	1975 = 100/Transformed
PXGMA	254	10.7	Deflator, exports of manufactures (excluding erratics)	1975 = 100/Transformed
QAFC	37	12.4	Adjustment to factor cost	£m 1975/ET
QCE	1	1.4	Consumers' expenditure	£m 1975/ET
QCND	2	1.1	Consumers' expenditure on non-durables	£m 1975/ET
QCURC	217	14.7	Notes and coins in circulation deflated by CPI	£m 1975/Transformed
QDK	9	2.8	Fixed investment, total	£m 1975/ET
QDKFEE	10	EXOG	Investment, fees	£m 1975/ET
QDKIS	12	EXOG	Investment, iron and steel	£m 1975/ET
QDKLAD	13	EXOG	Investment, public sector dwellings	£m 1975/ET
QDKLEASE	234	EXOG	Leasing to manufacturing industry	£m 1975/DOI
QDKMF	5	2.5	Investment, manufacturing	£m 1975/ET
QDKMP	7	EXOG	Investment, mainly public	£m 1975/ET
QDKOTH	6	2.6	Investment, other private	£m 1975/ET
QDKPD	8	2.1	Investment, private sector dwellings	£m 1975/ET
QDKPG	4	EXOG	Investment, petroleum and natural gas	£m 1975/ET
QDKPM	27	2.13	Investment, plant and machinery	£m 1975/ET
QDKSH	11	EXOG	Investment, shipping	£m 1975/ET
QDS	18	3.4	Stock changes, total	£m 1975/ET
QDSDT	16	3.2	Stock changes, distributive trades	£m 1975/ET
QDSMF	15	3.1	Stock changes, manufacturing	£m 1975/ET

VARIABLE	NO.	EQUATION	DEFINITION	UNITS AND SOURCE
QDSRST	17	3.3	Stock changes, rest	£m 1975/ET
QDURABLE	3	1.3	Consumers' expenditure on durables	£m 1975/ET
QEX	26	4.14	Exports, total	£m 1975/ET
QEXADJ	235	EXOG	Exports, OTS to BOP adjustment	£m 1975/Transformed
QEXFB	23	4.7	Exports, food and basics	£m 1975/MRETS
QEXMF	22	4.6	Exports, manufactures	£m 1975/MRETS
QEXNES	47	EXOG	Exports, rest (OTS)	£m 1975/MRETS
QEXOIL	223	EXOG	Exports, oil	£m 1975 MRETS
QEXOTH	24	4.13	Exports, other (BOP)	£m 1975/Transformed
QEXSER	25	4.11	Exports, services	£m 1975/ET
QGDP	39	12.1	GDP (expenditure estimate) at factor cost	£m 1975/ET
QGDPC4	187	12.3	GDP (average estimate) at factor cost	£m 1975/Transformed
QGDPMP	184	12.2	GDP at market prices	£m 1975/ET
QKOTH6	232	2.7	Capital stock, other private	£m 1975/Transformed
QLAP	112	1.2	Personal sector liquid assets	£m 1975/FS
QM	35	5.6	Imports, total	£m 1975/ET
QMADJ	32	EXOG	Imports, OTS to BOP adjustment	£m 1975/Transformed
QMG	33	5.4	Imports, goods	£m 1975/ET
QMGEO	221	5.3	Imports goods, excluding oil and gas	£m 1975/Transformed
QMMF	28	5.1	Imports, manufactures	£m 1975/MRETS
QMOILG	228	EXOG	Imports, oil and gas	£m 1975/Transformed
QMOTH	29	5.2	Imports, other	£m 1975/Transformed
QMSER	34	5.5	Imports, services	£m 1975/ET
QOIL	222	EXOG	Output of North Sea oil	£m 1975/MDS
QOILBR	261	EXOG	Baseline for QOIL in oil model	£m 1975/MDS
QPAC	36	EXOG	Public authorities' consumption	£m 1975/ET
QRDY	72	8.13	Personal disposable income	£m 1975/ET
QRES	244	EXOG	Foreign exchange reserves	£m 1975/Transformed

VARIABLE	NO.	EQUATION	DEFINITION	UNITS AND SOURCE
QRM	240	EXOG	Rate of tax on QMG	Transformed
QS	21	3.7	Level of stocks, total	£m 1975/Transformed
QSDT	20	3.6	Level of stocks, distributive trades	£m 1975/Transformed
QSMF	19	3.5	Level of stocks, manufacturing	£m 1975/Transformed
QXGER	253	4.5	Exports of erratic goods	£m 1975/MRETS
QXGMA	252	4.1	Exports of manufactures, excluding erratics	£m 1975/MRETS
QYGDP	195	8.17	GDP, income estimate	£m 1975/Transformed
RATEC	55	EXOG	Rate of employers' national insurance contributions	Transformed
RATES	152	9.19	Local authority rates	£m/FS
RATNIC	57	EXOG	Rate of employees' national insurance contributions	Transformed
RBL	119	14.12	Interest rate on bank loans	per cent/FS
RCNSL	118	14.15	Yield on 2½ per cent consols	per cent/FS
RCO	125	8.6	Rent, company sector	£m/BB
REU	123	EXOG	Euro-dollar rate	per cent/FS
RLA	115	14.14	Interest rate on local authority debt (3 month)	per cent/FS
RM	241	EXOG	Rate of tax on QMG	Transformed
RMORT	114	2.2	Building society mortgage rate	per cent/FS
RMPS	156	9.23	Income from customs/protective duties	£m/FS
ROCE	273	9.25	Income from 'other' customs and excise taxes	£m/FS
ROTH	160	9.22	Income residual from INDTX identity	£m/Transformed
ROYS	256	15.2	Royalties (North Sea Oil)	£m/BB
ROYSBR	257	EXOG	Baseline for ROYS in oil model	£m/BB
RPER	64	8.7	Rent, personal sector	£m/BB
RPI	126	10.2	Retail price index	1975 = 100/ET
RPUB	124	8.8	Rent, public sector	£m/BB
RRT	159	EXOG	Reduced rate of income tax	per cent/Inland Revenue
RSHR	116	14.16	Building society recommended share rate	per cent/FS
RTB	117	EXOG	Treasury bill rate	per cent/FS
RVAT	272	9.24	Income from VAT	£m/FS
S	107	12.16	Level of stocks, total	£m/Transformed

VARIABLE	NO.	EQUATION	DEFINITION	UNITS AND SOURCE
SA	238	12.17	Stock appreciation, total	£m/ET
SACO	239	12.18	Stock appreciation, company sector	£m/ET
SAPER	250	12.19	Stock appreciation, persons	£m/BB
SGDETPRI	193	14.9	Stock of debt sales to non-bank private sector	£m/Transformed
SOCE	211	EXOG	Share of goods subject to 'other' customs & excise taxes in CE	Transformed
SP	171	9.2	Aggregate single person's income tax allowance	£m/Inland Revenue
SPA	214	EXOG	Individual single person's income tax allowance	£/Inland Revenue
SRT	131	EXOG	Standard rate of income tax	per cent/Inland Revenue
SUBS	154	9.20	General government subsidies	£m/ET
SVAT	198	EXOG	Share of goods subject to VAT in CE	Transformed
TC	65	EXOG	Transfers from companies to charities	£m/BB
TMMF	93	EXOG	Tariff on imports of manufactures	per cent/Inland Revenue
TOCE	270	EXOG	Tax per unit; excise duties	Transformed
TRCE	108	EXOG	Tax rate on consumers' expenditure	Transformed
TRCORP	135	EXOG	Rate of corporation tax	per cent/Inland Revenue
TRCORPBR	263	EXOG	Baseline for TRCORP in oil model	per cent/Inland Revenue
TRX	109	EXOG	Rate of tax on expenditure other than CE	Transformed
TTAPER	69	EXOG	Transfers abroad, persons	£m/ET
TVAT	266	EXOG	Tax per unit; VAT	Transformed
TXCO	134	9.15	Tax of income, company sector	£m/ET
TXCOEFF0	176	9.5	Income tax coefficient	Internal definition
TXCOEFF1	177	9.6	Income tax coefficient	Internal definition
TXCOEFF2	178	9.7	Income tax coefficient	Internal definition
TXCOEFF3	179	9.8	Income tax coefficient	Internal definition
TXCOEFF4	180	9.9	Income tax coefficient	Internal definition
TXM	183	9.16	Tax on imports	Transformed
TXOIL	30	15.1	Total taxes paid by North Sea oil companies	£m/BB
TXOILBR	265	EXOG	Baseline for TXOIL in oil model	£m/BB

VARIABLE	NO.	EQUATION	DEFINITION	UNITS AND SOURCE
TXNO	31	9.14	Tax of company sector (non-oil)	£m/Transformed
TXPER	182	9.13	Tax of persons income	£m/ET
UNEMP	53	7.6	Unemployment in UK	Thous/DEG
URT	132	EXOG	Differential between higher tax rates and SRT	per cent/Internal definition
USIP	267	EXOG	Industrial price index (US) in dollars	1975 = 100/OECD(MEI)
UTIL	153	6.7	Capacity utilisation	CBI survey
UVIMMF	86	EXOG	UVI imports of manufactures (effective currency)	1975 = 100/Transformed
VATRATE	271	EXOG	Rate of VAT	per cent/customs and excise
VISBAL	200	11.4	Balance of visible trade	£m/Transformed
VSET	186	EXOG	Payments of selective employment tax	£m/ET
WAGERATE	169	8.1	Average wage rate	£ per week/Transformed
WPFB	203	4.10	World export price of primary products (US $)	1975 = 100/UNMBS
WPFBC4	202	4.9	World export price of primary products (in sterling)	1975 = 100/Transformed
WPFBE	231	EXOG	World export price of primary products (effective currency)	1975 = 100/Transformed
WPMF	204	4.4	World export price of manufactures (US $)	1975 = 100/UNMBS
WPMFC5	201	4.3	World export price of manufactures (in sterling)	1975 = 100/Transformed
WPMFE	230	EXOG	World export price of manufactures (effective currency)	1975 = 100/Transformed
WS	60	8.2	Wages and salaries	£m/ET
WTM	151	EXOG	World trade in manufactures	1975 = 100/UNMBS
WTTOT	207	EXOG	World trade total	1975 = 100/UNMBS
YG	181	9.10	Income definition for tax allowances	£m/Transformed

Recent publications

THE NATIONAL INSTITUTE OF ECONOMIC AND
SOCIAL RESEARCH

publishes regularly

THE NATIONAL INSTITUTE ECONOMIC REVIEW

A quarterly analysis of the general economic situation in the United Kingdom and the world overseas, with forecasts eighteen months ahead. The last issue each year contains an assessment of medium-term prospects. There are also in most issues special articles on subjects of interest to academic and business economists.

Annual subscriptions, £30.00 (home), and £40.00 (abroad), also single issues for the current year, £8.50 (home), and £12.00 (abroad), are available directly from NIESR, 2 Dean Trench Street, Smith Square, London, SW1P 3HE.

Subscriptions at the special reduced price of £12.00 p.a. are available to students in the United Kingdom and Irish Republic on application to the Secretary of the Institute.

Back numbers and reprints of issues which have gone out of stock are distributed by Wm. Dawson and Sons Ltd., Cannon House, Park Farm Road, Folkestone. Microfiche copies for the years 1959–82 are available from EP Microform Ltd, Bradford Road, East Ardsley, Wakefield, Yorks.

Published by

HEINEMANN EDUCATIONAL BOOKS
AN INCOMES POLICY FOR BRITAIN
Edited by FRANK BLACKABY. 1972. pp. 260. £ 8.50 net.
THE UNITED KINGDOM ECONOMY
by the NIESR. 5th edn, 1982. pp. 119. £1.95 net.
DEMAND MANAGEMENT
Edited by MICHAEL POSNER. 1978. pp. 256. £6.50 (paperback) net.
DE-INDUSTRIALISATION
Edited by FRANK BLACKABY. 1979. pp. 282 £9.50 (hardback), £6.50 (paperback) net.
BRITAIN'S TRADE AND EXCHANGE-RATE POLICY
Edited by ROBIN MAJOR. 1979. pp. 240. £14.50 (hardback), £6.50 (paperback) net.
BRITAIN IN EUROPE
Edited by WILLIAM WALLACE. 1980. pp. 224. £14.50 (hardback), £6.50 (paperback) net.
THE FUTURE OF PAY BARGAINING
Edited by FRANK BLACKABY. 1980. pp. 246. £14.50 (hardback), £6.50 (paperback) net.
INDUSTRIAL POLICY AND INNOVATION
Edited by CHARLES CARTER. 1981. pp. 241. £14.50 (hardback), £6.50 (paperback) net.
THE CONSTITUTION OF NORTHERN IRELAND
Edited by DAVID WATT. 1981. pp. 227. £15.00 (hardback), £7.50 (paperback) net.
RETIREMENT POLICY THE NEXT FIFTY YEARS
Edited by MICHAEL FOGARTY. 1982. pp. 216. £14.00 (hardback), £6.50 (paperback) net.
SLOWER GROWTH IN THE WESTERN WORLD
Edited by R. C. O. MATTHEWS. 1982. pp. 176. £14.50 (hardback), £6.50 (paperback) net.
NATIONAL INTERESTS AND LOCAL GOVERNMENT
Edited by KEN YOUNG, 1983. pp. 172. £15.00 (hardback), £7.50 (paperback) net.

RECENT PUBLICATIONS OF THE NATIONAL INSTITUTE OF
ECONOMIC AND SOCIAL RESEARCH

published by
THE CAMBRIDGE UNIVERSITY PRESS

ECONOMIC AND SOCIAL STUDIES

XXVI *Urban Development in Britain: Standards, Costs and Resources, 1964–2004*
By P. A. STONE. Vol. 1: *Population Trends and Housing.* 1970. pp. 436. £18.50
£18.50 net.

XXVII *The Framework of Regional Economics in the United Kingdom*
By A. J. BROWN. 1972. pp. 372. £22.50 net.

XXVIII *The Structure, Size and Costs of Urban Settlements*
By P. A. STONE. 1973. pp. 304. £22.50 net.

XXIX *The Diffusion of New Industrial Processes: An International Study*
Edited by L. NASBETH and G. F. RAY. 1974. pp. 346. £20.50 net.

XXXI *British Economic Policy 1960–74*
Edited by F. T. BLACKABY. 1978. pp. 710. £36.50 net.

XXXII *Industrialisation and the Basis for Trade*
By R. A. BATCHELOR, R. L. MAJOR and A. D. MORGAN. 1980. pp. 380.
£19.75 net.

XXXIII *Productivity and Industrial Structure*
By S. J. PRAIS. 1981. pp. 401. £20.00 net.

OCCASIONAL PAPERS

XXIX *Poverty and Progress in Britain, 1953–73*
By G. C. FIEGEHEN, P. S. LANSLEY and A. D. SMITH. 1977. pp. 192. £12.
net.

XXX *The Innovation Process in the Energy Industries*
By G. F. RAY and L. UHLMANN. 1979. pp. 132. £9.50 net.

XXXI *Diversification and Competition*
By M. A. UTTON. 1979. pp. 124. £10.50 net.

XXXII *Concentration in British Industry, 1935–75.*
By P. E. HART and R. CLARKE. 1980. pp. 178. £12.50 net.

XXXIII *State pensions in Britain*
By JOHN CREEDY, 1982. pp. 102. £10.50 net.

XXXIV *International Industrial Productivity*
By A. D. SMITH, D. M. W. N. HITCHENS and S. W. DAVIES. 1982. pp. 16
£13.50 net.

NIESR STUDENTS' EDITION

1 *Growth and Trade* (abridged from *Industrial Growth and World Trade*)
By A. MAIZELS. 1970. pp. 312. £5.75 net.

2 *The Antitrust Laws of the U.S.A.* (3rd edition, unabridged)
By A. D. NEALE and D. G. GOYDER. 1980. pp. 544. £9.95 net.

4 *British Economic Policy 1960–74: Demand Management* (an abridged version
British Economic Policy 1960–74)
Edited by F. T. BLACKABY. 1979. pp. 472. £8.95 net.

5 *The Evolution of Giant Firms in Britain* (2nd impression with a new preface)
By S. J. PRAIS. 1981. pp. 344. £7.50 net.